D0374987

Great Shipwrecks
of the Pacific Coast

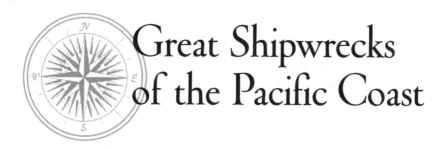

Great Shipwrecks
of the Pacific Coast

Robert C. Belyk

John Wiley & Sons, Inc.
New York • Chichester • Weinheim • Brisbane • Singapore • Toronto

Published by John Wiley & Sons, Inc.
Published simultaneously in Canada

This publication is designed to provide accurate and authoritative information in regard to the subject matter covered. It is sold with the understanding that the publisher is not engaged in rendering professional services. If professional advice or other expert assistance is required, the services of a competent professional person should be sought.

Library of Congress Cataloging-in-Publication Data:
  Belyk, Robert C.
    Great shipwrecks of the Pacific Coast / Robert C. Belyk.
      p. cm.
    Includes bibliographical references and index.
    ISBN 0-471-38420-8 (cloth)
    1. Shipwrecks—Northwest, Pacific. I. Title.

  G525 .B44 2001
  910'.9164'3—dc21

                                    2001024241

Printed in the United States of America

10 9 8 7 6 5 4 3 2 1

For Eryn

Contents

Preface

Writers have traditionally looked at Pacific Coast shipwrecks as isolated events. Each loss is seen as removed from other similar occurrences that have happened at different times and places on the West Coast.

Yet, many of these disasters share common antecedents. During the eighty years spanning the California gold rush to the beginning of the 1929 depression, many thousands of passengers and crews died on board Pacific steamships. A question that has been rarely asked is why were so many ships lost. My purpose in this book is to understand the dimensions of these human tragedies and attempt to reach a conclusion as to why they occurred.

Rather than preparing a compendium of coastal shipwrecks, I have chosen ten significant maritime disasters that took place from California to Alaska. The notion of "worst disasters" is subjective. The death toll is a poor gauge of the extent of the tragedy. It is impossible to equate a large steamer that went down during the night, slipping silently below the surface, to a smaller vessel whose passengers and crew were left clinging to a disintegrating superstructure for days before death finally took them. The choice of the greatest Pacific Coast shipwrecks is thus arbitrary and certainly open to argument.

The loss of a ship can be examined on many levels, but the passengers and crew are often done an injustice by simply looking at the obvious causes. While the weather conditions or human error are frequently blamed, there are often other, less public reasons that are omitted from inquiry reports. It is my purpose in this book to go beyond the superficial causes of the great shipwrecks of the Pacific Coast and look to other causes.

Acknowledgments

While the author may have his or her name on the cover, preparing a work of nonfiction is never an individual endeavor. There are many people who have offered their knowledge and experience to the development of this book from a concept to the finished project. I would like to thank specifically the following persons: Ruth Hoyem for the help and support that only a friend and fellow writer can offer; David Andrew and Lawrence Zellner for their suggestions regarding selling the concept; author John Kendrick, who kindly shared with me some of his vast knowledge of ships and the sea; Professor Randolf Arguelles, University of Southern California, whose knowledge of political history was most helpful. I am also grateful to Fred Braches and Nancy Greene Raine for their contributions to the completion of this work.

This book is more than simply words, and for that reason I am deeply indebted to Harold Allanson and Don Waldorf. They have given freely of their art, knowledge, and time. In a book about people and ships, illustrations and photos play an important role in making each chapter reach beyond the page to the reader's imagination.

The task of researching shipwrecks from California to Alaska has taken me to three states and one Canadian province. (Only Alaska was spared a personal visit.) I wish to express my appreciation to the following people, libraries, and repositories who have been particularly helpful in this task: Joyce Justice and the U.S. Archives and Records Service, Seattle; David Mattison and the British Columbia Archives, and Ron Clancy and the New Westminster Public Library.

I would like to thank the following libraries and archives for kindly sharing their resources: University of Washington Library, Seattle; Simon Fraser University Library, Burnaby, British Columbia; Bancroft Library, Berkeley, California; University of Oregon Library,

Eugene; University of British Columbia Library, Vancouver; Washington State Library, Olympia; California State Library, Sacramento; National Archives of Canada, Ottawa; San Francisco Maritime National Historical Park; London Public Library, London, Ontario; Puget Sound Maritime Historical Society, Seattle; British Columbia Institute of Technology Library, Burnaby; San Francisco Public Library; Vancouver Public Library; Tacoma Public Library; and Coquitlam Public Library, Coquitlam, British Columbia.

I would like to thank senior editor Hana Umlauf Lane for her faith in this project. Finally, it is not possible to express fully my gratitude to my wife, Diane, who has given up her own vacation time to accompany me to dozens of information repositories. Together we have strained our eyes before countless microfilm readers and catalog computer screens. She has read and made cogent comments on the draft versions of this work and completed the thousand small but time-consuming details that are necessary to complete a book. For her help, I cannot say enough.

Introduction

This is a book about the great passenger shipwrecks of the Pacific Coast. As the reader will discover, these accounts are filled with the drama of life and death on board doomed ships. They tell of the fortunate and the luckless, heroes and cowards. The threads of individual struggles are woven into the stories of ordinary people caught in extraordinary circumstances. Drawing heavily on contemporary sources, each account attempts to put the reader on board the vessel on her last run.

On another level, these are the stories behind the disasters. While to some degree accidents at sea are unavoidable, the golden age of travel on the Pacific Coast was not a time when marine safety could be taken for granted. The outcome of federal investigations into Pacific Coast shipwrecks pointed toward storms and fog or the failure of the captain and crew during critical moments as the causes of marine disasters. Such reports were frequently superficial and intended to direct blame away from the shipping companies.

It was also true that civil law favored the shipowners. Sheltered by a legal provision that rendered companies virtually immune from legal action, cut-rate firms frequently operated unsafe passenger vessels. In such an environment, shipping companies had little incentive to purchase newer and safer vessels, or even properly maintain their existing fleet.

PROBABLY THE MOST unseaworthy passenger steamship allowed to clear an American West Coast port was the 464-ton *Clara Nevada*, which cast off her lines from Seattle's Yesler dock on January 29, 1898. Built in 1872 for the U.S. Coastal Survey, the ship *Hassler* was by 1897 an aging steamer condemned by the government and put up for sale.

Her iron hull, engine, and boilers probably would have been sold for scrap, had it not been for the Klondike gold rush. She was purchased by the Pacific and Alaska Navigation Company and supposedly given an extensive refit at Ballard, Washington.[1] In fact, the ship received little more than a coat of paint before she was passed by the local steamship inspectors and allowed to begin service.

The account of the journey on the newly renamed *Clara Nevada* to Skagway, Alaska, was related by some of the passengers. Backing away from her Seattle dock, the vessel struck the revenue cutter *Grant*. At her ports of call, docks splintered under the crush of her iron hull. Passenger Charles Jones of The Dalles, Oregon, recalled: "We celebrated our arrival in Port Townsend [Washington] by running into the wharf and smashing our bowsprit, to say nothing of the damage done to the wharf. . . . After we left Port Townsend we got into rough water near Fort Simpson on the [Canadian] side, and blew out three flues from the boiler. We anchored in the bay off Fort Simpson and were compelled to remain there twelve hours before the damage was repaired."[2] Many of the 150 passengers who reached Skagway thought their arrival was a miracle.

The people returning on the vessel were not so fortunate. Soon after her departure on February 6, 1898, she met disaster. Witnesses on Lynn Canal saw a small ship burst into flames before she exploded. The steam launch *Rustler* found the remains of the vessel off Eldred Rock under four fathoms of water. There were no survivors. Her superstructure had been completely blown away, which suggested that her boiler had exploded.[3] The scale of the disaster was never certain, as there was no record of the number of people on board during the *Clara Nevada*'s return journey.[4]

While not every shipwreck can be blamed on the lust for gold, it is true that the precious metal was for many years the foundation of the maritime economy of the West Coast. In their haste to the gold fields, few passengers considered the seaworthiness of their vessel, at least until it was too late. The unfortunate *Clara Nevada,* her crew, and her passengers met the fate of many other ships.

THE YEARS BETWEEN 1849 and 1929 marked the period during which the Pacific coastal fleet played an important role in the economy of the West. The sea united the communities along the Pacific Coast from San Diego, California, to Skagway, Alaska. This time also witnessed many devastating shipwrecks.

In the wake of the discovery of gold in California's Coloma Valley in 1848, San Francisco emerged as the West Coast metropolis in an isolated hinterland. Although the rush was short-lived, later smaller gold discoveries in Oregon, Washington Territory, and British Columbia contributed to the development of San Francisco as the hub of north-south trade. In 1897 the important Klondike gold rush created new demands for ships to move miners and their equipment and supplies north. In the first decade of the twentieth century, the gold rush was over, but a new diversified economy continued to rely on coastal shipping for the movement of freight and passengers. Among the passengers on the ships were miners still exploring the more remote areas of the continent and San Francisco commercial travelers selling their wares in Los Angeles, San Diego, Portland, Seattle, Tacoma, and Vancouver, British Columbia, as well as other, smaller communities along the coast.

AMERICAN MERCHANT shipbuilding reached its zenith with the development of the wooden clipper ship, which firmly established the United States as a major trading nation. Ironically, it was the success of these vessels in the early nineteenth century that limited innovation in other areas of shipbuilding. The future of maritime transportation lay not with wood and sail, but with iron and steam. As Clinton H. Whitehurst has noted, "American owners and builders were late in accepting and developing iron (and later steel) hulls, compound engines, and the screw propeller."[5]

While American East Coast steamships were below the quality of European products, the vessels serving on the West Coast were often the castoffs of the American Atlantic fleet. The gold rushes in California and Alaska had contributed to a demand for marine transportation that outstripped supply. The result was that the Pacific Coast became the dumping ground for the rusting and rotting hulks that would otherwise have been consigned to the scrap heap. Once this precedent had been established, it continued well into the twentieth century. To a greater or lesser extent, the pattern of outmoded and unseaworthy vessels characterized the Pacific Coast passenger fleet during the period from 1849 to 1929. As Frederick E. Emmons observes, "The general unseaworthiness of many of the coastal ships, combined with the natural hazards of the routes on which they sailed, was reflected in marine insurance rates which were double those prevailing on the East Coast. In general, it could be said that the only reason they were not involved in more disasters was the experience and skill of the men who sailed them."[6]

Why had not the Pacific Coast shipping companies spent more money in modernizing their fleets? The *Portland Oregonian* blamed government policy. The newspaper wrote in a 1906 editorial: "Owing to our venerable navigation laws, which are more antique and out of date than the steamers which laboriously cover the Pacific Coast routes, it is impossible for our ship-owners to purchase modern economical carriers, which could be brought out here and put in service. . . . This embargo is the rankest kind of injustice. It forces the men engaged in the carrying trade to handle their business with more expensive but inferior vessels."[7] This was not entirely true. American shipbuilders and ship owners had been aided by government subsidies, but such programs never became part of a well-considered national policy.[8]

At the beginning of the twentieth century, more domestic orders were placed for new American passenger vessels, but these ships were destined for Cuban, Hawaiian, and Far East routes. The major ship-owners on the West Coast remained little interested in spending money to purchase new vessels.

By 1906, the decrepit condition of many of their ships did make it clear that newer and safer vessels were needed. Although a number of new ships were ordered from American shipbuilders, the Wall Street crash of 1907 slowed the interest of the shipping companies in modernizing their fleets.

Today, it seems surprising that Congress and the Department of Commerce, which was charged with enforcing maritime safety, so blatantly acted in the interests of the steamship companies. Difficult-to-understand safety laws and weak enforcement did not protect the traveling public. Since the beginning of regular coastal travel, the steamship owners had an effective lobby. Further, while the wreck inquiries of the government steamship inspectors continued to place the blame upon the captain and crew of the vessel, the steamship company itself escaped censure. With each new disaster, the public rose up in anger demanding that outdated and unsafe vessels be removed from passenger service, but little was done until the confidence in coastal passenger travel had been all but destroyed.

By the end of the 1920s, automobile travel was increasingly an alternative to ship and train passage. The most important reason for the demise of the coastal passenger service, however, was the 1929 depression. With less people and cargo to move, ships were sold or laid up. Ferries became the only regular passenger transportation on the American Pacific Coast.[9]

Today's travelers on cruise vessels may feel safe knowing that modern navigation and communication aids are at hand. It is well to remember, though, that it has not always been so. Less than a hundred years ago, a ticket to travel on a Pacific Coast steamship was an uncertain prize.

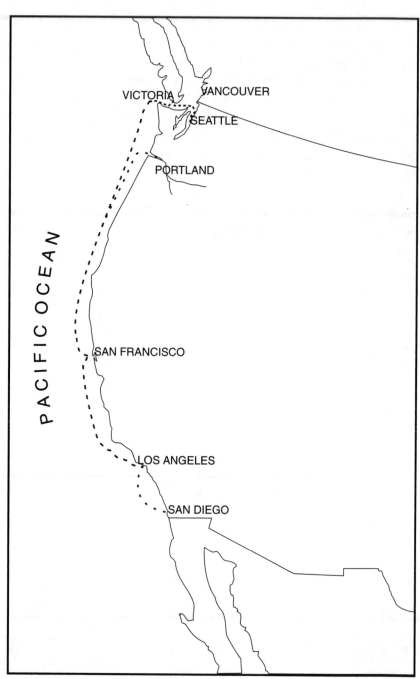

Steamship routes from San Francisco.

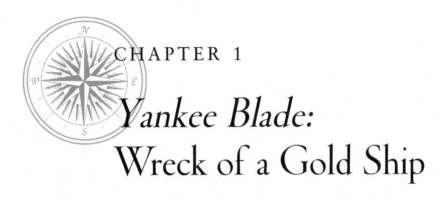

CHAPTER 1

Yankee Blade:
Wreck of a Gold Ship

Not every shipwreck is an accident. Maritime history has many tales of unlucky ships lured onto rocky shores by false beacons. Once aground, gangs of wreckers would move in and steal the ship's cargo. However, sometimes the reasons for the disaster were not so clear-cut. To collect insurance money, owners bribed their captains to put their ships on the rocks. At other times the ship's master would run his vessel aground so that he could plunder the cargo himself. While it may seem unlikely that Captain Henry Randall deliberately put the *Yankee Blade* on the rocks off Point Arguello, California, it is nonetheless true that he benefited substantially from this disaster.

In 1854 one of the companies transporting gold, people, and goods between New York and San Francisco via the Isthmus of Panama was the Independent Line, which was controlled by the shipping tycoon Cornelius Vanderbilt. The *Yankee Blade* was one of the most luxurious ships in the new Independent Line fleet. She was fairly large by the standards of the day—1,767 tons burden with a length of 275 feet, and a 21-foot beam.[1] Her 22-inch oak hull had been made to withstand the worst winter storms.

The ship's two boilers fed a cast-iron side-lever engine with two 78-inch steam cylinders, each with an 11-foot stroke. Her two 38-foot metal paddle boxes housed wheels that were 33 feet in diameter.[2] Each paddle or wheel float reciprocated so that it entered and left the water in a vertical position, thereby increasing its bite of the surface and decreasing its drag. With a cruising speed of about thirteen knots, the ship was considered fast for a steam-powered vessel. Important also were refinements in the beam-lever engine design—they gave the *Yankee Blade* an advantage over her older rivals.

For the comfort of her passengers, the *Yankee Blade* boasted large, square portholes, icehouses, and bath rooms. It may have also given the passenger some peace of mind to note in the company's advertisements that the Independent Line was "No. 1 with the insurance companies."[3] For the health of the passengers, the *Yankee Blade* was well ventilated and carried a surgeon whose services would be available free of charge. For safety the ship was equipped with six self-righting lifeboats as well as life preservers. The *Yankee Blade* was a cut above most of her competitors.

The speed records of the gold rush ships added to the prestige of the steamship companies. While beating a competitor by a few hours was hardly a worthwhile goal, the lines could advertise having the fastest vessel on the run, and such claims increased ticket sales. For the owners of these ships, it was particularly important to convince the public that their vessels were the fastest carriers on the east-west route, for they faced stiff competition. The Independent vessels had an advantage over those of its rival, the Pacific Mail Steamship Company, for the latter's ships were older and generally slower. The side-lever engine, though, was not fuel efficient and was falling out of favor with American shipping companies. In new ships, the cumbersome walking beam engine was replacing the standard side-lever design.[4]

IN COMMAND of the *Yankee Blade* was Captain Henry Randall, who had been employed by the Pacific Mail Steamship Company as master of the side-wheeler *Northerner* on the Pacific run until his retirement in 1852. Randall's familiarity with California waters made him an excellent choice for the master of the new ship, which was destined for the West Coast. Because of the premium placed on speed, Vanderbilt had promised Randall a bonus for record-setting voyages between San Francisco and Panama. This was a major incentive to Randall, for Vanderbilt had a reputation for paying his captains and crews less than other lines.

Drawing of the *Yankee Blade,* taken from contemporary sketches. (© 2000 Harold Allanson)

At noon on February 2, 1854, the *Yankee Blade* steamed out of New York to begin her trip around Cape Horn to San Francisco. On March 3, the ship dropped anchor in Rio de Janeiro harbor to pick up fresh supplies. Rounding the Horn proved not to be difficult, and the *Yankee Blade* arrived in the charming old city of Valparaíso, Chile, on March 23. There, she waited more than a week as she took on fresh supplies. After arriving in Panama City on April 14, the *Yankee Blade* took on 793 passengers, as well as coal for her bunkers that was of particularly poor quality.[5] It was indeed a seller's market for coal in Panama City. On April 18, she weighed anchor once more.

On April 25, the ship was low on drinking water, but found that her scheduled port of call, Acapulco, was under siege as Mexico was in revolt. Rather than allowing the *Yankee Blade* to fill her water tanks, the port authorities "arrested" her cattle, reducing the ship's food supply. As the sun was setting on May 4, the *Yankee Blade* entered the waters of San Francisco Bay and tied up at the Jackson Street wharf. The voyage from New York around the Horn had taken a little more than ninety days. The journey by way of the isthmus could be completed in less than one-third the time.

On June 1, the *Yankee Blade* began her regular run to Panama. Leaving at the same time was the Pacific Mail steamer *John L. Stephens,* which overtook and passed the Independent Line vessel. Fortunately for Captain Randall, the *Stephens* was detained four hours at Acapulco, which allowed his vessel to beat her rival into Panama harbor.[6] The *Yankee Blade* was not as fortunate during her return journey. She arrived in San Francisco on July 1, a few hours after the *Stephens*.

The *Yankee Blade*'s next run to Panama began from San Francisco's Jackson Street wharf at 3:30 P.M. on August 1. The *Sonora* departed from the Pacific Mail Steamship Company's Vallejo Street wharf fifteen minutes later.[7] On his second trip to Panama, Randall seemed even more determined to beat the Pacific Mail steamer. To achieve maximum speed, the captain did little at first to conserve coal. When he did cut back it was too late, for not far from Panama City, the ship ran out of fuel. When the *Sonora* neared, Randall ran up a distress signal and fired rockets, but the rival steamer simply acknowledged the summons for help and continued on her way. According to *Yankee Blade* Purser Samuel Vought, "We then found it necessary to run into Dumas Bay, Quibo [sic] Island, for wood, of which, by the assistance of our passengers, who displayed a genuine California zeal, we were enabled to procure sufficient in about 20 hours to take us to Panama. . . ."[8]

The *Yankee Blade* steamed into harbor barely in time to prevent another ship, the *Golden Gate,* from launching a search. For Randall, the entire incident must have been humiliating.

On September 29, an advertisement appeared in the *Daily Alta California* offering a $5,000 wager that the *Yankee Blade* would reach Panama in advance of the *Sonora*.[9] Although the person putting up the wager remained anonymous, it seems probable that Captain Randall was behind the challenge. Since the rival company regarded such races as dangerous, he could be sure that his ship would be officially unchallenged. Yet throwing down the gauntlet in this manner was certainly a provocation for Captain R. L. Whiting of the *Sonora*.

There is also some evidence as to why the wager may have been important to Randall. In the beginning of October, a Sacramento newspaper had reported that the Pacific Mail Steamship Company and the Nicaragua Steamship Company were negotiating to purchase the Independent Line, which included the *Yankee Blade* and *Uncle Sam* on the San Francisco–Panama run.[10] If Captain Randall had heard similar reports prior to his departure on September 30, the news would have been disturbing. One could not imagine that the Pacific Mail Steamship Company would take kindly to one of its "retired" masters commanding a rival company's ship. When the new company flag was raised on the *Yankee Blade,* Captain Randall would likely be out of a job. For this reason, winning the bet may have been doubly important.

At 4 P.M. on Saturday, September 30, 1854, the fore and aft lines holding the *Yankee Blade* to the wharf were cast off, and the vessel backed slowly into the main channel before heading toward the Golden Gate. Although the company's agent would claim a manifest of only 819 people,[11] there is little doubt that the *Yankee Blade* was carrying as many as 1,200 passengers.[12] Competition among a number of carriers on the route had lowered fares and made travel a bargain.[13] In addition, about 125 crew members were on board. Other ships were leaving at the same time, but only one was taking the same route to Panama: the Pacific Mail steamer *Sonora.*

The *Sonora* was only a few hundred yards to the stern of the *Yankee Blade.* The passengers on board the small coastal steamer *Goliah* watched the two big Panama ships close in on one another. As one of the *Goliah*'s passengers would later report, "Before reaching the Fort [Fort Point], the *Yankee Blade* stopped her engine, and allowing the *Sonora* to pass her, raised her flag as a challenge of speed, and then getting again headway, passed the *Sonora* at the bar. It was understood at San Francisco that a bet . . . was pending on the race to Panama."[14] Once beyond the bar, the *Yankee Blade* took a southward course that took her close to the coastline while the *Sonora* steamed farther out to sea.

At least $153,000 of specie gold in nine boxes, shipped by the bank Page, Bacon and Company, was on board the *Yankee Blade.* Additional valuables had been entrusted to the safe in the purser's office, but some of the passengers who didn't trust anyone or anything, including the ship's safe, carried large amounts of gold and coins on their persons.

As the *Yankee Blade* was now a dozen miles from the entrance to San Francisco harbor, the voyage settled into the usual shipboard routine. The splash of water against the floats, muffled as it was within the two big iron paddle boxes, made a throaty sound. Some male passengers went to the saloon to order a drink. The few women on board talked in the social room or walked on deck with their husbands, enjoying the fresh salt air. A few wisps of fog floated above the water, like shapeless ghosts haunting the ocean expanse. The air was already heavy with the coming of night.

CAPTAIN SAMUEL HALEY of the little *Goliah* was on a regular run between San Francisco and San Diego, stopping at a number of the smaller ports along the way. She had been originally built as a tug-boat—the second constructed in the United States—in 1849. After completion, she was sent around the Horn to Sacramento, where she served as a passenger steamer. A few years later, the *Goliah* was lengthened and used in the coastal trade. Captain Haley had steamed the waters off California since before 1852, first on the little steamer *Sea Bird* and later on the *Goliah,* and knew well the dangers of the coast south of San Francisco.

Since her departure, the *Goliah* had felt her way through the coastal fog that drifted in and out as they steamed south. Fewer than a hundred passengers had bought tickets and the *Goliah* was not overcrowded. Most were frequent travelers on the run and were accustomed to the vessel's slow pace. Not far out of San Francisco, the fog became so thick that it was necessary to heave to several hours before continuing. When they reached the port of Monterey on Sunday morning, the fog had thickened again, and it was not until late in the afternoon that they got under way for Santa Barbara.

ALTHOUGH THE *Yankee Blade* was crowded, the passengers did not seem to mind. For most, their journey on the ship was the first step in their return to friends and relatives in the East. A fresh late afternoon breeze blew gray mist away. At 9 P.M., Purser Samuel Vought saw the outline of a steamer off the starboard beam. He suspected it was either the company's sister ship, *Uncle Sam,* or the Pacific Mail's *John L. Stephens* returning from Panama.[15] It was in fact the small coastal steamer *Southerner* on her trip north to San Francisco. The *Southerner* passed the *Goliah* a few hours after her meeting with the *Yankee Blade,* and hailed Captain Haley. Captain Sampson, the *Southerner's* master, asked the *Goliah* to keep an eye out for the big side-wheeler, for she stood in danger of striking the rocks.[16] It seemed that Captain Randall had set a course sure to end in disaster. Concern for the fate of the *Yankee Blade* took Captain Haley close to shore, placing his ship in peril of running aground.

As WITH THE *Goliah,* the *Yankee Blade* encountered thick fog banks close in to the coast, but Captain Randall ordered no reduction in speed or change in course. With less distance to travel, the *Yankee Blade* had an advantage over the *Sonora.* Those on board who were familiar with this part of the coast were well aware that the vessel was close in to shore. Some passengers indeed claimed to have seen land before it was obscured by a fog bank, but Captain Randall said this was impossible.

G. A. Hart was on his way to New York State to visit his wife and family. Like many others, Hart did not buy passage for himself and a servant until after the ship was under way. About 3 P.M. on Sunday, October 1, he paid for his tickets at the purser's office. There he met Captain Randall, who invited him to the saloon for a drink. The ship's master noted that he was pleased with the progress the *Yankee Blade* was making. Her eleven-foot cylinders were stroking at thirteen revolutions a minute.[17] Immediately the ship shook from bow to stern.[18] Glasses flew off the bar and people were thrown to the deck. Those in steerage heard the ominous cracking of the oak hull.

The *Yankee Blade* had struck a rocky pinnacle jutting almost to the water line. For a moment, the fog lifted long enough to see that the ship was almost a mile from the mainland. Once Captain Randall reached the wheelhouse, he ordered full reverse but the great paddle wheels were useless: the ship didn't move. Forward, he could see that the *Yankee Blade* had run high up on the rocks. He quickly sent one of the mates and the ship's carpenter to survey the damage. After ordering the engineer to get the suction pump working, Randall went to inspect the damage and quickly found himself in water up to his waist. He noted a long gash running about twelve feet along the ship's stern below the waterline. As Randall stated later, "I saw at once that the ship was lost. . . ."[19]

The side-wheeler had been traveling at almost full speed when she struck, and the force had driven her bow sixty feet out of the water. Within thirty minutes the entire aft quarter was submerged. The bow anchors were dropped to make the ship less likely to slip off her perch into deep water while steam was vented to prevent an explosion. The *Yankee Blade* was firmly wedged high on the rocks, and while the forward quarter remained dry, the rise and fall of the waves worked the stern. It was obvious that the *Yankee Blade* would eventually snap in two. If the forward quarter slipped into deeper water, the death toll would be high.

Purser Samuel Vought was able to save the valuables entrusted to him and the express bags stored in his office, but when he and his crew approached the specie gold stored in the vault in the stern, he found that the safe was already under rapidly rising water. There was nothing they could do to save this valuable cargo.

Since the *Yankee Blade* carried so many passengers, there were not enough lifeboats for everyone. Each rescue craft would have to make many trips before everyone was removed. By now most of the daylight hours were behind them and the ship was some distance from shore. Even if the lifeboats landed safely, they could make only one or two return trips before darkness set in. Most of those on board would have to remain with the vessel through the night.

Although a large number of people crowded the decks, the loading of the three starboard lifeboats was orderly. The crew, responsible for making a safe landing, took their places. Women and small children were given seating preference, but a few single male passengers attempted to push them aside to gain a place. The boats were ready to be lowered.

Randall, with a crew of four sailors, took charge of the starboard quarter boat. C. W. Hewitt, the first officer, was in charge of one lifeboat and the second officer was in command of another. The captain left his son Henry Randall Jr. in charge of the *Yankee Blade*. The young man was only in his teens and entirely incapable of handling distraught passengers and an undisciplined crew.

Randall later claimed he was attempting to find a safe landing site for his lifeboats, but his action belied his words. The captain's desertion of his ship in one of the first boats was a matter of much controversy following the wreck. Seeking out a location to land the passengers was a task belonging to a boatswain or an experienced officer. Moreover, to leave in charge a relatively inexperienced young man seemed inexcusable. Purser Vought would claim that Randall's actions were the result of the lack of trust the captain had in many of his crew. Once the passengers were unloaded, he feared that the seamen would not return to the ship.[20]

The master also maintained that he gave no order to launch the other boats, but four craft were lowered. Randall's boat remained off-shore, making a survey of the coast to find a safe landing spot; two other boats turned their bows in the direction of the shore as the surf washed in behind them. One boat, with an unknown officer in charge, was hung up in its davits, and when the fall line was recklessly cut away, its crew and passengers tumbled into the ocean. The boat was eventually launched, and most of those in the water were picked up. A few, though, were lost before they could be rescued.

J. Moore and his young son Adolphus climbed into a boat under the command of First Officer C. W. Hewitt. There were thirty-one people on board. Because it was designed specifically to stay afloat, the little craft didn't go under when it was swamped by the waves, but many of the passengers were tossed into the cold Pacific waters. Some who had held on tightly and rode the boat to shore were badly in-jured. Moore lay unconscious in the breakers when a woman picked him up and carried him to higher ground, where he was revived. Others were not so lucky. Moore's son died in the pounding surf, as did twenty-five other people who had been on board his lifeboat.

The role of Captain Randall in subsequent events is a mystery. The master of the *Yankee Blade* claimed that he returned to the wreck to take on more passengers, while others stated that he did not go near his ship again. It was true that some boats returned with their crews to the *Yankee Blade* and took off more passengers, but later that evening Randall remained on shore rather than returning to his ship, where his presence might have reassured hundreds of passengers.

With most of the senior officers gone, a gang of San Francisco hood-lums who had come on board as steerage passengers came forward. Jim Turner, a well-known San Francisco crime figure, headed the gang. A week before the *Yankee Blade* steamed out of the harbor, a San Francisco grand jury had indicted Turner on a charge of assault with deadly weapons.[21] Those who had seen him on board the *Yankee Blade* had assumed he was attempting to flee the law, and few cared where he went as long as he left San Francisco.

During the chaos on deck, the beleaguered crew was not able to act against the "shoulder-strikers," as they were called, and these thugs were able to take large sums of gold and valuables from the passengers. Their activity was at first confined to below decks, but gradually they moved up among the first-class passengers. The Turner gang was aided by other crew members who joined in with the outlaws. "The miscreants on board attempted to get possession of all the boats," wrote the *San Francisco Daily Herald,* "and it was only when the passengers reduced to desperation, drew their revolvers, and threatened death to all who interfered, that they were able to get the women and children into the first boats."[22]

Life preservers became a valuable commodity as the panicked passengers realized that there were not enough of them to go around. Passenger G. A. Hart was given a preserver on boarding, but when he went to his stateroom, it was no longer there. He estimated that no more than one person in ten had a life preserver. Second steward J. Madison, who seemed to have acquired a large stock of "personal" preservers, sold them at a good price.[23] Other crew quickly followed, selling life preservers to the highest bidders.

After stealing from the passengers and breaking into the captain's bureau, which contained $1,200, some of Turner's gang commandeered one of the remaining lifeboats; but according to Horace Bell, one of the passengers on board the *Goliah,* "the boat swamped in the breakers and the pirates and their gold went down together."[24] Not all gang members had been in the boat. Many who didn't trust the surf remained on the *Yankee Blade* during the night.

By 6 P.M., waves had pulled away pieces of the promenade deck and aft superstructure above the waterline. The fog, which had retreated in the warmth of the afternoon sun, was thickening again. As evening approached, those on board could no longer make out the coast. First Officer C. W. Hewitt, despite being injured during the swamping of his lifeboat, had overseen the shuttle service between ship and shore. As the fog thickened, he decided it was too dangerous to continue that night. When the last boat pulled away from the ship's side, those on board the *Yankee Blade* were overcome by sadness. The action of the waves was relentless. There was no guarantee their ship would see the light of morning.

As darkness closed in, some passengers jumped overboard in a foolhardy attempt to swim to shore. Later their bodies were washed up on the rocks or were taken by the current into deeper water. G. A.

Hart jumped overboard and was picked up by one of the last lifeboats heading to shore. "It was so dark that I could hardly see," Hart wrote to his wife later, "but a sailor put out an oar and finally drew me on board the boat. . . ." [25]

Also sent overboard by the crew were eight or ten head of cattle. On shore, a passenger took the opportunity to shoot one of the animals for food. As the carcass was being butchered, the Turner gang moved in and began selling the meat to the hungry passengers. "If the rest of the passengers had turned upon them, and cut them to pieces," wrote the *San Francisco Daily Herald,* "they would have done the State a service and rid the world of monsters."[26] Many city residents who had been victims of San Francisco's large lawless element shared the same sentiments.

On shore, Hart and the other survivors shivered around a small fire. It was early October and the fog brought a chill that seemed to cling to the bones of the men and women. The fog was now as thick as wool. Eerily, the sound of the ship's bell echoed through the night. For many on shore, it was the beating heart of the stricken ship.

THE FOG, which had retreated in the afternoon, did not re-form until the early hours of the next morning, Tuesday, October 2. The *Goliah* was now feeling her way cautiously down the coast. Captain Haley had ordered his crew to keep a close lookout toward the fog-shrouded shore for the *Yankee Blade.*

At about 8 A.M., startled passengers and crew on deck heard the rumble of breakers off the port quarter. Immediately Captain Haley changed course to starboard, but the roar of the waves continued. Worse, a distant sound even more chilling could now be heard: terrified screams of hundreds of human voices echoing and reechoing through the dense fog. "Nothing is more solemnly terrifying than to be on shipboard near the breakers and in a fog bank," wrote Horace Bell, "but add to this the knowledge of being in close proximity to a wreck is awe added to terror, and is paralyzing to the bravest heart."[27] Captain Haley ordered a change in course and the voices subsided.

Suddenly, like a curtain, the fog lifted to reveal a wreck about seven hundred feet from the *Goliah.* It was the *Yankee Blade,* her aft partially underwater and awash by breakers and her passengers clinging to the rigging amidships and forward, the upper decks, and cabins. She was lying bow toward shore, hung up on the northwest side of Point Arguello. The magnificent ship had been reduced to a splintered wreck.

Captain Haley ordered the engines stopped and surveyed the scene. The *Yankee Blade* was at a forty-degree angle with the action of the waves threatening to break the vessel's back abaft her sidewheels. Already the mainmast had worked free from its place on the keel and crashed through the hull. Because of the difficult position of the ship, Captain Haley saw only one way to evacuate the men and women who remained on board. To do this, the *Goliah* had to be in close to the reef.

He put the ship's engines in reverse and backed in as close to the wreck as he dared. He then floated a buoy attached to a line in the direction of the *Yankee Blade*. Once the crew of the wrecked ship retrieved the line, a hawser was then attached and winched on board the *Goliah*. To keep the great cable as tight as possible, the *Goliah* dropped her anchors. To transfer those on board the *Yankee Blade* to the *Goliah*, Captain Haley connected one of his lifeboats to the taut hawser running overhead with a light bowline connecting the small craft with his ship. Then he floated a line attached to the opposite end of the lifeboat to the *Yankee Blade*. This lifeboat, secured to the heavy rope overhead, would transfer passengers. As the evacuation proceeded, the lifeboat would sometimes be stopped in midair as the rope slackened, but the removal of the passengers and crew was successful.

The first on board the boat were the mutineers who had intimidated and robbed many of the *Yankee Blade*'s passengers. When the story of their actions reached the captain, an armed squad of men on the *Goliah* confronted and disarmed them and put them under guard in the steerage.[28]

Many of the passengers had to be transferred to shore with provisions from the *Yankee Blade* because the *Goliah* was too small to accommodate all those remaining on the wreck. About three hundred people ferried from the *Goliah*'s boats joined those who already had been landed from the *Yankee Blade*. By sundown, the last man on board the steamer was removed. The rescue was finished just in time, for a few minutes later a gale began pounding the wreckage. As those aboard the *Goliah* watched, the hull of the *Yankee Blade* cleaved in two, sending the fore and aft quarters into deep water.

The *Goliah* completed her run to Santa Barbara, San Pedro, and San Diego, where she dropped off her passengers. It was not until late the following evening that the ship was ready to clear San Diego on her return journey to Point Arguello, where she would pick up the remainder of the stranded passengers. Near the entrance to the harbor, though, the ship went aground in a thick fog bank, and it was twenty-four hours before she was finally free. By the time the *Goliah* returned, some of the *Yankee Blade* survivors had reached Santa Barbara overland. An enterprising local resident had taken a string of horses to the wreck site and had sold rides for $25 per person.[29]

Most of the men and women were taken on board the *Goliah* and returned to San Francisco. The remaining passengers and crew who had been dropped off in the small coastal ports were picked up by the Nicaragua Steamship Company's *Brother Jonathan* and returned to the Jackson Street wharf—the same place where they had embarked on the *Yankee Blade* two weeks earlier.

Once in the city, passengers called a meeting that censured Captain Randall for "so quickly deserting the wreck and leaving the boat without a leading officer on board to quiet the passengers and prevent the plundering."[30] The choice of such a dangerous course so close to shore was also condemned. Had the ship followed the *Sonora*'s lead and plotted a course further out to sea, the wreck would never have happened.

Captain Randall was also unpopular with the San Francisco press. "It was the eager desire to make the quickest trip," the *San Francisco Daily Herald* wrote on October 11, "that induced Captain Randall to attempt the passage between the islands and the mainland. Herein he was culpable, and here the charge of recklessness applies."[31] Similarly the San Francisco weekly *Wide West* wrote, "No unprejudiced examiner into the facts can fail to come to the conclusion that the commander failed—whether from error of judgement or from other cause—in doing the duty devolving upon him before and at the time of the disaster."[32]

It would be wrong, though, to assume that everyone condemned Randall. Many passengers felt that he had done the proper thing by leaving the ship in the first boat to secure a landing site. In San Diego, where Randall went immediately after the wreck, he received considerable support in the press. "It is well known to all persons who have ever traveled by sea, that the officer of the deck is not supposed to be continually standing over the man at the wheel . . . but the man is sup-posed to steer the course laid down for him," wrote the *San Diego Herald*.[33] Of course, nothing could be further from the truth. The offi-cer of the watch and ultimately the captain was responsible for the ship. To blame the person at the wheel was only to admit that the cap-tain and his officers failed in their duty to ensure the ship was on her correct course.

The shipping company listed the number of dead as fewer than thirty, but there is little doubt the total was much higher. The com-pany agent had no accurate passenger manifest. Moreover, there was an unknown number of stowaways.

At the San Francisco meeting, the survivors freely showed their gratitude to some members of the crew who aided in the rescue. Pas-sengers began a collection for a gold watch to be presented to Third Officer William Quinn, the last man off the *Yankee Blade*. Other sailors were introduced with hearty applause.

Samuel Kenny, one of the most notorious of the robbers on board the *Yankee Blade*, was arrested in San Francisco, but apparently many of his companions, including the notorious Jim Turner, escaped. In San Francisco, law enforcement was at best uneven, and at worst cor-rupt. Another outlaw captured, though, was Rolla Powers, a desperado who had taken passage on board the *Yankee Blade* to flee California authorities. When the *Yankee Blade* sailed Powers was probably sure he had made good his getaway, but when the unfortunate ship was wrecked he found himself back in San Francisco. He quickly booked passage on another steamer, the *Golden Gate,* but San Francisco police came on board a few minutes before departure and arrested him, thwarting his escape.[34]

One recipient of instant California justice was second steward J. Madison, who had sold the *Yankee Blade*'s life preservers to passen-gers. He was discovered by some of the survivors working as a stew-ard on the ship *Sierra Nevada*. Before it sailed on October 24, Madi-son was grabbed by an irate mob and thrown off the ship.[35]

MANY CALIFORNIANS dreamed of striking it rich by salvaging the gold treasure lying in the wreck off Point Arguello. It was also certain that neither the insurance company, Lloyd's of London, nor the bank,

Page, Bacon and Company, were prepared to simply write off the loss. On October 12, 1854, Captain Randall had a new job. The underwriters had hired the Steam Tug Company to conduct salvage operations. The salvage vessel, the *Caroline,* was commanded by an officer of the U.S. Navy, but the former master of the *Yankee Blade* was taken on to direct the operation. Randall knew where to find the remains of the ship and was thus invaluable to the salvage. Two men in diving suits were lowered into the waters off Point Arguello at the place where Randall said his ship was wrecked. The attempt, though, was a failure. The *Caroline*'s crew, the *Daily Alta* noted, "found their submarine apparatus too imperfect to be of any avail, and it was found likewise utterly impossible to work at her with any security, on account of the heavy sea which rolled over the wreck continually."[36]

The general location of the wreck was no secret, for portions of the *Yankee Blade* were strewn along the beach. The stern, where the nine boxes of specie gold were kept, had broken off and slipped into about sixty feet of water. After Captain Randall reported that it would be impossible to secure the gold because of the heavy waves washing over the salvage site, Page, Bacon and Company withdrew its offer to finance the salvage, but it appears that the underwriters negotiated an independent deal with Randall and the Steam Tug Company.

On November 26, the refitted pilot boat *Dancing Feather,* under the command of a Captain Fowler, arrived at the wreck. To escape attention, Captain Randall arrived at the dive site some time later and took command of salvage operations. He recovered four boxes of gold valued at $68,000.[37] It seems, though, an additional two boxes of gold went unreported. Two salvage divers, Robert Wilson and Thomas Matthews, were charged with stealing $34,000 in gold. Captain Randall himself was charged with taking an undisclosed quantity of unreported gold dust from the wreck.

The incident touched off a complicated ownership battle between the bank, the Steam Tug Company, and Captain Randall. The court findings awarded 60 percent of the value of the four reported boxes to the salvagers. As salvage master, Captain Randall would receive the largest portion of this sum. The two boxes that had become the center of a criminal case were quietly turned over to Page, Bacon and Company, and the charges against the two divers were dismissed on

January 22, 1855. Four days later charges against Captain Randall were also dismissed.

A BOARD OF INQUIRY convened in San Francisco later that year found that Captain Randall was not responsible for deserting his ship. Many of those who sailed on board the vessel, not surprisingly, regarded these hearings as a whitewash. Adding to the anger of many, Captain Randall continued salvage operations at the site through 1855, and recovered the three remaining boxes of gold shipped on board the *Yankee Blade*. Randall had grown rich on the salvage of the ship he had taken to destruction.

Even more upsetting to many of the survivors was their treatment at the hands of Vanderbilt and his agents. After losing all the money they possessed on the *Yankee Blade,* many of those who returned to San Francisco were penniless. To make matters worse, the San Francisco agents for the Independent Opposition Line, Fretz and Ralston, failed to refund the value of the tickets. Eventually they paid each of the ticket holders 25 percent of the fare, but the remaining money was never returned. Vanderbilt claimed that the Independent Opposition Line had been sold to the Nicaragua Steamship Company, effective September 30, 1854, and therefore he carried no financial responsibility as of October 1. The question of moral responsibility was never addressed.

Did Randall purposefully wreck his ship? Before the incident with the *Yankee Blade*, Randall had a distinguished record as a mariner, and it seems difficult to believe he would have changed his behavior so late in life. Also sailing with him was his son Henry Jr. It is unlikely that he would have taken the young man with him if he intended to wreck the vessel. Yet there is no doubt that the master of the *Yankee Blade* behaved recklessly, putting the lives of his passengers and crew in extreme danger. Had the *Goliah* not come to the rescue when she did, the wreck of the *Yankee Blade* would have been one of the worst disasters on the Pacific Coast.

Whether the ghosts of those who died at Point Arguello haunted the master of the *Yankee Blade* is not known, but it is claimed that Captain Randall spent much of his later years working to increase the safe design of oceangoing vessels. It may have been that all the money he had made from the loss of his own ship could not ease his conscience.

CHAPTER 2

Brother Jonathan: In the Teeth of the Dragon

During his exploration of the western seaboard in 1792, Captain George Vancouver came upon a coastal headland located near present-day Crescent City, California, and named it St. George Point. The half-submerged basalt outcropping extending out from the point is called St. George Reef. Many have felt that the reef was misnamed. The dangerous, rocky ridge that only occasionally breaks the surface of the water reminds mariners more of the mouth of the dragon—the knight's fearsome opponent—than St. George himself. Like the teeth of the mythological creature, this reef has claimed many victims.[1] The greatest tragedy was when the treasure ship *Brother Jonathan* went down on July 30, 1865. A question long asked after her foundering was why the vessel was near the reef in the first place.

By 1865, the years were taking a heavy toll on the gold rush side-wheelers. Aging engines were less able to cope with a rough sea, and in an era when there was no enforced limit on the cargoes a ship could take, vessels frequently wallowed out of port showing only a few feet of freeboard.

The *Brother Jonathan* was a veteran of the West Coast. Built by Perrine, Patterson and Stack of New York City and bought by Edward Mills for his Independent Opposition Line, she was launched on November 2, 1850. At a length of 221 feet with a 36-foot beam, the

1,181-ton vessel was a formidable steamer. From their staterooms, passengers could either enter the spacious interior saloon or exit onto the deck for fresh air.[2]

Not everything on the ship was new, though, for the *Brother Jonathan*'s walking beam engine was salvaged from the steamer *Atlantic*, which had been wrecked after dragging her anchor in Long Island Sound in 1848.[3] Although it would become apparent that it was increasingly inefficient, the same engine served the *Brother Jonathan* throughout her career.

Another difficulty with the *Brother Jonathan* was that she was designed for the relatively tranquil waters of Long Island Sound. Although she was a beautiful-looking vessel, her shallow draft[4] meant that she was open to severe buffeting by the fierce storms on open water.[5]

The potential for acquiring huge profits on the California run during the gold rush, though, convinced Mills to place his ship on the New York–Panama route. After experiencing problems with other independent carriers on the Pacific side of the Isthmus of Panama—lines that were supposed to be coordinating their schedules with his ship were not arriving on time, if at all—Mills decided to sell the *Brother Jonathan* to the shipping tycoon Cornelius Vanderbilt.[6]

Under Vanderbilt's guidance, the vessel was rebuilt. To improve wind assist, a mizzenmast was added. The graceful bowsprit had been removed, the bulwark extended, and a third deck included. To add to profits, the number of berths on the vessel was increased from 350 to 750.[7] On December 31, 1852, the *Brother Jonathan* was sold to the Nicaragua Steamship Company, which sailed her between San Juan del Sur, Nicaragua, on the Pacific Coast, and San Francisco. The vessel continued on that run until 1856, by which time the gold rush was over. The *Brother Jonathan* was subsequently sold to Captain John T. Wright, who put her on the northern run between Puget Sound and San Francisco. By renaming her the *Commodore*, Wright defied an old nautical superstition. Once a ship was christened, it was considered bad luck to change her name. In 1857, the vessel paid her first visit to the British colony of Vancouver Island, where Indians at Fort Victoria were astonished by the size of the steamer.[8]

The next year, news reached San Francisco that gold had been discovered on the Fraser River in British Columbia. On April 25, resi-

Drawing of the *Brother Jonathan.* (Courtesy of New Westminster Public Library)

dents of Victoria were surprised to see the return of the *Commodore,* this time carrying a few hundred eager prospectors.[9] With them were the merchants, land speculators, cardsharps, prostitutes, and brothel keepers that were a part of all major gold rushes.

Transporting California gold seekers to the port of Victoria was a profitable business, but on a return trip to Vancouver Island in July 1858, the *Commodore* was almost lost. She encountered a severe storm and nearly foundered. To prevent the vessel from sinking, she had to turn back to San Francisco while her crew and 350 passengers had to throw the cargo as well as their personal belongings overboard. "On reaching the wharf," according to one newspaper, "the passengers seized on the owner, and with threats of hanging compelled him to return the passage money."[10] Wright sold out to the California Steam Navigation Company in 1861.

In that year the new owners began another refit of the side-wheeler. One deck was removed, rotten planks in the hull were replaced, and a new copper bottom was applied. Two new low-pressure boilers had been installed. (The vessel, though, retained the original eleven-foot-stroke walking beam engine salvaged from the sunken *Atlantic*.) The result seemed impressive. "The boat and all her appointments have an excellent repute among nautical men," noted the *Alta California*.[11]

By now the name of the ship had been changed back to the *Brother Jonathan*. Citizens of San Francisco recalled that in 1854 the *Brother Jonathan* played a role in the safe return of many of the *Yankee Blade* survivors. The name *Commodore,* by contrast, evoked unpleasant memories.

Between 1862 and 1865 the vessel continued to carry passengers and cargo between San Francisco and Victoria, taking a 110-mile side trip to Portland at the junction of the Columbia and Willamette Rivers. The northern route remained profitable, and the money the California Steam Navigation Company spent on her refit seemed a good investment. In the spring of 1865, though, the *Brother Jonathan* collided with a bark on the Columbia River.[12] No outward sign of structural damage was apparent.

CAPTAIN SAMUEL J. DE WOLF, an experienced West Coast sailor, was master of the *Brother Jonathan*. Born in Nova Scotia in 1822, De Wolf had been on the Pacific Coast since 1849. He joined the California Steam Navigation Company in the early 1850s and was master of the coastal vessel *Fremont* before taking over the *Brother Jonathan* in 1862. "As a commander," wrote the *Victoria Daily Chronicle,* "De Wolf was modest, yet capable; brave but not foolhardy; gentlemanly in his manners and considerate towards his passengers; he was a general favorite with travellers."[13]

An often-repeated story described an incident that was supposed to have happened the day before her final departure. To Captain De Wolf's consternation, the acting shipping agent accepted cargo beyond the tonnage the ship could safely carry. When the captain protested, the agent threatened to replace him with another master.[14] Captain De Wolf was reputed to have told a friend about the occurrence shortly before the ship cast off, but the evidence that the incident happened at all is thin. A successful and popular captain like De Wolf could not be easily replaced.[15]

There is no doubt that the ship was loaded beyond her capacity, for the activities of the renegade Confederate raider *Shenandoah,* which apparently did not know the Civil War was over, reduced the number of coastal runs. This created a backlog of cargo in San Francisco and other ports.

Licensed to transport 230 steerage and deck passengers, as well as an unlimited number in the first-class cabins, the *Brother Jonathan* was not overloaded with travelers.[16] The passenger list contained 124 names, but a few late arrivals were not noted on the manifest. She had a crew of 54.

AT 10 A.M. on Friday July 28, 1865, the *Brother Jonathan* cast off from San Francisco's Broadway wharf to begin her voyage north. The passengers included many men and women well known on the West Coast. Most famous of those on board was Brigadier General George Wright. He was born in Vermont in 1822, and had distinguished himself during the Mexican War in 1848. Wright had spent most of the Civil War on the West Coast, away from the bloody battlefields that were the making or undoing of many army officers. Before being replaced by General Irvin McDowell in 1864, Wright had commanded the Department of the Pacific. Orders in July of 1865 had sent General and Mrs. Wright on board the *Brother Jonathan* to Fort Vancouver, where he was to begin his new assignment as commandant of the Columbia District. The Wrights were traveling with the general's aide-de-camp, Lieutenant E. D. Waite, and his wife.

Also journeying to Fort Vancouver was paymaster Major F. W. Eddy, who had joined the army in 1861 and was now probably expecting his release to civilian life. With him was $200,000[17] to pay the troops stationed in the Northwest. Eddy would not have normally been sent to accompany the army payroll to Fort Vancouver, but for some reason he requested the assignment. Even more surprising, the officer had a premonition of the disaster that was to befall him. Not long before he sailed, Eddy told friends he had a feeling the voyage of the *Brother Jonathan* would end tragically. Yet he was prepared to follow fate. Before leaving, he made sure that the government account books were brought up to date, completed and signed his will, and then paid all his outstanding debts.[18]

Another traveler on board the *Brother Jonathan* was editor James Nesbit of the *San Francisco Daily Evening Bulletin.* During time off from the newspaper, Nesbit was taking a four- or five-week tour of Oregon, Washington, and British Columbia.[19] He apparently planned to sell the property he had acquired in the Northwest a few years earlier.

Nesbit was a man of considerable writing talent who regarded the day-to-day routine of the newspaper boring. He was born in Glasgow, Scotland, in 1817 and had studied law, but was drawn toward writing. His first and only novel, *The Siege of Damascus,* was not a success. He traveled extensively before arriving in San Francisco in November 1852, where he joined the staff of the struggling *Dramatic Chronicle.* In 1856, he was offered a job at the *San Francisco Bulletin.* Although he was well liked, even among his newspaper colleagues he had few intimate friends, preferring to keep his own company.

Victor Smith, the former collector of customs for the Puget Sound District, was returning to Washington Territory. Smith was onetime editor of a Cincinnati newspaper, and an influential supporter of Abraham Lincoln during his election campaign. As a reward, in 1861, the president, on the advice of Treasury Secretary Salmon P. Chase, gave Smith the job of customs inspector for the Puget Sound District. Smith's lean, long frame, straw-colored hair, and fair complexion gave him a passing resemblance to a scarecrow. Such an image, though, was misleading, for Smith was anything but harmless. A man of considerable power in the frontier communities, he frequently acted quickly and ruthlessly.

Smith's decision to move the customhouse from Port Townsend, Washington, to Port Angeles, Washington, raised the ire of the citizens of the former community. When the Port Townsend customs records were not given to Smith after his return from the nation's capital in 1862, he became incensed. If they were not handed over in one hour, Smith threatened, he would turn loose on the city the lighthouse tender *Shubrick*'s three small cannons.

Civic leaders had little choice but to comply. However, the customs collector had gone too far, and many influential residents of Washington Territory requested, through Surveyor General Anson G. Henry, that the overbearing official be fired. Lincoln reluctantly agreed—the customs collector had been a loyal supporter—and Smith returned east. His government career, though, was not over. Secretary

Chase promoted him to the position of special federal treasury agent for the Pacific Coast.[20]

In 1865, Smith was on his way back to the Northwest to take over his new duties, but fate had something in store for the person who had made so many enemies. Smith was on the Atlantic side-wheeler *Golden Rule* when she wrecked on Cayos de Roncador, a barren reef off the Nicaraguan coast, stranding 635 people. After rescue, he had spent several weeks in San Francisco recuperating from the disaster before booking passage on the *Brother Jonathan.*

Dr. Henry, the former U.S. surveyor general and longtime enemy of Smith, was on his way north where he was to take up his appointment as governor of Washington Territory. Some have claimed that it was Henry who was responsible for Smith's firing as collector of customs. By a strange circumstance both had taken passage on the same ship.[21]

Mrs. John C. Keenan, late of San Francisco, had returned to that city to bring back seven young women to entertain the customers at Victoria's Music Hall Bar, which was located in the Fashion Hotel–an establishment owned by her husband. It has been claimed that Mrs. Keenan was, until shortly before her trip, a well-known San Francisco madam.[22] Among those in her party were Martha Stott and her young son, and Mina Bernhardt and her baby.

ONCE BEYOND Point Bonita, the steamer met strong headwinds and faced a heavy swell. Never a fast ship, the *Brother Jonathan* was making only a few knots an hour. The vessel was taking a severe pounding as water spilled over her bulwark. For the remaining hours of Friday and all day Saturday she struggled on her northerly course.

About noon on Sunday, the side-wheeler *Sierra Nevada* passed Crescent City, and as was her usual practice, kept a lookout for the *Brother Jonathan.* The ship, though, was not in sight. There was a stiff wind and a light fog toward shore with visibility to about two miles.[23]

On the *Brother Jonathan,* Quartermaster Jacob Yates was on watch and took the wheel at noon with Captain De Wolf beside him. "The sea was running mountain high," Yates recalled, "and the ship was not making any headway."[24] The sun, though, did break briefly through the clouds, allowing Captain De Wolf to calculate his position. They were five miles beyond St. George Point, a rough piece of land that jutted out into the Pacific northwest of Crescent City.

De Wolf continued on his heading for a few more minutes, but it was clear that the ancient walking beam engine was no match for an overburdened ship in a moderate to heavy swell. He realized that his only choice was to turn back and seek shelter at Crescent City. He ordered the helm hard to port. The ship came around well, and then he ordered a southeast course. It was now about 12:45 P.M.

The noon meal had been served, but few passengers were well enough to enjoy it. Most stayed in their berths, seasick. Mrs. Keenan had been too ill to watch over her entertainers; she had remained with the covers pulled up around her all morning. Also in his berth was Third Officer James Patterson. He was off watch and catching up on his sleep.

Beyond St. George Point are the Dragon's Teeth, stretching out about six miles in an arc toward the northwest. The reef formed part of a long-extinct volcano, the rim of which was near the surface of the water. The captain was familiar with St. George Reef, and under other circumstances would not have approached the jagged rocks, but De Wolf had to find shelter as quickly as possible.

No one on board the *Brother Jonathan* saw the danger until it was too late. The haze toward shore restricted visibility, while the rocks themselves were frequently covered in sea spray. Steward David Farrell later described the shipwreck: "She struck very hard, apparently about half way between her stem and foremast. She did not appear to strike her stem, but raised on the swell, and settled directly on the rock. The next sea that struck her carried her as far on to the rock as her foremast. Her bottom was badly torn to pieces and her foremast dropped through until stopped by the yard-arm."[25]

"The captain stopped and backed her," Yates said, "but could not move the vessel an inch. She rolled about five minutes, and then gave a tremendous thump, and part of the keel came up alongside."[26] The first passengers to reach the deck were knocked down as the ship worked her way up onto the rock. Men and women took firm hold of the bulwark. Like a bird impaled on an arrow, the *Brother Jonathan* twisted against the rocky wedge that pierced her belly. The damage, though, had been done, and it was only the sharp pinnacle, which minutes earlier had mortally wounded her, that now kept her above the surface. It would not be long before the forces of wind and water would transform the *Brother Jonathan* into a floating bed of wreckage.

The deck was chaotic, with people rushing about frantically. The almost four hundred cork life preservers that were supposed to be on board were difficult to find by frightened passengers. Martha Stott, one of the entertainers hired by Mrs. Keenan, was standing talking to two men who had acquired life preservers.[27] Yet these devices provided passengers with nothing more than the illusion of safety; they could not prevent death from exposure, the greatest killer at sea. Both men drowned.[28]

Among the confusion, one man sat apart, as if he was personally detached from the human drama swirling about him. Editor James Nesbit was scribbling in a small notebook. He was calmly writing his will and a few final letters to his family.

The first wooden lifeboat got away from the side of the ship, but so many men had crowded onto it that within a dozen yards the craft overturned, spilling everyone into the icy waters. David Farrell recalled his last sighting of the lifeboat: "When we last saw her, there was one man sitting astride of her and she was upside down."[29]

At about this time, Captain De Wolf yelled down from the hurricane deck to David Farrell to put the drainage plugs in the bottom of one of the portside lifeboats, which was still on its davits. The port boat was one of the smaller, iron self-righting types. Farrell later claimed he was ordered to remain with the boat to ensure that the crew did not rush it. The ship's storekeeper, John Hensley, helped by dragging two women to the lifeboat, but they begged to be freed. Hensley released them.

Others passengers were not as reluctant to leave the ship. Martha Stott saw the small craft as the only salvation for her and her child. Also on board the lifeboat was a Mrs. Lee, with her infant child, and Martha E. Wilder, as well as an older woman, Mary Tweedale, who was traveling to the Northwest to visit her son.

On the panorama that was the wreck of the *Brother Jonathan*, an ironic little scene emerged. The wife of General Wright had been persuaded to enter an iron portside lifeboat, but Martha Stott watched as Captain De Wolf came over and escorted her across the deck to a wooden lifeboat under the command of Second Officer J. D. Campbell.

Since the starboard was on the lee side, he probably felt that this boat had a better chance of surviving the waves. Also a longtime seaman—he had been a sailor since he was sixteen years old—De Wolf may not have trusted the iron design of the port boats. They had none of the beauty of wood and were unwieldy and heavy.

First Officer W. A. H. Allen began loading Campbell's boat with female passengers, one of whom apparently was Mrs. Keenan, who had managed to stumble from her berth onto the deck. Allen began lowering the boat, but before it was clear of the davits the craft's bow struck the *Brother Jonathan*. In moments the little boat was smashed and survivors were being pulled back on board. Captain De Wolf's effort to save the wife of an important figure cost the woman her life. Mrs. Wright was pulled from the water onto the deck,[30] but the ship had only a few minutes remaining.

When last seen, General Wright was standing on the deck, a life preserver in his hands. Martha Stott saw Mrs. Keenan, wearing two life preservers, struggling in the water. Someone later claimed that she was stunned when something struck her on the head.[31]

Third Officer James Patterson was in charge of David Farrell's boat, which contained four women and three children. As the boat was lowered, they noticed Mina Bernhardt with her baby around her neck, attempting to climb into the boat as it passed the main deck. A member of the crew leaned forward, grabbed the mother, and pulled her and her child into the boat.

At the moment the launch hit the water, the *Brother Jonathan* suddenly rolled in the boat's direction, and the craft was almost crushed. As it was, the port thole pins (oar crutches) were lost and the lifeboat was more difficult to control. Because they were on the windward side of the ship, it was necessary to maneuver around her stern. As Farrell recalled: "We started immediately for shore. We were running quartering with the waves, which broke over us on nearly every crest, at times nearly filling the boat, and had it not been for the [fire bucket they had been given by John Hensley], there would probably never been a soul saved to give tidings of the terrible disaster."[32]

As he and the other survivors made for shore, Farrell watched the *Brother Jonathan* fire two cannon shots. Although the distress signal was hanging from the mizzenmast, it was apparently seen by no one on shore, and the sound, although heard, was thought to be only a conventional signal sent by a passing ship.[33]

Farrell did not see the death of the *Brother Jonathan*, but it no doubt came quickly: "We were again let down into she [*sic*] trough of the sea, and when we came up again, the ship had entirely disappeared. I think the waves drove her over the rocks and that she went down stem first."[34] After striking the reef at 1:30 P.M., the *Brother Jonathan* was probably gone in forty-five minutes.

It was only when the lifeboat with its occupants touched shore at Chetco Harbor, Oregon, about 5 P.M., and the survivors walked eight miles to Crescent City, that the residents of that community were aware of the disaster.[35] About 8 P.M., a fleet of small boats was sent to St. George Reef, but returned with no survivors. The U.S. Army's Camp Lincoln, six miles inland from Crescent City, was notified and soldiers were sent to search the beaches for bodies.

At 10 P.M. on August 1, a soldier from Camp Lincoln rode up to the closest telegraph office, which was at Jacksonville, Oregon, with the news of the disaster. When the story reached San Francisco, it received front-page coverage, but given the remote location where the *Brother Jonathan* went down, details of the disaster were lacking. Jacksonville, more than a hundred miles northeast of the wreck site, was a long and difficult journey by horse, so the outside world was slow to receive news. In his dispatch dated July 31, Camp Lincoln's commander, Thomas Buckley, sent only a brief message: "At 2 P.M., yesterday, the steamer *Brother Jonathan* struck a sunken rock, and sunk in less than an hour, with all on board, except 16 persons, who escaped in a small boat, the only survivors of the ill-fated ship. No trace of the vessel is left."[36]

Only the next day did the names of the survivors appear in the press. The California Steam Navigation Company released a list of passengers,[37] but many people boarded at the last minute, making the manifest incomplete.

"Our citizens are again called upon to mourn the wreck of one of our coast steamers with the probable loss of nearly all on board," the

San Francisco Bulletin observed.[38] Flags over the city flew at half-mast as news of the disaster spread throughout the community. With the Civil War not long over, and the exploits of the Confederate cruiser *Shenandoah* against Union ships still continuing, the *San Francisco Alta California* regretted "that not a Government vessel of any description is now here, except the revenue cutter *Joe Lane*, either to protect our commerce or render assistance. . . ."[39] Ironically, one of the passengers to lose his life on the *Brother Jonathan* was Captain John Chaddock, who was formerly the master of the *Joe Lane*.

Mrs. Keenan did not survive, but two of the entertainers she had hired did. Martha Stott and Mina Bernhardt, together with their children, had made it to shore. Without her, Mrs. Keenan's husband John had little interest in the Fashion Hotel. Within a month he had leased it to two Victoria entrepreneurs.

San Francisco merchant James R. Richards had taken the *Brother Jonathan* to meet his wife in Victoria, where she had arrived from Honolulu on board one of his company's sailing vessels.[40] However, he did not pass beyond the Dragon's Teeth.

Captain A. C. Brooks had arrived at Portland from Hawaii. He was master of the bark *Cambridge,* which sat at anchor awaiting his wife, who was traveling on board the *Brother Jonathan*. The couple looked forward to sailing the islands of Hawaii aboard his ship. From Portland to Victoria, there were many more friends and relatives who would be waiting in vain for the arrival of the vessel.

Gradually the dead began to return. James Nesbit's body, with the notebook containing his will tied to his clothes, was found floating seven miles out to sea. Of the perhaps 170 lives lost, according to one estimate, fewer than 75 bodies washed ashore.[41]

The remains of General Wright and his wife were identified, but many bodies were not. The action of the water against the rocks removed clothing and scraped away features so that it was impossible to recognize the victims. Further, in this remote location, the victims were subject to predation by animals.

IT WILL NEVER be known whether the shipping agent played a role in the sinking of the *Brother Jonathan* or whether such a charge was constructed by Captain De Wolf's friends to divert blame from the ship's master. As Third Officer James Patterson pushed his boat away from the side of the ship, the officer claimed that Captain De Wolf yelled, "Tell them that if they had not overloaded us we would have got through all right, and this would never have happened."[42] No one else on board the boat, though, apparently heard the captain's last words. It is also difficult to believe that the captain would have considered this grievance in the face of more immediate concerns, such as the survival of his passengers and crew.

St. George Reef was not one of the sixteen lighthouses originally approved by Congress for the Pacific Coast in 1852. Few mariners disagreed, though, that such a warning beacon was necessary to prevent more disasters like the *Brother Jonathan*. Even the highest of the rocky promontories of St. George Reef was underwater during the worst winter storms. It was not until 1883 that work actually began on a lighthouse. A massive concrete foundation and imposing granite tower rising 134 feet above its base made the station the most expensive lighthouse ever built in the United States. It was completed in 1891, and remained operational until 1975.[43]

FROM ALMOST THE DAY the vessel struck the reef, the ship has captured the interest of treasure hunters. "The *Brother Jonathan* had a considerable sum of money on board to be used to pay the troops in the Northwest," E. W. Wright noted in 1895, "and from this fact have sprung a great number of wild tales of fabulous wealth supposed to have gone to the bottom with the vessel."[44] By then, many attempts had already been made to rescue the ship's precious cargo of gold. In 1933, a local fisherman snagged a twisted piece of wreckage that had once been a lifeboat. Under the seat, in a deteriorating case, were eleven bars of gold.[45]

In 1993, Deep Sea Research Incorporated located the wreck near Jonathan Rock, a basalt pinnacle of St. George Reef that has been named after the doomed ship. Not surprisingly, the California State Lands Commission, which has jurisdiction over the coastal waters, soon raised questions concerning the ownership of the *Brother Jonathan*. The protracted court case between the state and the salvors has been recently settled, with the California State Lands Commission acquiring 20 percent of the treasure and all the artifacts. The remainder of the valuables, including jewelry, became the property of Deep Sea Research. By April 1999, approximately a thousand gold coins had been found.[46]

With so much attention given to the wealth on board the *Brother Jonathan,* it is easy to forget that many people perished. In terms of the numbers, the shipwreck was the third worst sea disaster on the West Coast. Many of the bodies were buried at Crescent City, the safe haven that Captain De Wolf never reached on that stormy summer day in 1865.

CHAPTER 3

Pacific: The Final Whistle

While the polished brass fixtures and fresh paint may have impressed those people who boarded the old side-wheeler, the *Pacific* was an unseaworthy vessel that should never have been permitted to ply the waters of the North Pacific. A minor collision with the square-rigger *Orpheus* about eighty miles south of Cape Flattery, Washington, on November 4, 1875, was a major catastrophe. The *Pacific* sank in under an hour, taking with her an estimated 260 to 300 souls. It remains the worst sea disaster on the Pacific Coast of the continental United States.

To a large extent, the press of the day seemed inured to the corruption going on around them. Following the disaster, newspapers professed shock and bewilderment that such a stout ship had gone down. "The vessel has been considered one of the very best sea-boats on the coast," wrote the *San Francisco Chronicle*.[1] According to the *San Francisco Alta California*, she had only recently been in dry dock, "where she was examined and found to be as sound and staunch as a new boat."[2] The same sentiments were echoed by the *Olympia Standard,* which wrote, "The *Pacific* was an old vessel . . . but was deemed entirely seaworthy. . . ."[3] Nothing was further from the truth.

LIKE THE *Yankee Blade* and the *Brother Jonathan,* the *Pacific* was part of the California gold rush fleet. Built in New York in 1850, the vessel was sold almost immediately to the fast-expanding United States Mail Steamship Company. Her ten-foot-stroke walking beam engine made her one of the fastest steam vessels in the Americas. On her first voyage south, she broke the record for the greatest distance covered in a twenty-four-hour period.[4]

Early drawing of the *Pacific*. (Courtesy of New Westminster Public Library)

She had, however, a major shortcoming. The *Pacific* was only 876 tons and 225 feet long with a width of 30 feet. In 1851, she was sold to Cornelius Vanderbilt and placed on the San Francisco–San Juan, Nicaragua, route. Over the next eleven years the *Pacific* changed owners many times. In 1872, the Pacific Mail Steamship Company acquired her for service between San Diego and Mexico.[5] As the company knew, it was the owner of a fleet of rapidly aging ships that were expensive to maintain and operate. The *Pacific*—now the oldest steamship in service—was soon consigned with other ancient vessels to the San Francisco mudflats.[6] In a time of rapidly changing marine technology, the *Pacific* had become a relic from a bygone era.

The vessel would have probably remained rotting in the company scrap yard if a gold rush in the Cassiar District of northern British Columbia had not placed a new value on all steamships capable of carrying passengers and cargo. The *Pacific* and three other ships in the Pacific Mail's fleet were purchased by a new company, Goodall, Nelson and Perkins of San Francisco, in 1874, and plans were made to ready her for the Northwest route. Later, it was claimed that the company spent $40,000 rebuilding the *Pacific*.[7] In the 1870s this was a considerable sum.

• • •

THE *Pacific* left San Francisco on October 26, 1875. After an uneventful trip, the vessel entered Victoria harbor on the morning of October 30, where she discharged her passengers and 185 tons of cargo. The *Pacific* then steamed south as far as Tacoma, where she loaded 2,000 sacks of oats, 128 bales of hops, 18 casks of tallow, as well as assorted dried hides and buckskin.[8]

She took on board more than thirty-five passengers from Puget Sound ports, including prominent Steilacoom merchant J. T. Vining, who was to oversee the sale of his consignment of hops. Another passenger, E. L. Hastings of the San Francisco wholesale liquor firm of Crane, Hastings and Company, was on a business trip to the area and had telegraphed his wife that he would be sailing on the *Pacific*. Also traveling south were six members of the Rockwell and Hurlbert equestrian troupe, which had been performing in Seattle. With them were their six trained horses and two dogs. The troupe was on its way to its winter headquarters in Binghamton, New York. Returning as far as San Francisco was the troupe's advance agent, thirty-eight-year-old J. D. Crowley.

On her return journey to Victoria, the *Pacific* anchored off shore at Port Townsend while a small steamer carrying sacks of oats pulled alongside. In all, it took the vessel three trips to transport the cargo to the other ship and the *Pacific*'s crew more than sixteen hours to stow the sacks below deck.[9]

She reached Victoria about 7:30 A.M. on November 4, and took on board coal that was stowed below and a quantity of potatoes, some of which were lashed in their sacks to the deck. In addition, she took on some hides, two cases of opium, six horses, and two buggies.[10] The sky had taken on a leaden appearance and rain was falling lightly.

David Higgins, editor of the *Victoria Daily British Colonist,* who had last-minute business to conduct with advance agent J. D. Crowley, had come down to the E. Engelhardt and Company wharf where the *Pacific* was moored. Many of her passengers were already on board. The weather had brought an end to mining activity in the Cassiar area, and hundreds of people were streaming into the city. In his memoirs, Higgins recalled, "I found the boat so crowded that the crew could scarcely move about the decks in the discharge of their duties."[11]

Many late arrivals were American prospectors returning to their homes in California and elsewhere. For Francis Garesche, private banker and agent for the Wells Fargo Company, the journey was business. Wells Fargo was shipping nearly $100,000 in gold to San Francisco. Although working in Victoria where he had recently completed a new office building, Garesche maintained his home in California. Two men who made their fortune in the north were Richard Lyons and Dennis Cain, the discoverers of the Cassiar goldfields. They had booked a first-class cabin on board the ship. Also taking the voyage south was J. H. Sullivan, the gold commissioner for the Cassiar district, who had taken a leave of absence to visit his aging mother in Ireland. He planned to take the train from California to New York, where he had booked passage on a transatlantic steamer. A large man with dark hair and an outgoing nature, Sullivan knew the names of many of the miners and prospectors traveling south.

Captain Otis Parsons, who had arrived from San Francisco in 1858 with little more than the shirt on his back, had profited from the British Columbia gold rush. Realizing there was more money to be made carrying passengers and freight than panning for gold, Parsons made his fortune in the transportation business. After selling his interest in a river steamer for $40,000, he booked passage on the *Dakota,* which was to sail to San Francisco the day before the *Pacific.* When he discovered that his old friends Sullivan and Garesche were taking the later ship, he decided to stay an extra day and travel with them. Before he left Victoria, Parsons telegraphed the Cosmopolitan Hotel in San Francisco to make reservations for himself, his wife, Jennie, and their eighteen-month-old son. Also traveling to California were Jennie's sister Alicia, her brother Cal, and her sister-in-law, Belle Mandeville. Members of the family were well-known entertainers on the West Coast; Parsons had met and married Jennie while she was on tour in British Columbia.

Elizabeth Moote, daughter of James E. McMillan, the editor of the *Victoria Daily Standard,* was on her way back to her husband in San Francisco. She had attended the christening of her nephew in Victoria. Other passengers were simply tourists and knew no one in the area. San Franciscans Lizzie Keller, her husband, and their child were on an excursion through the Northwest that ended in Victoria. They had spent the previous evening in a local boardinghouse before taking passage home.

Cabin passenger Thomas J. Ferrell was visiting several old friends in Victoria. Ferrell, who had been born in Australia but had spent most of his life on the West Coast, was in his mid-twenties, of slight build and fair complexion. He made his home in San Francisco, where he worked in a bag factory. His friend, J. P. Miller of Victoria, had come down to the wharf that morning. The last glimpse he had of Ferrell was about fifteen minutes before departure. Ferrell was standing in the crowd on the hurricane deck.[12]

On his way to California on a business trip was Sewell P. Moody, a native New Englander who was now the principal owner of a large British Columbia sawmill. Moody had a reputation as a kind and generous employer. He had funded the construction of a library for his nearly one hundred employees and their families and donated a large sum for the purchase of books.

Another first-class passenger was Henry F. Jelly, a civil engineer who had spent the summer with the survey crew working on the British Columbia portion of the new Canadian Pacific rail line. He was short and thin with dark hair parted down the middle in what was then the popular style. Although twenty-two years old, and having moved to Canada from his native Ireland nine years earlier, Jelly still retained his brogue. The journey on the *Pacific* was the first leg in his return trip to his home near London, Ontario. Before the first transcontinental passenger trains began service on the Canadian Pacific Railway (CPR) in 1886, the only practical route was through the United States. Jelly was traveling with his friend A. Fraser, who also came from the same Ontario town.[13]

For some passengers, the journey was an opportunity to see loved ones separated by almost a thousand miles. Fannie Palmer planned to visit her two sisters who had married and moved to California. Her father, Digby Palmer, had arrived in Victoria in 1862 to teach music. His wife, Jane, taught dance, and together the couple held an exalted place in the city's cultural circles. Fannie, their youngest daughter, was a popular young woman. On the day of her departure, many admirers came to the wharf to see her off.[14]

Samuel Thomas Styles, a partner in the contracting firm of Kinsman and Styles, which operated a stone quarry on Newcastle Island near Nanaimo, British Columbia, had also planned to go to San Francisco.

Newcastle stone had an excellent reputation among builders and had been used in the construction of the U.S. Mint at San Francisco.[15] Styles, like many other travelers, would be looking forward to escaping the rainy tedium of late fall in Victoria.

There were a number of ships on the San Francisco–Victoria run and it was difficult to choose a favorite. Like many other residents of the city, Styles was likely impressed by the *Pacific*'s fresh paint and the officers' blue uniforms with brass badges reading "GN&P" attached to their caps. Obviously, these trappings were intended to inspire confidence in the minds of travelers. A new coat of paint, though, told a passenger nothing about the soundness of the vessel.

At the beginning of November, Styles had stopped by the office of E. Engelhardt and Company, Goodall, Nelson and Perkins Steamship Company's Victoria agent, to learn the cost of cabin fare. He was told that a first-class ticket was $10, an amount he regarded as fair. When he discussed the plans for his journey with his wife that evening, she persuaded him to let her go in his place and to take their son. Styles agreed to the delay, planning to take a later vessel and meet his family in San Francisco. He went back to the agent's office the next day, but was told the price had gone up to $15. When he asked why, Engelhardt replied that the cabins were almost all booked, but that he could probably find room for Mrs. Styles and her child. Suspicious, Styles asked if there were restrictions on the number of passengers the *Pacific* was permitted to carry. Engelhardt answered that there were no regulations and that he could book as many people as he wished. Not wanting to disappoint his wife, Styles went ahead and purchased the tickets.[16]

Engelhardt's claim that he could load the ship as he wished was not entirely true. The vessel's inspection certificate, of which the agent was supposed to keep a copy, stated the number of passengers the ship was permitted to carry. Because the *Pacific* was an American ship, he was not legally required to ensure that she met these capacity limits, yet on her return voyage, the vessel would be traveling through American waters and be subject to the requirements of the inspection certificate. When the ship arrived at San Francisco, the regulations were not enforced. Englehardt, otherwise, would not have maintained such a cavalier attitude toward American law. He would testify before the Victoria inquest that he lost his copy of the certificate and was unfamiliar with the contents of the document.[17]

The ship had berths for 115 passengers in cabins and 88 in steerage, along with its complement of 50 crew members, making a total of 253 people. The cabins, though, were overbooked, with many first-class passengers sleeping on the floor. (Last-minute arrivals that had not yet bought tickets simply jumped on the ship as she was pulling away from the wharf.)

At 9:30 A.M. on November 4, 1875, the *Pacific* wallowed slowly out of Victoria harbor, her decks crowded with passengers. While she was still in the harbor, the crew observed that the vessel heeled to starboard, and they set about trimming the ship by moving sacks of potatoes to the port side. By the time she reached the harbor entrance the "list" had not been corrected.[18] The crew on board a harbor dredge also observed the incline of her decks. She steered so poorly that one of the dredgers remarked that something must be wrong with the steamer.

David Higgins had walked up from the waterfront when he saw Jane Palmer, Fannie's mother, gazing at the *Pacific* as she steamed out of the harbor. "I'm seeing the last of Fannie!" her mother said.[19] Her words were indeed prophetic.

At the *Pacific's* wheel was her master Jefferson D. Howell, a native of Natchez, Mississippi, who was revered in some quarters as the brother-in-law of the South's Jefferson Davis. Howell had been a midshipman in the Confederate navy. He had been on other West Coast vessels about nine years, but had been the captain of the *Pacific* less than a dozen weeks. Some months earlier he had been an officer on board the Goodall, Nelson and Perkins steamer *Los Angeles* when she had run aground off Tillamook Head, Oregon, and at great personal risk had managed to reach land and bring rescuers from the city of Astoria. (The *Los Angeles* was later refloated.) Howell was given command of the *Pacific* as a reward for his heroism. Well liked by his crew, Howell, at thirty-four, would have been looking forward to a long and distinguished career at sea.

As FAR AS passenger Henry Jelly was concerned, there was something seriously wrong. The ship was unstable, tending to heel to one side or the other. Later the crew would ask the passengers to move to one side of the vessel, to help keep her trim. The deckhands also took a

Captain Jefferson D.
Howell of the *Pacific*.
(Courtesy of New Westminster
Public Library)

questionable action to keep the ship on an even keel. Jelly recalled
later:

> As we were about four or five miles out of the harbor, they com-
> menced to put water into the [lifeboats] to keep the vessel steady.
> The first water was put in the boat on the port side; the boat was
> swung in on the davits; the vessel was listing to the starboard, when
> they put the water in the boat. She kept steady for a while, and
> then listed over to the port side; [I] saw one of the officers pull the
> plug out of the boat on the port side to let the water run out; and
> put the hose in the boats on the opposite side, one forward of the
> paddle box and one abaft; this kept the vessel even for a while;
> it is my opinion this changing was of all along.[20]

Jelly said that the vessel would never reach San Francisco.

Gold commissioner J. H. Sullivan wrote in his diary, "Passed Cape
Flattery about 4 P.M. Some of the miners drunk; some ladies sick."[21]

Beyond Tatoosh Island the wind had freshened from the south. As evening fell, the lights on the ship were all that broke the blackness of the night.

Quartermaster Neil Henley took the wheel at 6 P.M. and continued on a south-southwest course. A twenty-one-year-old Scot, Henley was one of four quartermasters. Captain Howell, Henley recalled later at the inquest, came to the wheelhouse briefly, but he did not order a change in course or speed. (Signals were passed from the wheelhouse to the engine room by a primitive bell system.) Henley saw no lights in the distance at any time. For him and the second officer, A. Wells, it had been a routine watch. They remained at their posts until 8 P.M., when J. M. Lewis, the third officer, and another helmsman relieved them.

As Henley left the wheelhouse, he instinctively checked the ship's running lights to make sure they were lit. The port and starboard sidelights mounted on the paddle boxes marked the borders of the night, as did the lamp high on the mainmast. The sails remained furled to their yards. A few passengers remained on deck in the lee of the wheelhouse, seemingly enjoying the cold sea air. A dozen men could undoubtedly be found in the saloon where a steward tended bar, but almost everyone on board had retired early, lulled to sleep by the throbbing of the ancient walking beam engine. Henley went below to his bunk in the forecastle. He noted few empty beds except for those on watch. The seamen had worked a twelve-hour day, from 6 A.M. to 6 P.M., which had included stowing the cargo taken on at Victoria. Henley, too, was tired and he was soon asleep.[22]

SAILING IN THE opposite direction, off the Washington coast, was Captain Charles A. Sawyer of the square-rigger *Orpheus.* His ship was in ballast, bound for the coal-mining town of Nanaimo, British Columbia, where she was to pick up a cargo. Sawyer's 1,100-ton vessel was built on the Atlantic Coast in 1856 and had sailed around Cape Horn to San Francisco.[23] Unlike the *Pacific,* the *Orpheus* was a stout ship. Captain Sawyer had part ownership in the vessel and therefore had an interest in keeping her well maintained. In personality, the master of the *Orpheus* was the opposite of the sociable Jefferson D. Howell. Sawyer was an austere individual who took pains to distance himself from his officers and crew.

Captain Charles A. Sawyer of the *Orpheus*. (Courtesy of New Westminster Public Library)

The freshening wind from the south had meant that the *Orpheus* was making good time hugging close to shore. Although he had sailed these waters before, the captain was still uncomfortable being this far north. By dead reckoning, he estimated his position as not far off the Cape Flattery Lighthouse at the entrance to the Strait of Juan de Fuca. A master had to be particularly careful, for to miss the beacon could mean destruction on the rocks of Vancouver Island. It was raining now, and Sawyer, together with six or seven members of his crew, stood on the deck in their oilskins peering into the darkness.

About 9:30 P.M., Sawyer turned the vessel over to Second Officer James G. Allen with orders that if a light was seen, he was to take the ship toward port and away from the coast. (Allen, coincidentally, had been first officer on the *Pacific* some time earlier.) Sawyer had gone to his cabin and was studying the charts when he heard the second officer order a change in course: "I immediately went on deck and asked the officer what was the matter, and he said there was a light on the port bow; said it was Flattery light. I told him it was impossible to have Flattery light on that bow, and just then I saw the light on the starboard bow."[24] According to Sawyer, Allen's order had put the square-rigger directly across the path of an oncoming vessel. Sawyer watched the approaching side-wheeler through his glass, expecting her captain to order a change in course.

From out of the darkness the lights on board the approaching vessel were clearly visible. The watch on the side-wheeler must have been asleep, for the ship kept coming, her bow pointed a little forward of the *Orpheus*'s starboard beam. Just before she struck, the *Pacific* gave one blast on her whistle.[25] The blow was a comparatively light glancing one, which resulted in the vessels swinging around and striking each other side-on. Much of the *Orpheus*'s rigging and her rail on the starboard side were carried away.

As the two ships passed each other, Sawyer claimed he hailed the side-wheeler and asked her to stand by, but the steamer didn't reply. Then, believing the *Orpheus* was in danger, he turned his attention to his own ship. When it was obvious that his vessel was not sinking he did not turn back to ensure the other ship was uninjured. This single act was to cost many lives. The next day, a large piece of the *Pacific*'s bow was discovered hung up in the rigging of the *Orpheus*.[26]

HENRY JELLY had retired to his cabin on the starboard side about seven o'clock. "While I was in the cabin in bed, I heard a crash," Jelly recalled, "and felt a shock as if we had struck a rock or something of the kind, and heard something fall, as if a lot of rocks had broken into and fallen in her starboard bow."[27] Jelly immediately heard the engine room bell ring once, which signaled a full stop, followed by the signal to reverse the paddles.

He quickly rushed on deck, where he heard reassuring voices saying, "It is all right: we have only struck a vessel."[28] Looking off the starboard beam, Jelly saw three navigation lights already some distance away. With the impression that the damage was only slight, he went back to his cabin and was about to retire when he noticed the ship was listing far to port. Even more disturbing was the sound of rushing water coming from below. He quickly returned to the deck, where he heard one of the crew say, "She is making water very fast forward."[29]

Jelly went forward, where he saw the captain coming out of his cabin directly behind the pilothouse. He approached Captain Howell and asked him if there were any blue signaling flares that could be lit. "He told me I would find blue-lights in the pilot-house," Jelly recalled. He went into the pilothouse and, to his surprise, found one of the passengers was steering the vessel. He asked Jelly what was the course for shore. After searching the pilothouse, Jelly said, "[we] found six blue-lights and set five of them off, losing the other one."[30]

QUARTERMASTER NEIL HENLEY was awakened by a crash. Although enough to bring him to consciousness, the noise was not very loud. His mattress was about twenty-four feet from the stem of the ship, and there were two rows of bunks between him and the bow. In seconds water was rushing into the forecastle. He and the men around him scrambled to put on their clothes. Grabbing his jacket, he hurried up the companionway as water washed over the floor of the crew's quarters. When Henley arrived on deck the scene was chaotic, with the passengers running back and forth wildly. None of them had been told what to do or where to go. Some of those on deck were only half dressed, many without shirts or even shoes.

When Henley reached the pilothouse he heard Captain Howell order, "Hard a starboard!"[31] The captain had obviously been in his bunk, for he was dressed only in his underwear. The engines were still turning, but moments later a stoker came on deck and told the captain the fires were out. By now several distress flares had been launched, but no ship answered their signal.

HENRY JELLY heard the purser ask the captain to which lifeboat he should go, but in the din he did not know what the captain said. The crew, it was later revealed, had never been assigned lifeboat stations nor drilled in how to launch the craft. Some passengers crowded around the five lifeboats, while others wandered around aimlessly. About forty Chinese passengers traveling steerage stood under the ship's funnel at the spot to which they had hauled their baggage. They huddled together, talking excitedly.

Jelly went to the starboard longboat, which was forward of the paddle box, where a group of men were attempting to launch it. Someone said that two of the smaller metal boats abaft the side-wheel boxes had been launched successfully, but he didn't know whether this was true. It was later discovered that the boats had been lashed to their davits, which prevented them from being lowered quickly. No trace of these smaller metal boats was ever found.

Giving up on the starboard longboat, Jelly made his way to the portside craft, which was under the command of H. F. Houston, the chief engineer. With Houston were T. H. Bigley, the freight clerk; O. Hyte, the purser; Neil Henley, the quartermaster; and a steward. Although hung from davits, the port longboat rested on the deck and had filled with passengers before it could be swung over the side. As the angle of the decks increased, it was becoming difficult to swing the port longboat over the side. The chief engineer was attempting to fill the boat with women and sailors to handle the oars. Some of the male passengers tried to get in, but the crew, who made it clear that they were there to row the women, removed them.

A number of women crowded around the craft. Jennie Parsons was weeping, as was her sister Alicia. Mrs. Parsons's little son had been crushed to death when the ship suddenly rolled and a large man had fallen on him. According to Jelly's description, Fannie Palmer, the young Victoria woman, was also there. The ship was sinking so quickly that Fannie had not had time to dress and had slipped her waterproof cloak over her nightdress. As the women stepped on board the lifeboat, they found their feet and legs immersed in water—apparently the craft was partially filled with the water used for trimming the ship.

By some means Jelly secured a place in the longboat, but none of the crew seemed to know how to release the boat from its complicated tackle. However, as the ship settled, the boat eventually swung free and someone took an ax and cut away the falls. Given an opportunity, a number of men who had crowded around now jumped on board.

The crew had rowed only a boat length away from the *Pacific* when the overcrowded launch began to capsize. Jelly went under with the boat. A minute or two later he came up beside the overturned launch. With some effort he and four other men succeeded in climbing on top of the boat, while Houston, the engineer, was able to clamber back on board the *Pacific*. Many of the women who had been in the boat were weighed down by the layers of their Victorian clothing. Before they came to the surface, their lungs had filled with water.

The *Pacific* was now on the edge of extinction. From his place on the overturned boat, Jelly watched the vessel's funnel break loose and tumble into the sea. With her bow down and listing heavily to port, she seemed to lurch several times, and then split in two with her super-structure separating from the hull. There was a tremendous explosion of compressed air, then both sections disappeared underwater. Those passengers standing amidships who had escaped the crush of the ship's funnel were sucked down with the *Pacific*. Others swam desperately to avoid the undertow. Some of those in the water were able to grab onto pieces of the ship that had floated free.

NEIL HENLEY was also on Jelly's lifeboat. Before the launch had rolled over, Henley jumped clear and into the cold water. By now the hull of the ship was gone and only fragments of the upper works remained. For about ten minutes after the sinking of the *Pacific,* the air was filled with agonized cries. Then the voices fell silent. The survivors, huddled on pieces of wreckage, were unable to see into the darkness. Each felt the bite of the November wind and the slap of the rising sea. Henley swam until he found the skylight that had broken free when the ship went down. It was fragile protection from the wash of the waves, and to make matters worse, the waves were rising.

IN THE STARLESS NIGHT, Jelly and his companions rode precariously atop the longboat until another piece of wreckage drifted by. It was the top of the pilothouse. He and another man swam over to it and hung on. His fellow traveler had obviously spent some time in the water. He told of being sucked down many fathoms and when he opened his eyes, he saw hundreds of bodies suspended lifeless in the depths. From Jelly's description, the man was probably Frank McCormick, who spent the year prospecting in the Cassiar District. Despite his terrible ordeal, the man retained his sense of humor and did much to buoy up his companion's spirits.

That first night clinging to the pilothouse was the longest Jelly had ever spent. "Next morning I got some life-preservers floating near the house, and with their ropes lashed myself and my comrade on to the house."[32] During the next day, Jelly saw a few pieces of wreckage carrying human passengers. Jelly and his companion were constantly exposed to the wash of the high seas and about 4 P.M. the man died. Jelly cut the body loose.

Not long after the man's death, Jelly saw a vessel passing. He heard the sound of voices in the darkness. He attempted to hail the crew, but she sailed on into the night. At eight o'clock the next morning the ship *Messenger,* out of San Francisco, saw Jelly still lashed to the top of the pilothouse, where he had been for almost thirty-six hours. He was suffering from exposure and, as a result of his attempts to stay on the raft, his legs were severely lacerated. The ship sent out her own boats to search the area where he was found, but discovered no one else.

AFTER THE *Pacific* went down, Neil Henley clung to the skylight until he was able to see another piece of debris, which was the part of the hurricane deck that had once supported the pilothouse. It already carried seven people, including the captain, the second officer, a cook, and four passengers, one of whom was a woman. The disaster apparently had shocked most of the small band of survivors into silence. The captain did say they were fifteen or twenty miles from land. Their makeshift craft, though, was at the mercy of wind and wave. There was nothing anyone could do but to hold on and hope for rescue. Henley was able to sit on the raft with his feet dangling in the water, but his hold was precarious and the weather was deteriorating rapidly. "At 1 A.M. the sea was making a clean breach over the raft. At 4 A.M. a heavy sea washed over us, carrying away the captain, second officer, the lady and another passenger, leaving four of us on the raft. At 9 A.M. the cook died and rolled off into the sea."[33]

With the coming of daylight, the thick weather obscured any sight of land, but by late afternoon the mist had lifted enough for a glimpse of the coast some miles away. They also saw another piece of wreckage holding two men. There was no sign of a rescue ship, though, and the wind and waves were continuing to take their toll. "At 5 P.M. another man expired," Henley recalled, "and early the next morning the other one died, leaving me alone."[34]

Sometime later Henley managed to snag a box that floated by. Using it as a windbreak, it allowed him to sleep a few hours. Early on the morning of the fourth day after the sinking, the U.S. revenue cutter *Oliver Wolcott* found what was left of the hurricane deck with its one survivor.

THE FIRST WORD of the disaster came with the arrival of the *Messenger* at Port Townsend, Washington Territory, on Sunday, November 7, with Henry Jelly on board. In the cities along the coast, the news was met with shock and disbelief. Wrote the *Victoria Daily British Colonist:* "The catastrophe is so far-reaching that scarcely a household in Victoria but has lost one or more of its members. . . ."[35] The *San Francisco Chronicle* observed, "The truth of the old saying that 'he who sets sail invests in a lottery' seems to be abundantly proven by the fate of the 200 souls who so suddenly stepped from the staunch deck of the steamer *Pacific* into an awful eternity."[36]

In ports along the West Coast, worried relatives and friends of anyone thought to have sailed on the *Pacific* crowded the offices of Goodall, Nelson and Perkins and its agents. When a list of the victims on board the *Pacific* was posted at the San Francisco Merchants' Exchange, a crowd gathered. While the list of those traveling first-class was generally accurate, no manifest for the steerage passengers was complete, for many had caught the ship moments before it cast off from the wharf. Yet there was still hope, for it seemed impossible that such a fine-looking vessel could take everyone, or almost everyone, to his or her death.

THE IRON-HULLED side-wheeler *Gussie Telfair* had likely been spotted before she passed the narrow entrance to Victoria harbor, for when the ship tied up on the evening of November 10, a crowd had already gathered. The vessel ran a regular route between Portland and other Northwest ports. Her captain and crew had interrupted their regular run to search the seas off Cape Flattery for more survivors.[37]

"We've got two men and a woman, dead, and no one else," said a deckhand.[38]

Not waiting for the lines to be made fast, men and women hastened over the gunwale and were led back to where three tarpaulin-covered forms were laid out on the deck. A member of the crew carrying a lantern leaned forward and drew off the rough shrouds. His light revealed two middle-aged men and a young woman, about twenty-five years old with fair hair. At first there was not a murmur as the crowd took in the faces. After a few moments a man came forward.

"That lady slept at my house, and with her husband and child on Thursday morning last, sailed in the *Pacific* for San Francisco."[39] After his short speech, there was little to add and the crowd drifted away silently. The body was that of Lizzie Keller of San Francisco. The remains of her husband and child were never found. One of the other victims was J. T. Vining of Steilacoom, Washington Territory, who left a wife and eight children. The third body was that of an unidentified crew member.

On November 5, the *Orpheus* also came to an unfortunate end. She ran aground on Tzartus Island in Barkley Sound. The reason apparently had been that since the square-rigger's last visit to the Northwest, the Canadians had added a lighthouse at Cape Beale, Vancouver Island, which Second Officer Allen mistook for the Cape Flattery Lighthouse. On November 11, the *Oliver Wolcott* found Captain Sawyer and his crew camped out near the remains of their stricken ship. The revenue cutter took them to Port Townsend.

AT FIRST, the San Francisco press had difficulty accepting Henry Jelly's account of the sinking of the *Pacific*. "The entire accuracy of the story of Jelly, the survivor, is doubted by some persons acquainted with the coast, who believe that a number of the passengers and officers and crew have been saved in boats and on pieces of the wreck," concluded the *Alta California*.[40] The *San Francisco Chronicle* noted that "some think he is laboring under an hallucination in that matter."[41] That Jelly's account was questioned is not surprising given the supposed condition of the *Pacific*. After all, Charles C. Bemis, San Francisco's supervising inspector of steamships, had claimed the vessel was safe. Moreover, had anything happened to the *Pacific*, Bemis proclaimed, she carried two lifeboats capable of holding two hundred people each and six large self-righting metal craft, which were more than enough to accommodate everyone on board.[42] (In fact the ship had two wooden longboats capable of carrying about sixty people and three smaller metal craft able to hold no more than twenty people each.)

The *Victoria Daily British Colonist* was one of the few West Coast newspapers prepared to accept Jelly's account of a crumbling ship. It wrote: "In our ignorance of marine architecture we have always looked with suspicion upon old ships that come from the builder's hands 'as good as new' . . . But to claim that a ship has been rebuilt when decayed timbers only are removed, old bolts driven a little closer to bind the old planks, and a new coat of paint donned is simply to attempt a fraud."[43]

Only when Jelly's account was largely substantiated some days later by Neil Henley was the seaworthiness of the ship and its lifeboats reconsidered. On November 16, the *San Francisco Chronicle* noted:

> The *Pacific* was built in the year 1851. How many times it has been rebuilt, refitted, recaulked, recoppered and repainted we have no means of knowing; but that it was a sound and seaworthy ship the incidents of the collision, at least, do not prove. It struck a sailing vessel amidships, and in a way that ought not to have injured the steamer, but ought to have cut the *Orpheus* in two. . . . If the *Pacific* had been a staunch, sound and well timbered ship, built in compartments and officered by cool, brave and competent seamen, this accident would not have occurred, or if it had, would not have been attended with such frightful consequences.[44]

The master of the *Orpheus* faced his share of criticism. The following day, after reaching Port Townsend, four members of the crew swore a statement charging Captain Sawyer with placing his ship in the path of the *Pacific* and then failing to go to the aid of the steamer. Rumors circulated in the communities along the West Coast that were even more damning. It was said that he ignored the cries for help of those on board the *Pacific*. "It is awful to think of the havoc that a single turn of a man's wrist in the wrong direction [on the wheel] has caused; but . . . it is more terrible still to believe that the Captain of the *Orpheus* heard the pitiful cries of the sinking people; cursed them and left them to their fate," wrote the *Colonist.*[45] Similar sentiments were expressed by the San Francisco newspapers that had generally been less willing to place the blame for the disaster on the captain and officers of the *Pacific* or the ship's owners.

MORE BODIES were carried into the Strait of Juan de Fuca by the prevailing currents. A dead man wearing a life preserver was seen in the water off Waddy Island, Washington Territory. He was identified as Richard Jones, a steward on board the *Pacific.* He was buried at Neah Bay.[46] The body of E. L. Hastings was found on the beach not far from the mouth of the Elwha River near Port Angeles. A gold piece and a watch engraved with the initials "E.L.H." were found in the pockets of his suit.

On November 18, another body was recovered washed up on the shores of Vancouver Island not far from Victoria. He was Thomas J. Ferrell, the employee of a San Francisco bag factory.[47] The remains of J. D. Crowley of San Jose, California, were found about two miles from Victoria's city center. Two men strolling along the beach by Beacon Hill spotted a body tangled in a kelp bed. Although the action of the waves against the rocks had obliterated his features, personal papers confirmed him as the advance agent for the Rockwell and Hurlbert equestrian troupe.

Some time later the bloated corpse of a white gelding belonging to the troupe was found saddled and bridled floating in the strait. It was believed that one performer had attempted to ride the animal to shore, but given the condition of the sea and the fact that the nearest land was many miles away, the horse and rider perished.

The remains of J. H. Sullivan, the Cassiar District gold commissioner, were washed up on the rocks near Beechy Head on November 18, and taken to Victoria. He had several large bank drafts in his pocket as well as personal items.[48]

Pieces of the doomed ship continued to wash up on the American and Canadian sides of the Strait of Juan de Fuca, including doors, windows, and even a companionway ladder. The wreck of one of the black wooden longboats was found near Clover Point on Vancouver Island. The end had been ripped away and one side was stove in. In it was a girl's shoe.[49] A message from almost beyond the grave was picked up near the same area. Written on a piece of a cabin support was "S. P. MOODY. ALL IS LOST."[50] Moody apparently had expected no one to survive and was recording the *Pacific's* epitaph.

The Victoria coroner's office inquest into the death of Thomas J. Ferrell and other victims was convened soon after the first bodies arrived. Because of its limited jurisdiction, few witnesses could be compelled to testify; however, many of those familiar with the vessel came to Victoria to tell their story. Captain Sawyer, who had been threatened with arrest by Canadian authorities, chose not to attend. Nor did the principals of Goodall, Nelson and Perkins, although they had counsel present.

Among the first to testify were members of the *Orpheus's* crew. The early rumors that Sawyer sailed into the night, actually ignoring the cries of drowning passengers and crew, were not supported. Indeed, the captain had hailed the *Pacific*, asking her to lower boats, but received no reply. Yet Sawyer did not escape accusations of negligence. Charles Thomson, the seaman at the wheel at the time of the collision, testified that it was the master of the *Orpheus* and not the second officer who had put the ship in the path of the oncoming vessel. (Sawyer apparently wanted to approach the ship to learn his exact location.)

After discovering his vessel was in no immediate danger, Sawyer ordered his ship to keep on her course. This was only a few minutes after the collision. Thomson saw the *Pacific* alter course and come after the sailing vessel, but she was slipping further behind, and about fifteen minutes later the lights astern were no longer visible. Another seaman, August Hartrigg, testified that he was on watch at the time and was sure that it was the *Orpheus* that was seriously damaged and in danger of sinking. Yet it was true that Captain Sawyer had violated maritime convention, which required both vessels to stand by after a collision. According to Hartrigg and other members of the crew, Sawyer was a hard-drinking, overbearing individual who was disliked by almost everyone under his command. Once rescued by the *Oliver Wolcott*, Sawyer had branded his men a set of scoundrels, which did not increase his support among the crew. The ship's steward would go so far as to testify that he believed the captain and officers contrived to wreck the ship.

Although neither a representative of the San Francisco dry dock where the *Pacific* was supposedly rebuilt nor the steamship inspectors testified, others came. William Collings, a ship carpenter in San Francisco, noted that before the last rebuild, it was said along the waterfront that a person could pick up a digging tool and shovel out the rotten sections of the ship's frame. Although he could not claim to know what had been done to the hull of the vessel during her last refit, he stated that no staunch ship would go down after so little damage. James Wallace, a boilermaker from San Francisco, testified that he did not believe the engine had been removed in twelve years.

James G. Allen, second officer, late of the *Orpheus* and formerly first officer of the *Pacific,* testified that prior to being run up on the mud flats the side-wheeler was unsound. "They were always calking [*sic*] her because she spit the oakum out of her seams; the machinery had not been taken out of her for the last 5 years to my knowledge."[51] The witness claimed that during inspections, fire hoses and water buckets were borrowed from other company vessels. He also said that the ship's poorly maintained lifeboats were removed and good ones, kept in a shed simply for use during the inspections, were hung from the davits. The ever-shifting boats and buckets did not mislead the inspectors. In exchange for such cursory examinations, Allen claimed that the officials were given champagne lunches on board the ship.

As officer of the watch at the time the *Orpheus* collided with the *Pacific,* Allen was hardly an impartial witness. Yet in sum, the evidence against the *Pacific*'s owners was damning. J. P. Goodhue, Victoria agent for the Oregon Steamship Company, revealed that no customs officer in Portland would allow a steamship to leave port without a valid inspection certificate and that such certificates required a thorough investigation into the seaworthiness of the vessel: holes were bored into the hull to ensure the ship's soundness, and her lifeboats were inspected as to their fitness. However, Goodhue admitted that this was the way in which the procedures were carried out in the Oregon city, and he was not familiar with how the San Francisco inspectors performed their duties.[52]

At 4:50 P.M. on November 23, the Victoria coroner's jury came down with their verdict. After noting the circumstances involving the collision, the findings concluded "that the *Pacific* struck the *Orpheus* on the starboard side with her stem a very slight blow, the shock of which should not have damaged the *Pacific* if she had been a sound and substantial vessel."[53] As damning perhaps were the lack of competent lookouts on board the *Pacific* and "that the boats were not and could not be lowered by the undisciplined and insufficient crew."[54]

Captain Sawyer's understandable refusal to testify in his own defense certainly weakened the master's position before the jury. "The captain of the *Orpheus* sailed a way [sic] after the collision and did not remain by the *Pacific* to ascertain the amount of damage she had sustained," the jury concluded.[55] Not mentioned in the verdict, but nonetheless blamed by most Victoria citizens, was Goodall, Nelson and Perkins Steamship Company's Canadian agent, E. Engelhardt and Company.

IN LATE NOVEMBER, the Board of Steamboat Inspectors announced in San Francisco that it was conducting an investigation into the loss of the *Pacific*. It was to take place under Captain Bob (Bully) Waterman, the hull inspector, and James Hillman, the boiler inspector. "The investigation is held with closed doors," the *Chronicle* noted, "at the express desire of Captain Waterman, who did not wish to be annoyed by outsiders."[56]

Goodall, Nelson and Perkins Steamship Company stated publicly that the firm was eager for an open hearing to clear its name, as it had been treated unfairly by the press. Wishing to repair the damage to its image, the company claimed it was singularly absurd to conclude that the enterprise would risk people and property on an unseaworthy ship.

NOT LONG AFTER the sinking of the *Pacific,* the West Coast narrowly escaped another shipwreck tragedy. On November 29, 1875, the Goodall, Nelson and Perkins Steamship Company steamer *Los Angeles* pulled away from her wharf at San Francisco with ninety-eight passengers bound for Puget Sound and Victoria. She was a condemned revenue cutter that the steamship company purchased and rebuilt by adding a new superstructure. At 9 A.M. on December 1, about ninety-five miles south of the Columbia River, she developed engine trouble, with the result that she had to rely on her auxiliary sails. As she progressed north, she met the full fury of a gale, and passengers would later claim it was the seamanship of Captain Charles Thorn that saved the vessel from certain destruction. As it was, on December 5, one sailor was washed overboard.

For the residents of Puget Sound and Victoria, the long overdue *Los Angeles* seemed a terrible repeat of the *Pacific* tragedy. Finally, though, on the morning of December 8, the ship was seen by a British man-of-war and towed into Victoria harbor. The voyage from San Francisco that usually took four or five days to complete had taken nine.

On December 11, the report of the San Francisco steamship inspectors Captain Bob Waterman and Jim Hillman was made public. Most of the blame was placed on the master of the *Orpheus,* who had crossed the path of the oncoming *Pacific.* That the latter ship failed to get her lifeboats away was attributed to frightened passengers interfering with the duties of the crew. That the bow of the *Pacific* was ripped off during the collision was the result of the lighter construction of steam vessels vis-à-vis sailing ships. According to the report, the *Pacific* would have gone down just as quickly had she been new.

In Victoria, there were many questions about the handling of the San Francisco inquiry. Indeed, the entire procedure was simply a whitewash, the *Colonist* proclaimed: "When it is remembered that Waterman was a member of the Commission, that serious charges of corruption were preferred against him in connection with the *Pacific* disaster, and that the commission sat with closed doors, the result is not surprising. To appeal to a commission of which the chief culprit was the chief member was like appealing from Caesar to Caesar. How could Capt. Waterman be expected to convict himself?"[57]

Yet in British Columbia no charges were laid against the owners of the *Pacific,* its agent, or Captain Sawyer as a result of the coroner's verdict. In San Francisco, on January 6, 1876, the master of the *Orpheus* found himself under arrest. He was accused of deliberately wrecking his own ship, but there was little evidence and the charges were quickly dismissed. Sawyer retired to Port Townsend, where he continued to complain about his unfair treatment by the press.

Some officials appeared to emerge from the *Pacific* tragedy unscathed. George Clement Perkins, one of the owners of the *Pacific,* ran for the office of governor of California in 1879, and despite opposition from the *San Francisco Chronicle,* which regarded him as a tool of the transportation interests, he won easily. Perkins went on to serve as a U.S. senator from 1893 to 1915.[58]

In 1877, Goodall, Nelson and Perkins Steamship Company reorganized as the Pacific Coast Steamship Company. Although the name may have removed the taint associated with the *Pacific,* the truth was that little had changed. New feathers did not make a new bird. The Pacific Coast Steamship Company continued to make huge profits by operating questionable vessels with ill-trained crews.

ONE OF THE LAST bodies to be identified was Fannie Palmer, whose remains, clad in a life preserver, were found on San Juan Island, Washington Territory, on November 25. She had come ashore only 10 miles from the wharf the *Pacific* had sailed from three weeks earlier. Fannie's body had drifted 110 miles, floating past her parents' home. Her steamer trunk had been found on the beach at Whidbey Island and a box containing her sheet music was discovered near Cape Flattery. Fannie and her belongings finally arrived only a few miles from home.

Her funeral cortege was one of the largest in the city's memory. Among the mourners were her many friends who, less than a month earlier, had come to wish her a good voyage. By the time the procession reached the cemetery, Victoria was experiencing a rare snowstorm. As the coffin was lowered into the ground, men and women shivered in the cold blast of the wind blowing in from the Strait of Juan de Fuca. Fannie's was one of only a dozen or so bodies recovered from the ocean. Others, including entertainers Belle and Cal Mandeville, his sister Alicia, and Jelly's friend A. Fraser, were never found.

During a time when families depended solely on the husband and father for support, the loss of so many men rippled through West Coast communities. As David Higgins wrote nearly three decades after the tragedy: "About fifty families were broken up and scattered, and many came upon the public for maintenance. There were two suicides at San Francisco in consequence of the disaster, and there were many instances of actual distress of which the public never heard."[59]

For most friends and families of the victims, there were no tangible remains upon which to grieve. All that were left were pieces of the

Pacific. On January 22, 1876, a resident of the community of Sooke, east of Victoria, came upon the large gilt eagle that had once adorned the *Pacific*'s pilothouse. It was put on display with other pieces of the *Pacific*'s frame that had washed ashore at Gonzales Bay near Victoria. It was said that the remnants of the ship were so rotten that they could be pulled apart by a person's fingers.[60]

QUARTERMASTER Neil Henley returned to the sea after his ordeal and in 1877 settled in Steilacoom, Washington. If his obituary is to be believed, he held many jobs during his lifetime, including that of the captain of the doomed *Pacific.*[61] He died in 1944.

Passenger Henry Jelly returned to the family farm near Port Stanley, Ontario. Despite his experiences at the mercy of the sea, Jelly was to make two more ocean voyages not long after his return home. He sailed to Ireland, where he was married, and then he and his new bride took a steamer to Canada. He worked the family farm and fished commercially in the waters of Lake Erie. He was seventy-seven years old when he died in 1930.

For Charles A. Sawyer, the master of the *Orpheus,* it was impossible to escape the memory of his brief encounter with the *Pacific.* It continued to burden his soul. According to one account, shortly before Sawyer's death in 1895, he was engaged in a game of whist with several friends when he abruptly stopped what he was doing and turned as if trying to hear something. "There it is again! Didn't you hear it?"[62]

What was he talking about, his friends wanted to know.

"The whistle of the *Pacific!*"[63]

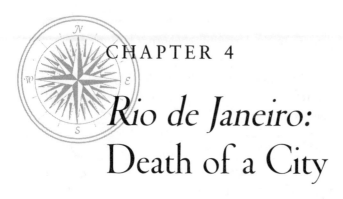

CHAPTER 4

Rio de Janeiro: Death of a City

Before the 1906 earthquake and subsequent fire, the worst disaster to befall San Francisco was the sinking of the passenger ship *City of Rio de Janeiro* at Fort Point. On a fog-shrouded morning, the Pacific Mail Steamship Company's transoceanic liner struck a rocky outcropping that guarded San Francisco Narrows. Her loss at the city's doorstep was ironic. "Other ships had sunk at sea in the midst of frightful storms," observed the *San Francisco Call*. "Others had foundered because of their own incapacity to struggle against the elements, but the *City of Rio de Janeiro,* after a journey of thousands of miles, through storm and violent weather, struck upon the rocks and went down in its home port."[1]

On the morning of Friday, February 22, 1901, San Francisco residents awoke to news that bodies and debris were floating in the waters off the Golden Gate. Among the flotsam were pictures and letters, luggage and odd pieces of clothing: pathetic remnants of lives ended only hours earlier. In the obscenity of death, nothing remained private. Within hours, looters were gathering near the scene.

AT ABOUT 5 P.M. a day earlier, the *City of Rio de Janeiro* was near the nine-fathom buoy when Frederick W. Jordan stepped from the cutter *Gracie S.* and climbed the ladder onto her deck. The signal for the anchor to be dropped had been given and only a few muffled voices broke the fog-enveloped night. A portly man in late middle age, the pilot had never suffered an accident during the more than a dozen years he had taken ships across the bar into port. Nevertheless, Jordan

Early promotional drawing of the *City of Rio de Janeiro.* (San Francisco History Center, San Francisco Public Library)

and his fellow San Francisco pilots were inclined to underestimate the dangers of their job. The thought of a warm meal at home and the comfort of their own bed was a strong inducement to risk the fog. Indeed, many vessels went safely through the thick gray cover to their berths. But it was not to be the case on this morning.[2] Jordan's exemplary record would soon come to an end. Now, though, the ship pulled lightly at her anchor cables like a pony gently tugging at her reins. Except for the fog, there seemed little reason for concern.

The vessel was almost three days overdue because of weather and mechanical difficulties. But now, anchored four miles northwest of Point Lobos, the *City of Rio de Janeiro* was almost home. Only the cold, cloying white vapor kept the ship from the harbor.

Shortly after the pilot boarded, the fog cleared. The anchor was raised and the ship got under way. Point Lobos lookout John Hyslop, whose job it was to provide the San Francisco Merchants' Exchange with news of incoming vessels, heard the sound of a big ship steaming toward the narrows.

A few minutes later, though, the noise told a different story. A deep-throated splash followed by the screech of cables made it clear that this voyage was short. The ship had crossed the bar during a brief break in the weather, but the fog closed in again. The vessel would not be making port this evening. And the passengers and crew on board the *City of Rio de Janeiro* prepared to spend another weary night at sea.

Although the ocean surface was as gentle as a pond, the fog was thick around the ship. When the big iron-hulled collier *Czarina,* out of Seattle, approached the Golden Gate about 7:30 P.M., the night was so thick that her captain could see only a few yards in any direction. Through the gray of evening, the ship's master suddenly saw lights emerge. At first he was confused as to where he was, but the sound of the fog bell and the position of the anchor lights soon convinced him that he was near one of the big Pacific Mail ships. The *Czarina* also dropped her anchor.[3]

As evening slipped by, time on board the *City of Rio de Janeiro* was measured by the rhythm of the fog bell. At the lookout tower at Point Lobos, John Hyslop would catch occasional glimpses of the anchor lights of a big ship. At about 5 A.M., Hyslop heard the sound of the anchor cables as they were winched up, and then the call of a fog whistle. There was no doubt that a big ship was hidden in the fog, and Hyslop knew she had to be the *City of Rio de Janeiro.* He telephoned the Merchants' Exchange with the news that the Pacific Mail ship would soon be arriving.[4]

Fog often delayed a ship's entry into San Francisco Bay. Many of the passengers who had sailed the coast or taken a liner back from Asia were prepared to wait for a change in the weather. Some, though, were less willing to wait. During dinner at the captain's table, Rounseville Wildman, the U.S. consul general in Hong Kong, and his wife, Letitia, made their displeasure clear. Kate West, a Red Cross nurse, recalled, "Both the Consul and Mrs. Wildman were impatient because the ship was three days overdue and twice on Thursday evening I heard them tell the Captain that the delay had greatly interfered with their plans."[5]

They were a well-connected family. Wildman, thirty-seven, was the son of a Methodist minister. As a young man he attended Syracuse University, and later traveled west to become editor of the *Statesman,* a successful Boise, Idaho, Republican newspaper. Wildman was sent as a delegate to Washington and it was largely through his efforts that

Idaho was admitted to the Union on July 3, 1890. Wildman did not remain there to enjoy the fruits of his labor. In 1889 he was appointed U.S. consul to Singapore.

Consul Wildman met Letitia Aldridge in Washington, D.C., in 1889 and the two married shortly after. His wife was the daughter of a former San Francisco judge and a niece by marriage of a U.S. senator. The Wildmans were influential people in their own right. In Hong Kong, the *San Francisco Bulletin* noted: "Mrs. Wildman at once became a leader in society. Her home was regarded as one of the most hospitable in the colony, and it was regarded as an honor to be one of her set. Admiral Dewey made the Wildman residence his headquarters when he was in Hongkong [*sic*], and Mrs. Wildman gave a dinner in his honor the night before he sailed for Manila."[6]

Wildman served briefly in Bremen, Germany, before representing Borneo and the Straits Settlements at the 1893 World's Columbian Exposition held at Chicago. After a short break, during which he edited a San Francisco magazine, the *Overland Monthly,* Wildman was appointed to the Far East, where he took up his duties as consul general in Hong Kong.

Wildman was returning to the United States for a three-month leave of absence. The war with Spain had placed substantial stress on the consul, possibly the result of his own questionable activities in the region. In 1898, Wildman was part of a scheme to supply guns and ammunition to the Filipino rebels battling Spain. On one occasion, Wildman failed to deliver the guns for which he had been paid, and although there was no strong evidence of personal gain, some rebels believed he simply pocketed the money.[7]

Leaving for the United States on the *City of Rio de Janeiro* on Tuesday, January 19, 1901, Wildman took his wife, two children, and their servant back to the United States. Kate Nichols, who had been hired as governess by the Wildmans in the Unites States four years earlier, was not looking forward to her return home. Three days before her departure, the then Kate Reidy married a sergeant in the Royal Welsh Fusiliers stationed in Hong Kong. When she confided her plans to leave service to Letitia Wildman, Mrs. Wildman urged her to accompany the family as far as San Francisco, where she could take a ship returning to Hong Kong. Although her plans were not revealed to Consul Wildman, she did tell others on board the ship.

Wildman was experiencing other problems. He had not counted on the turbulent Pacific weather, the aging ship's mechanical difficulties, or the San Francisco fogs that frequently obscure the entrance to the harbor for days at a time. The delay was more than irritating, for he had business and political meetings in the East. "What seemed to annoy the Consul was that the delay would prevent him from reaching Washington in time for the inauguration of President McKinley," West recalled. "He said that he had been put to considerable expense in bringing his family from the Orient and that the object of his coming home would be lost if he failed to get to Washington in time."[8]

Captain William Ward listened carefully to what Consul Wildman and his wife said. He would not regard the Wildmans' displeasure lightly. As consul, Wildman would have had considerable influence within Hong Kong's European community and could turn much business either toward or away from a shipping line. Until now, he preferred Pacific Mail ships and the *City of Rio de Janeiro* in particular. Rounseville Wildman's brother Edwin recalled: "It is a remarkable thing that this steamship was my brother's pet and he always made it a point to sail on her when crossing the Pacific. When I was last in Hongkong [sic] he wanted me to sail on her too—he was so fond of her. I sailed, however, last November on the *Coptic*."[9]

On the surface at least, the iron-hull 4,548-ton *City of Rio de Janeiro* had little to recommend her. Launched on March 6, 1878, at Chester, Pennsylvania, by the large American shipbuilder John Roach and Son, the *City of Rio de Janeiro* was one of two ships built for a business consortium headed by Roach himself. Their goal was to establish a strong link between Brazil and the United States, but the operation was unprofitable and soon the vessels were on the market.

Bought in 1881 by the Pacific Mail Steamship Company, the vessel was refitted for the long Pacific run to Honolulu, Yokohama, Japan, and Hong Kong. She did not escape her share of close calls. On August 5, 1890, she collided with the British ship *Bombay* in Hong Kong harbor. With the ship badly damaged, the Pacific Mail Steamship Company made emergency repairs at that port before returning her to San Francisco.

Five years later, the *City of Rio de Janeiro* struck a reef near Nagasaki, Japan, ripping a large hole in her side. The damage was so severe that the steamer was laid up on the beach to prevent her from sinking.

The steamer *City of Rio de Janeiro,* seen in Nagasaki, Japan, in 1894.
(San Francisco Maritime National Historical Park, J. Porter Shaw Photographic Collection
[H6.4135n])

In 1897, on her voyage from Japan to Hawaii, the vessel encountered
a typhoon so severe that it pounded the ship for twelve days. Her fight
for life had cost her all the coal in her bunkers, and she made the last
few miles by burning what had once been the furnishings of the after
cabin.[10]

In 1898, the vessel was for a brief time leased to the government
as a troop ship, transporting military personnel during the Spanish-
American War. In that same year, she steamed into Manila harbor
with almost a thousand men on board. In 1900, the *City of Rio de
Janeiro* was back to her familiar run between San Francisco and Asia.

Thirty-eight-year-old William Ward cut a dashing figure in his
blue captain's uniform. He had a reputation as a genial host at the
captain's table and an amiable deck companion for those wishing to
indulge in their last cigars of the night, and for this reason his ship
remained popular with travelers who could afford first-class fares.
Born in Raleigh, North Carolina, he entered service with the Pacific

SS *City of Rio de Janeiro*: ship's officers at the captain's table, Hong Kong, 1894. This rare picture of the ship's interior shows William Ward, then the apprentice captain, seated on the far right. (San Francisco Maritime Historical Park, Tichenor Photographic Collection [H10.28739n])

Mail Steamship Company in 1883. After serving as apprentice captain on board the *City of Rio de Janeiro,* Ward was given command of the ship in 1897.

On this night, the safety of the ship remained very much on Captain Ward's mind. He had a reputation as a cautious navigator, and was not one to take chances. On Thursday evening, February 21, 1901, freight clerk George Englehardt recalled him saying that he was prepared to sit at anchor an entire week rather than run through the channel in the fog. Passenger William Brandon Jr., a member of a wealthy Edinburgh family who was on board the ship enjoying a world tour, spoke with Captain Ward on the *City of Rio de Janeiro*'s last night. Ward had said he did not wish to "risk taking his ship through the Gate in the dense fog."[11] He also told journalist Russell Harper that he did not want to take chances with his ship.[12] Ward had reason to be concerned, for eight years earlier the Pacific Mail ship the *City of New York,* outbound from San Francisco, had wrecked on the rocks at Point Bonita. Like now, the harbor was shrouded in fog. It was a hard lesson to forget. In 1901, what was left of this once-splendid passenger liner still remained visible above the water.

R. H. Long, a first-class passenger en route from Honolulu to his home in Petaluma, California, also remembered being told by Captain Ward that the ship would not enter port during foggy weather. On this point, Pacific Mail policy was very clear; no unnecessary chances were to be taken.

A YEAR EARLIER, the Pacific Mail Steamship Company had been taken over by the Southern Pacific Railroad,[13] but the principals so far had made few changes. If there had been friction between Ward and his new employers, he had not mentioned the fact openly. The Southern Pacific had plans, not only for Pacific Mail's transpacific service, but for its coastal steamship subsidiary, the Oregon Railway and Navigation Company, which the railroad intended to expand.

On this, her last voyage from Asia, the *City of Rio de Janeiro* carried a mixed cargo, including 1,800 rolls of grass mats, 1,750 bales of hemp, 2,423 slabs of "pig" tin (a commodity that would become more valuable in later years), as well as raw silk, tea, sugar, curio cases, and other general merchandise.[14] The insured value of the silk and tea alone was estimated to be more than $250,000.[15] Yet often the most profitable items were not listed on the ship's manifest. "Its long career was eventful," observed maritime historians James P. Delgado and Stephen Haller. "Frequently the vessel was involved in customs cases, as smugglers used the *City of Rio de Janeiro* to bring a variety of items, usually opium, into the United States."[16]

At one time the Asian route had supplied large numbers of Chinese to build railways and to labor in the mines of the West. The Pacific Mail Steamship Company, as the major transporter of Chinese labor, made large profits. Given that it was not required to take on an American crew, most of the deckhands, oilers, and other unskilled jobs on board Pacific Mail vessels were filled by Chinese, who were paid far less than their American counterparts.

Almost from the beginning of the California gold rush, resentment against America's open immigration policy festered among the laboring classes. Increasingly, social unrest was finding a political voice. By the turn of the twentieth century, the United Labor Party was becoming an active force against the financial and transportation establishment, including the shipping tycoons.[17] The rich, it was claimed, became richer through their exploitation of the workingman.

Yet it was not only the wealthy that were seen as the enemy. The fact that the Chinese had come from a "backward" country and now worked for lower wages seemed to confirm to many Californians that Asians were racially inferior. They did not belong in a society evolved from the rich tapestry of European culture.

It was in this way necessary for the Pacific Mail Steamship Company to maintain two steerage sections: one for Asians and one for European passengers. As if to emphasize the inferiority of the former, their section was on a lower and less well-ventilated deck. Racial segregation was so entrenched that when, in 1900, a large number of American horse handlers who were returning to California after delivering a shipment of horses to China were placed in Asian steerage on the *City of Rio de Janeiro,* they filed a suit against the Pacific Mail Steamship Company. "When the *Rio de Janeiro* pulled out of the harbor of Nagasaki," the lawyer for the complainants argued, "the men discovered that they had been assigned to the Asiatic steerage and were herded in with Chinese, Japanese, Filipinos and other denizens of the unsavory quarter."[18]

Since the mid-1890s, barriers to immigration made it increasingly difficult for the Chinese to enter the United States. In 1901, many of the Asians traveling to the United States on the *City of Rio de Janeiro* were on academic or cultural scholarships. In some cases, the Chinese were simply passing through the United States en route to European destinations. Yung Ching, a wealthy student, was on his way to England, where he would further his education.[19] Another traveler from Asia, Zenji Yamada, a well-known painter in his native Japan, was on his way to study in New York. The young man would later paint a dramatic picture of the last moments of the *City of Rio de Janeiro.*

The process of Asian exclusion once under way had not run its course. A little more than a year after the sinking of the *City of Rio de Janeiro,* the U.S. Congress passed legislation that all but barred the Chinese from entering this country. It received presidential approval.[20]

• • •

THE WILDMANS RETIRED about 10:30 P.M. on February 21. The two children, nine-year-old Rounseville Jr. and two-year-old Dorothy, and nursery governess Kate Nichols were probably already asleep. With the fog as thick as ever, Captain Ward retired to his cabin sometime after dinner. Pilot Jordan, too, sought out his berth.

At 4 A.M. on February 22, Graham Coghlan, the second officer, called first Jordan and then Ward to the bridge. (Jordan had left word that if the weather changed, he was to be awoken a few minutes before the captain.) The pilot gave orders to First Officer C. J. Johnson to heave the anchors, but before the flukes were free of the water the fog thickened again and Jordan halted the operation. He then left the bridge for what was probably a conference with the captain in his cabin. Jordan returned and gave the order to finish heaving the anchors and start the engines. A few minutes after that, Captain Ward arrived, still in his nightclothes.

Later, the question of who was in charge of the *City of Rio de Janeiro* during her last fateful hour would be a contentious issue. "The captain took no part in issuing orders," Coghlan declared. "The pilot seemed to be in command."[21] Neither the captain nor the pilot gave orders for depth sounding; it was an accurate way to navigate in poor visibility, but the process was slow. Instead, the engine room was signaled to reduce to half speed, and the quartermaster was given a course as the big ship moved sightlessly ahead. The only sounds were the regular blast of her fog whistle and the deep-throated tones of the foghorns onshore. Then the mist lifted and suddenly the sky opened ahead, but this was only for a moment. Before they had time to determine their position, the mist hid them again.

Lookout Frederick Lindstrom was standing watch when he suddenly saw a white-and-red light beyond the bow of the ship. He braced himself. "I felt my heart stand still. I knew what was coming."[22]

The aging ship met her end literally at the gate to her homeport. At 5:30 A.M. on Friday, February 22, 1901, the *City of Rio de Janeiro* struck a rocky reef jutting out from the south side of the narrows.

SHIP'S CARPENTER Frank Cramp was one of those detailed to haul the anchors up. He was still stowing the cables when the ship struck. "We're on the rocks," Cramp said to a man working with him.[23] He headed belowdecks to check the water in the bilges. When Cramp reached the bridge, he told Captain Ward there was ten feet of water in the forward hold and twenty amidships.

There could be little doubt that the force of the collision had ripped the starboard forward quarter of the *City of Rio de Janeiro* open as far back as her boiler room. The signal to take to the boats was followed by the distress signal. Then Captain Ward tied down the whistles so they blew continuously. The cacophony would continue for the last minutes of the vessel's life.

In the confusion, Captain Ward's actions were not entirely clear. Lookout Frederick Lindstrom claimed that it was the pilot who gave the order to abandon ship and that Captain Ward simply went into his cabin and closed the door as the ship began to sink.[24] (In the face of many eyewitness reports that Ward had taken an active role in the evacuation of passengers, Lindstrom was forced to recant his story.) "The brave captain rushed below to arouse the passengers," observed Frank Cramp. "He kicked and banged at the doors and shouted to every one to get on deck as soon as possible, and remained below till every cabin passenger had turned out and preceded him to the deck."[25] His absence was so brief, apparently, that few others on the bridge noticed he was gone.

Unknown to the passengers and many of the crew on board, the vessel's hold on the rocky ledge at Fort Point was precarious at best. As the stern of the *City of Rio de Janeiro* filled with water, she was in increasing danger of slipping into greater depth.

In charge of the No. 9 boat, port side aft, was Dr. Arthur A. O'Neill. The ship's surgeon had apparently slept through the collision and resultant commotion, and had to be awoken by one of the quartermasters. O'Neill quickly dressed and was met by Frederick Jordan, who told him to launch his lifeboat, which had been reserved for the Wildman family. O'Neill, Quartermaster Lindstrom, and some seamen were in the boat, letting the craft down by the davits, when suddenly the forward fall was allowed to run and foul the tackle. The stern swung down as the crew tried to free the davit. The lifeboat struck the water with a splash. It was still connected to the davit and held by the forward fall. Partially swamped, the boat was laboriously maneuvered back to the side of the *City of Rio de Janeiro*. All the while, the crew on No. 9 worked to bail out the craft.

At first there was little panic among the passengers. Obviously something serious had happened, but the *City of Rio de Janeiro* seemed like such a solid vessel. She had a reputation for weathering the worst typhoons. It appeared incomprehensible that she would meet her end at the entrance to this safe harbor. Unlike some of the passengers, William Brandon Jr. was still asleep when the *City of Rio de Janeiro* made her last run in. "I was awakened by a terrific shock, which caused the steamer to tremble all over."[26] Still in his night attire, Brandon rushed up on deck and was told by a crew member that they had grounded, but that it was nothing serious.

On deck he met passenger J. K. Carpenter, a mining engineer who was returning to his home in Oakland from a job in Sumatra. Carpenter told him that it was more serious than the crew was letting on and that he should go back to his stateroom and change.[27] Brandon felt his stomach tighten. "I ran to my cabin and partially dressed. I could not find my shoes. . . . I also put on an overcoat. Luckily I also had on my waistcoat containing my money and letter of credit."[28]

Patrick Henry Herlihy, the chief engineer, was in his berth when the ship struck. A veteran of many years at sea, he had been on the *City of New York* when she grounded in 1893. He had not gone to his post when the *City of Rio de Janeiro* had got up steam. Herlihy had earlier been on deck when he noted the thickness of the fog. He had decided that it was too dangerous for Captain Ward to sail in before it lifted, so he took extra time in his bunk.

Yet as chief engineer, he was expected to be in the engine room when the ship got up steam, and the fact that he was not was a serious breach of company rules. Herlihy later provided an account of his actions at the time of the sinking:

> When she struck I rushed from my room to the engine-room and stopped the machinery. I gave orders to start the pumps. There [was] four feet of water then under the plates. The whistles were blowing in long blasts. I sent word to the captain by the second officer of the situation in the engine-room. Then I ordered my men up from below. The steam escape valves were opened, so as to prevent bursting pipes. The escaping steam made a loud noise. . . . I was with my men by the donkey engine on deck when the ship sank.[29]

For whatever reason, Herlihy did not dismiss his men so that they could go to their lifeboat stations. This action meant that there were fewer skilled crew members to launch the boats. And time was important, for the life of the *City of Rio de Janeiro* was now measured in minutes.

J. K. Carpenter had been awake in his stateroom on the morning of February 22 and heard the anchors being winched up. "At 5:10 this morning the weather was perfectly clear. . . . Fifteen minutes later the fog bank was again upon us and the speed of the vessel was slackened. Then came the shock."[30] Carpenter would retain vivid memories of the ship hitting the rocks. "If you ever were struck by a ball from a six-shooter," he told a reporter, "you know how it felt when she struck. I knew it was all off and wasted no time in getting to deck."[31]

When R. H. Long heard the raising of the anchors, he assumed that conditions had cleared. Long, a horse dealer who frequently made the trip between Hawaii and San Francisco on the *City of Rio de Janeiro,* dressed and went on deck. Within minutes of the anchors breaking the calm surface of the ocean, the fog came down again. "The vessel, however, started up, and she ran about twenty-five or thirty minutes when she struck hard," Long recalled. "She piled up on the rock."[32] The ship had hit on the starboard side of her forward quarter and the vessel immediately canted slightly toward port.

Also traveling on board the ship was Harry Guyon, Long's friend and a fellow Petaluma resident. Guyon was a painter who had recently completed a large contract in Honolulu. He was now returning to his wife and three children.

Robert Holtz, a Shanghai merchant, was returning to Germany from China. With him was his friend Captain Max Hecht, an officer in the German navy stationed in China. "I heard the noise and knew that something was the matter," Holtz recalled. "I did not think, however, that it could be anything serious, and, to tell you the truth, I took my time about dressing."[33]

When the anchor was weighed, many passengers arose and began to pack. First-class passenger Zenji Yamada was awakened by the commotion made by his fellow travelers, who were obviously pleased that this long and difficult voyage would soon end. He put on his clothes and left his stateroom to see the ship come in. "It was less than one hour from that time that the steamer struck. I was on the upper deck then and felt the jarring of the vessel on the rocks."[34]

Steerage steward Harry Donohue had arisen about 5:20 A.M. and was about to dress. "Suddenly I heard a crash and felt a heavy jar. Then the boat trembled under my feet and I knew we had struck something."[35]

Nurse Kate West, who was on her return trip after taking a patient to Hong Kong, later recalled the collision. "I was awake at five o'clock when the *Rio* steamed up, and was in my berth partially dressed when she struck upon the rocks. The concussion was terrible and it seemed to me that the whole vessel was going to pieces."[36] Minutes later the electric lights were out and she and the other passengers who were not yet on deck were thrown into the dark. People became confused and unsure of what to do. Some made it to the first-class saloon on the upper deck, but did not know where to go after that.

For artist Zenji Yamada, the panicking passengers added to his fright. "I tried to get down from the hurricane deck, but many persons were coming up in the opposite direction, shouting that the steamer was wrecked."[37] He was pushed back to the top deck by the press of people.

Storekeeper E. W. Borg was up until 4 A.M. finishing the paperwork he was required to present to the company:

> I went to bed and had barely got there when I heard the winches going and the anchor coming up. I went to sleep and did not awake until I felt the shock of the ship striking on the rocks. I got up and went to the door. One of the officers went by and I asked what was the matter. He said, "Don't you know enough to know that we are aground?" I pulled on my trousers over my pajamas and started for the deck, and then went back and dressed completely in my uniform, putting on my underclothes and my collar.[38]

Like Borg, George Englehardt, the freight clerk, failed to realize the seriousness of the situation. At the time of the impact he was in his berth. "The jar was not severe," he remembered. "It seemed to me like three dull thumps in regular succession. I wondered for a moment whether the ship was going over the bar or whether we had gone on the rocks. I quickly decided we must have struck the rocks, and I thereupon got out of my berth and went on deck and awakened the purser whose room was next to mine. I told him the ship had run aground and I thought he ought to know it."[39]

Englehardt, though, didn't believe that the *City of Rio de Janeiro* was in danger of sinking. He returned to his stateroom and dressed with his usual care, putting on his uniform and lacing up his shoes. Despite the fact that Captain Ward called for all boats to be lowered, he did not think the *City of Rio de Janeiro* was in imminent danger of sinking, for her bow seemed to be well wedged in the rocks.

As the crew went to their lifeboat stations, Second Officer Graham Coghlan moved to the upper deck to cut the ropes that held the life rafts in place. That task, he discovered, was already done.

Coghlan would later state that the Chinese deckhands did little to assist the launching of the lifeboats. Almost none of them spoke English, and they relied on a bilingual boatswain to translate the orders from the officers. Now, though, the voices of passengers and crew were at a fevered pitch, and it was not possible to follow the usual lines of communication. "Orders shouted from the bridge through this babble of tongues were not obeyed," Coghlan claimed. He added, though, that "the Chinese, when they did understand orders, obeyed them with promptness and courage."[40]

Early on, there were individual acts of bravery. Steerage passenger Frances Ripley risked her own life for the safety of others. The seamstress was returning on the *City of Rio de Janeiro* with her father, George Ripley, to San Francisco from Honolulu. While her father apparently slept, Ripley arose early to see the ship's passage through the Golden Gate. She quickly dressed as soon as the ship was moving and made her way to the deck. "I had been there but a few minutes when the vessel seemed to recede for a second and then make a wild plunge forward. It quivered from bow to stern and then began to turn on one side."[41]

Many passengers had not appeared on deck after the collision. Some, like Rowena Jehu of Alameda, California, were never seen after the ship struck the rocks. It was reasonable to assume that many on board were too confused or frightened to leave the security of their berth, or that a few may have even slept through the ordeal.

Sarah Wakefield, the widow of a prominent San Francisco stockbroker, and her daughter Naomi were returning home after a vacation in the Hawaiian Islands. Naomi was a high-strung girl, and her mother had hoped she would find a sea voyage rejuvenating. The Wakefields were last seen alive on deck struggling with their life preservers.

R. H. Long prepared for the end. "The shock of the collision threw me upon my face. . . . It didn't take me any time to realize we were in danger, and after recovering my balance, I went down to my cabin to get my valises. I packed my clothes into the bags hurriedly, but then the electric lights all over the ship went out, leaving us in total darkness."[42] Before going on deck he went to the saloon, where he received a life preserver.

After the lights failed, all was confusion around seamstress Frances Ripley. Terror-stricken passengers ran about without direction. Ripley, who was on deck, remained remarkably calm. "Thinking some of the ladies of the cabin would need aid I ran down to the saloon and found Mrs. West who was bewildered and frightened."[43] According to Kate West, "Miss Ripley . . . literally pushed me up the stairs to the deck. We had no life preservers and Miss Ripley went down into the cabin and came back with one for each of us."[44]

Steerage steward Harry Donohue also was well disciplined during the first minutes after the *City of Rio de Janeiro* grounded. "I went on deck at once and reported to the captain. He ordered me to get the passengers on deck, and with others of the crew I assisted in this task. I got fifty-eight steerage passengers on deck."[45] Unfortunately for the Chinese steerage passengers, few of whom could speak English, the panic on deck produced even greater confusion. The death toll among this third class of passengers was particularly high. A total of thirty-seven Asian steerage passengers lost their lives. Only nine survived.[46]

By now the forward quarter of the *City of Rio de Janeiro* had slipped below the water as far as the first cabin on the main deck. Coghlan supervised the lowering of the lifeboats. After the difficulty with Dr. O'Neill's boat, he had likely been given orders to make sure Consul Wildman and his family were safely evacuated from the ship. "The vessel was then listed far over, but I entered the social hall, off which Consul Wildman and family had their staterooms. I am sure I know where their rooms were, but when I reached them they were empty. All of the rooms on that side of the vessel were empty. I then crossed the hall and found all of the rooms also vacant."[47]

According to freight clerk George Englehardt, Wildman had other concerns. After finishing dressing, Englehardt walked down to the parcel room to get the dispatch pouch. By now the lights had gone out, and Englehardt had taken a kerosene lamp with him. After returning to the deck, he met Consul Wildman. "He wanted me to get a tin box out of the [ship's] safe. I couldn't open the safe and referred him to the purser [John Rooney]. The purser . . . was still dressing."[48]

Knowing their social station gave them assured boarding for the lifeboats, the Wildmans were oblivious to the danger they were facing. Mining engineer J. K. Carpenter remembered his final encounter with Letitia Wildman. "I saw Mrs. Wildman and her child just before the ship went down. They were down below and the maid wanted me to go to their cabin for the baby's shoes. No one seemed to realize how short a time there was in which to act."[49]

A few minutes before the *City of Rio de Janeiro* went down, Frances Ripley saw Rounseville Wildman belowdecks at the purser's office "looking for a box of valuable papers. He was very much exercised because he could not find them and remarked that he couldn't go off without them."[50]

After dressing in his uniform, storekeeper E. W. Borg left his room. "As I went toward the deck I saw the purser working at the safe, trying to get it open."[51] The list had probably jammed the tumblers. According to Borg, Wildman and another passenger, Alfred Hart, were on deck assisting in the launching of one of the lifeboats.

William Brandon Jr. walked to the stern of the ship, where he saw Letitia Wildman and Kate Nichols with the two children. A few moments later Rounseville Wildman joined him. Noted Brandon, "From his action he evidently was looking for some means to save his family. He was looking over the side of the ship endeavoring to attract the attention of some sailors who were out in a boat."[52]

At this point, No. 11 boat, under the command of Charles J. Holland, the third officer, had been launched and a side ladder had been lowered. On the deck, merchant Robert Holtz recalled, "I was told to put on a life preserver by my comrade, Captain Hecht, and was ready for the worst. All this time I did not think that it was anything serious, but I soon saw I was mistaken."[53]

Once on the hurricane deck, Ripley and West met the captain, who directed them to one of the boats. This lifeboat, though, had already been lowered to the main deck, which was below them. "The captain called down 'Be sure to get all the ladies in the boats!' and then he disappeared and I did not see him again. He seemed stunned and acted as though he was in a trance."[54]

After the impact, R. H. Long's friend Harry Guyon had apparently panicked. "He was without a preserver or other means of escape and it was too late for him to go inside to get one," Long said. "I did all I could to encourage him, and was trying to cheer him up when the water shot over the decks."[55]

There were many differences in the versions of the last few minutes of the *City of Rio de Janeiro*. Some on board recalled after the collision that the ship started to turn on her side almost immediately. According to most crew members, the cant was not severe. Only after she began to slide off the reef was the list marked, and once free, she began to capsize.

UNABLE TO USE Dr. O'Neill's craft, the Wildmans were taken to Third Officer Charles Holland's boat, which was now launched with six Chinese crewmen at the oars.[56] A rope ladder was thrown over the side, and Consul Wildman was given a seat on the boat. Letitia Wildman and their son Rounseville Jr. had been entrusted to Frederick Jordan,[57] who then escorted them through the crowd. Jordan recalled later that before she started down the ladder, Letitia Wildman "gave [the boy] to me. I held him in my arms and the little fellow had his arms around my neck."[58]

On deck behind Jordan was Kate Nichols with little Dorothy, waiting to follow Mrs. Wildman and the others into the lifeboat. Mrs. Wildman had been reluctant to leave the apparent security of the ship for the lifeboat, and her passage down the side ladder was slow. "The woman [Letitia Wildman] and I were about half of the way down the ladder," Jordan said later, "when the *Rio* gave a tremendous pitch. I was flung off the ladder. I saw nothing then of the woman or boy. I went down with the ship about fifty feet. I worked my way up to the surface and got hold of some wreckage."[59]

The ship had lurched free of the rocks that had held her and now slid quickly into deep water and then keeled over. In a parting gesture, one of the *City of Rio de Janeiro*'s booms struck the Wildmans' boat, cleaving it in half. The *Rio* did not leave silently. A tremendous explosion rocked the surface, turning wooden pieces of the deck and cabins into pieces of shrapnel.[60]

At the end, passengers like mining engineer J. K. Carpenter concluded that it was every man for himself. "Suddenly I saw the vessel give a lurch forward, and, knowing that it would mean certain death to remain longer on board, I rushed aft and slid down the davit ropes into a boat manned by the third officer of the ship. As the *Rio* started to settle forward the third officer gave the order to pull away fast."[61]

The fate of those on board the lifeboat was already sealed. "As the ship went down she keeled over on her side and the aftermast struck our boat, shattering it to splinters," J. K. Carpenter remembered. "All were thrown into the water and I managed to keep afloat by grasping an oar."[62]

For Dr. O'Neill, his first thought was to put as much distance between his lifeboat, No. 9, and the vortex created by the sinking of the *City of Rio de Janeiro*. "We pulled around and got away from the wreck, but we did not see any one floating around to save."[63] The lifeboat drifted aimlessly in the fog until they sighted a Russian ship, the *Harbinger*, heading into port. "I am only too glad to say that I am alive," exclaimed O'Neill, "and it all seems as a dream to me to get so near home and then to meet with this awful disaster."[64]

The third boat launched, No. 10, was under the command of Frank Cramp. Freight clerk George Englehardt was at the stern of the ship helping to lower the lifeboat. Turning around, Englehardt saw Frances Ripley and Kate West on the deck behind him. "I grabbed them and we literally threw them in the boat. Some others got into the boat, but I was excited and wanted to get away. I just jumped into the boat in time, when the ship began to sink. We had to row like mad to get away from the spot as soon as possible, as I knew that otherwise the suction would draw us down."[65] Cramp and his crew pushed off from the side of the ship. "For God sakes," Cramp cried, "shove off! She's sinking!"[66]

For Second Officer Graham Coghlan, it was clear the *City of Rio de Janeiro* had only minutes left.

> As the ship began to show signs that she was ready to founder, I hurried on deck. Captain Ward was standing aft: still directing the lowering of boats and the disposition of passengers therein.

> My boat, No. 10 commanded by Frank Cramp, was standing off
> from the vessel a short distance, and I could see that others had
> been pulled aboard her. Suddenly the *Rio* gave a lurch and I sprang
> for my boat. I struck a piece of wreckage and painfully injured my
> ankle, but was soon pulled aboard the boat.[67]

Kate West also vividly recalled the last moments of the *City of Rio de Janeiro*: "As soon as our boat pushed away from the vessel I saw to my horror that the mast of the steamer was falling our way. The men in charge of the boat saw it too, and our salvation was due to the heroic, almost superhuman efforts they made in sending our craft out of its way. Our escape was marvelous. The mast . . . fell on and shattered the other boat and we were almost engulfed in the whirlpool that followed."[68]

One other female passenger, Gabrielle Lehrahen, a young French woman living in Van Ness, California, was on board the lifeboat. Little is known about her. She may have been traveling with Alfred Hart and his wife, neither of whom survived.

Harry Donohue, the steerage steward, obediently followed the captain's orders to load the passengers and didn't attempt to escape himself in one of the lifeboats. As he recalled later,

> All at once I felt the water under my feet and I made a dive for the
> rigging. As I started to climb I noticed Captain Ward on the bridge
> of the pilot house yelling something to a number of the crew who
> were trying to get a boat away. I climbed as far up the rigging as I
> could, but she settled faster than I climbed, for in a minute more I
> again felt my feet in the water. When the sea was up to my waist I
> let go and struck out for safety. I floated around for about fifteen
> minutes and was then picked up by the carpenter's boat.[69]

Storekeeper E. W. Borg was probably the last person to see Captain Ward alive. Borg went on deck and witnessed the captain coming aft toward him. "Following was what looked like a heavy sea sweeping along the deck from the bow. Instead of a sea as I thought, it was the steamer sinking bow first and leaning slightly to starboard. Everything seemed to be ripping apart."[70]

Not surprisingly, the accounts of surviving witnesses were not always in agreement. The estimates of the length of time it took the ship to sink varied. Second Officer Graham Coghlan testified, "The ship went down in ten minutes after striking."[71] Charles J. Holland, the third officer, placed the sinking at five minutes. Chief Engineer Patrick Henry Herlihy, who had survived other sinkings, estimated the time to be about twenty minutes.[72] Given that men and women had time to dress, obtain life preservers, and reach the deck, it would seem that the *City of Rio de Janeiro* remained above water for at least twenty minutes.

Passenger R. H. Long was pulled down with the ship. When he surfaced, gasping for air, he saw only two lifeboats. "One I know had been launched for Consul General Wildman and his friends from Hongkong [*sic*]."[73] Exhausted, he was too tired to swim. Neither boat seemed close enough. "Then I saw the ship's life raft, but I was so heavily weighted down that it must have been fully ten minutes before I got on the raft. I saw one boat break up. She was loaded with people."[74]

Artist Zenji Yamada pulled himself into a lifeboat but there were no crew members to let out the tackle. Yamada recalled that the end of the *City of Rio de Janeiro* came suddenly when she finally keeled over:

> I went down with her. I had not even time to reach for a life preserver, so fast did she sink. I was drawn way down into the water and lost consciousness, but soon drifted upward and came to the surface. I saw people floating and struggling in the water, trying to reach some wreckage to cling to. I managed to keep afloat until I reached a piece of floating wreckage. It must have been part of a cabin or stateroom, and I climbed on top of it. I found four Chinese floating on that raft. I was chilled all through and exhausted when I got on the float. We drifted about for fifteen or twenty minutes when one of the steamer's lifeboats picked us up. . . . After drifting and rowing about for a time we were picked up by a passing vessel that sailed into the harbor.[75]

Robert Holtz recalled the last seconds of the *City of Rio de Janeiro*:

> All of a sudden the ship gave a sudden lurch and I had just time to put my foot on the rail of the vessel when I found myself launched into the water. I went down with the ship, and in some way I was held with ropes. I got a terrible smash on the head, and then I came up to the top of the water. I swam to a capsized boat that three

Chinamen were holding on to. I got hold of the boat and held myself up. The water was awfully cold, and I thought that I would die with the cold. A raft came along with Captain Hecht and others on it and the boat was righted. We then all got in it and were soon after rescued by Italian fishermen.[76]

Storekeeper Borg was pulled down with the ship but managed to swim to the surface. "I grabbed a settee to buoy me and all around was wreckage with persons clinging to it all yelling as loud as they could. I was numb with cold when I crawled on a larger piece of wreckage on which I found [water tender E. H. Lane]. We managed to keep warm until we were taken off in [No. 10] boat."[77]

Cramp had waited until the water settled and then returned to the spot where the ship sank and here had picked up Borg and Lane. Freight clerk George Englehardt was unsure of what was taking place around him: "We came close upon another boat that was crowded with both men and women. I don't know what happened but there was an explosion and the boat upset and all were thrown into the water. The screams of these people were terrible. We rowed to the spot where this boat upset, but there was not a trace of them anywhere and I am confident that they were all drowned."[78] Englehardt had witnessed the destruction of the third officer's boat, which had been taking on the Wildman family and Frederick Jordan when struck by the aftermast. The blow was so severe that the freight clerk thought the craft had blown apart.

Englehardt recalled the hours spent on that sea of horror: "We also saw people on rafts. We shouted words of encouragement to them. Finding that they were getting exhausted and that we might possibly drift out to sea we decided to pull for the shore, where we landed. This wreck was the most awful experience I ever want to go through. I think I shall always hear the shouts of those drowning people in my ears."[79] The fog remained thick and no one on board the lifeboat had a clear notion of direction. As a result, Cramp and his crew rowed around for hours without sighting land.

Contrary to what Englehardt believed, Third Officer Charles Holland survived the destruction of his boat. He was apparently in a state of shock and suffering from a partial loss of memory following the sinking. Holland did not recall that the aftermast struck his lifeboat, but he remembered being carried under by the suction and managing to take hold of a life preserver. He was eventually picked up by a fishing vessel and taken to shore. He did not announce his rescue to anyone, remaining instead an anonymous face in the crowd at Meiggs wharf.[80]

AT 7:40 A.M., M. J. Fitzgerald, an employee of the Merchants' Exchange, was waiting for news of the *City of Rio de Janeiro,* which was long overdue. Bored, he balanced precariously on the edge of the wharf and stared off into the dirty white fog. The visibility had improved slightly since the previous night, but he could not see very far beyond where he was standing. Fitzgerald was surprised to see a fishing boat towing a craft with the neat letters CITY OF RIO DE JANEIRO on its bow. Fitzgerald quickly notified the Merchants' Exchange, which in turn informed the lifesaving stations.

Soon eighty survivors were picked up by the many small fishing boats in the area and taken to Meiggs wharf. As the events of the night before were circulated among city residents, people, wearing anxious expressions, made their way to the wharf. A few happy scenes were played out as friends and relations found those believed lost. But this was all too infrequent. Only three of the more than twenty-five women on board the vessel escaped death. Frances Ripley, one of the women to survive (the others were Kate West and Gabrielle Lehrahen), observed that the men always managed to take care of themselves.

THE JUT OF LAND forming the northern end of the Golden Gate is Fort Point. The San Francisco Narrows is particularly dangerous at this spot, for the point gives way to reefs and pinnacles that drop away to deep water not far off shore. While in the daytime and in good weather that massive monument to pre–Civil War defense planning, Fort Point Fort, provides ample warning of land ahead, the Golden Gate is often shrouded in fog. For that reason, a twenty-seven-foot iron lighthouse with foghorn was built above the bastion guarding the entrance to San Francisco Bay. It was completed in the late 1860s.

On February 22, 1901, the Fort Point barracks was home to Battery E, Third Artillery. Sometime after 5:30 A.M., Private Harry Taylor had drawn sentry duty on the wall perimeter of the old fort. Taylor paced off the steps on the parapet until he reached the area directly below the lookout tower. He heard a strange sound: the steady note of a steam whistle ending with a gurgling noise. "It was different from any whistle I ever heard on the bay."[81] As Taylor strained to listen, he could hear the sound of excited voices penetrating the fog. He was not alone: others also heard the noises. Privates S. O. Bridgens and F. M. George, who were on sentry duty, corroborated Taylor's testimony.

A mile down the beach from the barracks was the Fort Point Life-Saving Station, which was operated by the U.S. Life-Saving Service. Established in 1878, the service was intended to reduce the terrible death toll of shipwrecked sailors and passengers. At Fort Point, Captain Joseph Hodgson and his men spent hours practicing so that their boat could be launched at a moment's notice into the roughest sea. There was an esprit de corps among the men that is today common among highly skilled lifesaving units. When battling the sea, each man depended on the others in his boat for survival.

Every station was supplied with the latest in safety gear, including flares as well as Hunt and Lyle guns, which were rescue devices used to propel a light line from a ship to the shore or vice versa. In desolate areas, houses were constructed and maintained for shipwrecked seafarers to take refuge. The stations on the points of land entering San Francisco Bay had another important role. They patrolled the beaches, ensuring that no vessel was in difficulty.

In the lookout tower on the bluff overlooking the fort, Mark Ellingsen maintained his lonely vigil from 4 A.M. until 8 A.M., when another crewman would take over. The time clock required that the lookout punch in every half an hour. Although the tower was above the surface layer of fog, all below him dissolved into the dark-gray night. It was so thick that it was impossible to see the ships in the harbor. The fog blended the night noises into a timpani of bells, whistles, moans, and groans.

About 5:30 A.M., a new and disturbing cacophony broke through the background sounds. It was two long followed by a number of short blasts on a ship's whistle, repeated at least twenty times. Then voices and shouts were heard coming out of the fog. All Ellingsen had to do was pick up the telephone and call the lifesaving station, but he did nothing. At 7:20 A.M. as the fog lifted, Ellingsen observed the presence of a large number of ships off Fort Point and wondered if some incident had occurred.

Only a call from the Merchants' Exchange alerted Captain Hodgson that a huge liner had sunk about a mile from where they slept. The service had saved many a shipwrecked sailor from almost certain death, but on that cold, foggy morning something had gone terribly wrong. Other lifesaving stations in the area also should have been aware of the disaster. As the *San Francisco Call* noted:

> Golden Gate Life-saving Station is located on the ocean front,
> three-quarters of a mile south of Point Lobos, the Southside station
> is situated three and three-eighths miles south of the Golden Gate
> station and Fort Point station stands three-quarters of a mile east
> of Fort Point light. The testimony of the survivors of the *Rio de
> Janeiro* shows that the siren of the steamship was kept sounding
> during her fatal trip inside the bay. If the crews of the life-saving
> station were keeping vigilant watch, both on the ocean's edge and
> in their station houses, they must have heard the *Rio's* siren as she
> crept her way toward port.[82]

Although Ellingsen apparently admitted to his superior officer, Captain Hodgson, on February 29, 1901, that he heard the ship's distress signal and cries for help, he denied this confession under oath. But the testimony of the soldiers was damning for Ellingsen. As far as the residents of San Francisco were concerned, he had failed to do his duty, and many on board the unfortunate steamer paid a terrible price.

ON THE MORNING of the disaster, the hours must have passed slowly for those who had friends and relatives on board the *City of Rio de Janeiro*. Many people on the passenger manifest remained missing. The sea was reluctant to give up its dead. It is likely that most victims were swept against the bulkhead and held there as the ship sank.

The bodies of the victims found by search boats or whose remains were cast on the shore were taken first to Meiggs wharf. Dozens of people crowded the dock to get a quick glimpse of the bodies as they were passed into the care of morgue attendants. As each boat came in, the excitement of the crowd rose. Men and women pushed against police lines that cordoned off the area. One of the first to arrive contained the remains of three Asians and one European. After several hours, her nephew identified Oakland socialite Sarah Wakefield. The body of her daughter, thirteen-year-old Naomi, was never found.

The racial barriers that separated Asians from the European majority were no less apparent in death than in life. At Meiggs wharf, "in the hurry, which such a catastrophe must of necessity entail, [officials paid] slight attention . . . to the bodies of the Chinese which were picked up in the bay," wrote the *Examiner*. "Early in the morning five lay side by side on the wharf, while the Coroner's deputies were on their way to the scene."[83]

In a society that regarded the Chinese as clearly culturally inferior to Europeans, it seemed to come as a surprise that these people exhibited the same feelings of grief at the loss of loved ones as would be expected of the racial majority. Thus, on the occasion of the transfer of the Asian bodies from a tug to the wharf, a journalist for the *Examiner* found it newsworthy to report that several Chinese "of the better classes" were among the throng watching the grim event: "The crowd strained and jostled for a better view. As one of the dead Chinese was being carried across the gangplank a scream startled everyone. A tiny figure in Oriental costume dodged by the policeman, and catching the dead man's head in her arms the Chinese girl moaned and cried, plaintively calling aloud in her native tongue. The Chinaman who was with the child stepped out and caught the girl in his arms and carried her away."[84]

Few of the Asians on board the vessel had relatives in San Francisco. Members of the Chinese crew identified their shipmates. Surviving Chinese steerage passengers identified their unfortunate fellow travelers.

Along the shores of Bakers Beach, bonfires were blazing so that light was cast on the ebb and flow of the tide. Everyone waited in grim anticipation: scores of people remained unaccounted for. Where were the bodies? After midnight, a heavy rain began to fall and the men and women who maintained a vigil pulled their collars up to ward off the water. Toward the sea, the weather remained thick. It was as if the darkness had closed in, masking everything beyond the light of the fire.

During the night the police maintained watch over the items taken from the sea. Some were of value. Captain Ward's Masonic medals, still in their case, were retrieved. Other items were simply a remembrance of the tragic event. A suitcase containing the clothes of the two Wildman children was brought to the wharf by a fisherman. Throughout the next day more than a dozen bodies arrived at Meiggs wharf. On the body of steerage passenger Mrs. Alfred Hart was found several hundred dollars worth of jewelry. Her husband, a former jewelry salesman, apparently wished to go into business in San Francisco[85] and had used his wife as a courier. One of the most unusual items recovered, on February 23, was a painting of a battleship in Manila Bay signed "E. W. M." The ownership of the piece of art remained a mystery.[86]

On February 25, a strange ritual was enacted. A crowd of people gathered at Fort Point and stared across the water. There was nothing to see. Not even an oil slick marked the surface where the vessel slid back into the sea. However, for many this was the burial place of so many friends and family. It was the place to pay one's last respects.

A letter addressed to "Master R. Wildman," which was dated Monday, February 11, 1901, and contained an invitation for a tea party, was found floating in San Francisco Bay on February 26. Also found were a few Hawaiian coins wrapped in yellow foolscap.[87]

The sinking of the *City of Rio de Janeiro* brought forward a number of strange stories. Among the grief-stricken relatives and friends was Miss Lena Jackson, who claimed to have been betrothed to Captain Ward for nine years.[88] Whatever Miss Jackson and Captain Ward's relationship, other members of his family stated they had no knowledge of such an engagement.

THE FINAL DEATH LIST had not been completed before the residents of San Francisco were speculating about the cause of the terrible tragedy. John B. Roach, president of the company that had built the ship twenty-three years earlier, claimed that the major problem was her age and lack of modern safety features: "The *Rio* was a staunch and steady ship, splendidly constructed and had proved her seaworthiness in a dozen typhoons: but the lack of watertight bulkheads was a fatal defect in case the ship struck a reef."[89] As with vessels of similar age and construction, the *City of Rio de Janeiro*'s hull was divided across its width by watertight metal partitions intended to prevent the ship from sinking if her plates were ruptured below the waterline. On this steamer, though, there were only two main watertight bulkheads dividing the ship into three compartments.[90] These were certainly not enough to keep a vessel so severely damaged from sinking.

A source of continued complaint among many survivors was that tule life preservers were not effective. Many people believed that tule—the California bulrush material that went into making preservers—tended to become waterlogged quickly. The use of tule instead of cork would be a matter of continuing controversy in later years.

For newspapers like the *San Francisco Bulletin,* it was almost a given that the Chinese crew would not hold their posts. Commenting on the confusion on board ship, the newspaper wrote, "A few cool-headed [white] men could have held in check the crowd of fear-crazed Chinese that poured over the sides and into the boats."[91] However, within two or three minutes of the collision, the ship was in total darkness. Unless a person was one or two feet away, it was impossible to see who anyone was. The notion of who maintained their stations and who did not was largely a matter of supposition. Writing about northern European prejudice in his book on the *Titanic* disaster, Walter Lord noted, "To the survivors all stowaways in the lifeboats were 'Chinese' or 'Japanese'; all who jumped from the deck were 'Armenians,' and 'Frenchmen,' or 'Italians.' "[92] These same ideas were prevalent on the *City of Rio de Janeiro* eleven years earlier, only the main focus of prejudice was the Asians.

Probably for insurance reasons, the Pacific Mail Steamship Company wanted to lay most of the blame for the disaster upon its own captain. The company vice president, R. P. Schwerin, argued that the pilot was simply an adviser while the captain retained command of the vessel. Between the handsome Captain Ward, who went nobly down with his ship, and the portly, aging Pilot Frederick Jordan, who survived, the public had little difficulty assigning blame. "Mr. Schwerin is taking advantage of a dead man," opined the *San Francisco Call,* "a privilege he is perhaps pleased to exercise, but his loud assault upon the master of a ship who bravely died at his post will not release responsibility from Pilot Jordan."[93] The *Bulletin* argued in favor of Captain Ward from a point of law: "The pilot gains his authority from the Legislature, the sovereign body of the State. . . . Under the law he is master, in every sense, of the vessel he is guiding into port."[94]

One important explanation for the high number of deaths was the lack of proper training of the crew. While Captain Ward had scheduled lifeboat drills at night, they were not held in total darkness, as was the case when the *City of Rio de Janeiro* went down. Third Officer Charles J. Holland could not recall a time when the lifeboats were lifted and hung suspended in their davits in preparation for lowering. Other members of the crew described the drills as simply a farce.

ON FEBRUARY 23, 1901, San Francisco coroner Thomas B. W. Leland and his jury met to view the body of Sarah Wakefield and then adjourned to the following Wednesday, February 27. Once commenced, the inquest was measured in hours rather than days. Jordan told his version of the sinking, as did Second Officer Graham Coghlan. Schwerin testified that he had complete faith in his Chinese workers and would trust his life to their care. Gabrielle Lehrahen, one of the three women survivors, testified that it was so dark on deck that she was unable to tell what the Chinese were doing.[95] Jordan made the case that the reason for his risky run into the harbor was that Captain Ward was eager to take his ship home. Dr. O'Neill testified that the sailor who fouled the tackle while lowering his lifeboat was Chinese. Each witness was only briefly examined.

According to the jury, the accident was caused "by criminal negligence on the part of both Captain Ward and Pilot Jordan." Seemingly almost as an afterthought, the jurors added: "And we most strenuously censure the Pacific Mail Steamship Company for employing incompetent Chinese crews for saving human lives."[96]

Given that so little evidence was introduced, it is difficult to know how such a far-reaching verdict could be decided. Obviously the daily newspapers had more influence on the jury than anything that could have taken place in the inquest's short session. The hearing provided ammunition for the anti-Asian element in society. Their actions on the *City of Rio de Janeiro*, it was claimed, proved that they were unreliable. Two weeks after the inquest, the San Francisco Labor Council adopted a resolution condemning the Pacific Mail Steamship Company for employing Chinese workers and demanded that Congress "enact a law prohibiting the employment of any Asiatic in any capacity on any vessel of the United States."[97]

Other boards of inquiry would continue their investigations. O. F. Bolles, the inspector of hulls, and his counterpart John K. Bulger, the inspector of machinery, under the supervision of John Birmingham, the general inspector for San Francisco, began a federal maritime hearing. The impartiality of the federal inspectors, who no longer included Captain Bob (Bully) Waterman, seemed possible to the *San Francisco Call.* As it noted two days after the disaster:

> The Federal inspectors have already begun their inquiry, and their method indicates that the investigation will be of some benefit. In times past the Pacific Mail Steamship Company has taken care to interview survivors of wrecks before the officers of the law could see them, and the result has been not infrequently advantageous to the Pacific Mail Steamship Company. The Federal inspectors probably do not intend that this happen again, for yesterday they had one important witness, the surviving officer of the *Rio de Janeiro,* Graham Coghlan, before them.[98]

Apparently, the newspaper was not aware that Inspector Birmingham was formerly superintendent of the Pacific Mail Steamship Company, the enterprise whose ship his employees were investigating. It is difficult to explain why such a blatant case of conflict of interest did not seem to raise an eyebrow among the public. On March 27, the federal commission rendered its decision. Captain Ward and Pilot Jordan were censured for the *City of Rio de Janeiro* wreck.[99] But since Ward was dead and Jordan out of federal jurisdiction—pilots were regulated by a state board—the government could take no action against either man. Only Chief Engineer P. H. Herlihy faced the inspectors' sanction. He had failed to dismiss his men so that they could assist with the evacuation of the ship. Herlihy was severely censured and his license as engineer was revoked.

About the same time as the federal inspectors were conducting their hearing, Major Thomas J. Blakeney, superintendent of the Thirteenth Life-Saving District, was holding an investigation into the alleged negligence and inefficiency of the stations ringing the narrows. While it was supposedly called to gather information about the role of the service in the *City of Rio de Janeiro* tragedy, the hearing's real purpose was to clear the sullied name of the Life-Saving Service in the San Francisco area. Blakeney, it soon became evident, was not interested in examining the problems within the U.S. Life-Saving Service, but simply to discredit witnesses who testified against it. The crew and passengers of the *City of Rio de Janeiro,* as well as Pilot Frederick Jordan, were called and cross-examined as to whether they actually heard the ship's distress whistle. Despite his attempts, Major Blakeney found it difficult to shake the witnesses' testimonies.

Seemingly to confuse the issues, Blakeney attempted to make the case that Captain Ward and Frederick Jordan were at fault. The point, of course, was irrelevant. The reason for the accident was up to other boards to investigate.

Similarly, the soldiers from Fort Point were subjected to rigorous cross-examinations. After interviewing a number of soldiers who swore under oath to hearing the distress whistle, and being unable to shake their stories, Blakeney was becoming increasingly exasperated. After dismissing the last soldier on March 7, 1901, he told the hearing, "They can't tell the truth. T'would kill 'em if they did."[100] In the end, the Live-Saving Service investigation proved nothing that was not already clear: Mark Ellingsen and other lookouts had not recognized the *City of Rio de Janeiro*'s distress whistle. Instead of clearing its name, the inquiry further tarnished the image of the lifesaving program.[101]

Concerned that the wreck-strewn entrance to the city may turn away potential business, the Chamber of Commerce called for the upgrade of fog whistles and sirens near the narrows. Their appeal, incidentally, was sent to Senator George C. Perkins, a partner in the firm of Goodall, Nelson and Perkins, onetime owners of a fleet of dilapidated coastal steamships. Through Perkins's initiative, the money for a better foghorn was soon forthcoming.

The sinking of the *City of Rio de Janeiro* turned the press's attention to new ways of preventing sea disasters. Edwin Fabion took out a patent for electric bulkhead doors that closed after the hull struck an object.[102] As it stood, Fabion's invention did not leave much time for the firemen, oilers, and engineers to escape what would soon be watery prisons, but similar devices were soon in place on many large liners. The *San Francisco Call* noted that experiments were then under

Drawing of Pilot Frederick
W. Jordan from the *San
Francisco Call,* February
28, 1901.

way using radio waves for communication: "Recent successes obtained
in experiments with wireless telegraphy give reason to believe that
within a time comparatively short science will devise a means by
which the officers of a ship proceeding along a dangerous coast or
through a narrow channel will be able to know exactly how near they
are to the coast."[103] While the newspaper was correct, it did not recognize the full impact of the role of radio on board ships.

As was the usual practice after the loss of a ship, the Pacific Mail
Steamship Company petitioned the U.S. District Court on March 19,
1901, for limitation of liability. If granted, such limitation meant that
claims against the carrier were restricted to the value of the passenger
tickets, the money the ship made from the freight it carried on that
voyage, and the value of the ship. In the case of the *City of Rio
de Janeiro,* this was an appallingly small figure. The shell of the ship
had slipped into deeper water, and in the face of numerous attempts
to find her, she remained lost. The total value of freight and passage money was about $25,000—an amount to be shared among the
passengers.

Shipping companies normally had little difficulty sheltering under the limitation of liability legal provisions, for in order to overturn the ruling it was necessary to prove the company was negligent. Despite that final perilous run, both Captain Ward and Pilot Jordan were regarded by their professional boards as competent individuals, so it would be difficult to prove that the company would have expected such an attempt.

However, Ruth Miller, executrix of Sarah Wakefield's estate, filed a petition against the limitation of liability, claiming that the *City of Rio de Janeiro* was not seaworthy and was poorly equipped. She also claimed that the captain and pilot were negligent, and that the ship lacked sufficient trained crew. Others joined Miller with claims against the company.[104]

The petition went to a hearing on November 25, 1902, with William Denman as the lawyer representing the claimants. Denman's case hinged on the failure of the company to provide a sufficient crew, one that understood the officers and could follow orders. He called among others R. H. Long and Kate West, both of whom testified that after the ship struck, there was enough time that the passengers might have been saved.[105]

On April 10, 1903, Judge De Haven, although observing that the captain and pilot were grossly negligent, found that the ship had sufficient crew and that officers' giving orders through the boatswain was standard maritime practice. Since the company could not be held responsible for the actions of the captain and the pilot, the court refused to overturn the company's petition for limited protection.[106]

The case was reargued before the U.S. Circuit Court of Appeals for the Ninth Circuit in 1904. In his presentation to the court, Denman had made it clear that the difficulties on board the *City of Rio de Janeiro* were not the result of deckhands being Chinese per se, but that it was the language difficulties between the officers and the sailors that created problems. However, for many that harbored deep-seated resentments against this foreign and apparently unfathomable culture, anything that brought shame to the Chinese was regarded as a victory.

The California Court of Appeals had earlier rejected the Pacific Mail Steamship Company's petition for limitation of liability. Although the case would not be settled until it reached the U.S. Supreme Court, the Pacific Mail Steamship Company was the big loser. As far as is known, this was the first time that a petition for limited liability by a major transoceanic carrier was refused by the courts.[107]

WHILE PARTS OF the ship's superstructure, pieces of her cargo, and even the occasional body came to the surface, the hull of the liner *City of Rio de Janeiro* has never been found. Soon after the sinking, stories that the vessel carried fabulous wealth in her cargo holds and in her safe began to circulate, but the ship's manifest lists goods of a more prosaic nature. Over the years, many efforts to uncover the rusting remains of the ship were made, all without success.

The disappearance of the *City of Rio de Janeiro* off the face of the earth[108] has contributed to the strange stories about a jinxed ship and her crew. After the sinking, the *San Francisco Call* referred to her as a "hoodoo."[109] It appeared she was a cursed vessel.

Typical of doomed ships, the fate of the *City of Rio de Janeiro* was apparently clear to those who could sense the future. Returning from Hawaii to California, Mr. and Mrs. John Spencer had booked passage on the vessel. However, as the day of the departure approached, Mrs. Spencer had the undeniable fear that something was going to happen to the ship. She asked her husband to return the tickets, which he did, but the only other ship to the Pacific Coast at that time was the *Warrimoo,* which ran to Victoria, British Columbia. Since the Spencers lived in Los Angeles, they would disembark far from their final destination. When the couple arrived at Tacoma, Washington, they received the news of the *City of Rio de Janeiro* disaster.[110]

On February 20, two days before the accident, the wife of Robert J. MacCoun, a twenty-eight-year-old first assistant engineer, was suddenly struck by the notion that she would not see the *City of Rio de Janeiro* or her husband again. As it turned out, her fears were well founded: he was one of the crew who was lost.

The wife of another member of the crew, Purser John Rooney, had a presage of death. On the night the *City of Rio de Janeiro* was due to arrive, his wife went to bed, and after falling asleep dreamed that her husband faced a terrible fate. Rooney was last seen in his office attempting to open the safe.[111]

The myth of the hoodoo ship was again given wider press coverage fifteen years later when a water cask belonging to the *City of Rio de Janeiro* floated to the surface of San Francisco Bay.[112] The ship was cursed, some mariners claimed, because of an incident that happened during an earlier voyage to the city. As she steamed for port, one of the crew members went insane, but before he could be restrained he escaped; and taking advantage of the confusion, broke into the cabin of a young female passenger and assaulted her. The crewman was taken in irons and chained to the rail for the remainder of the voyage. In his fury, the man cursed the *City of Rio de Janeiro,* calling on God to sink the ship with her entire crew.[113]

God apparently acceded to the wishes of the crewman, but contrary to his desire some of the crew escaped. It is not surprising in this atmosphere, where a large vessel together with many of her crew and passengers disappear at the very gate of the city, that such stories take shape.

MAJOR SHIPWRECKS like the *City of Rio de Janeiro* are played upon an enormous stage, for the cast includes not only the crew and passengers on board, but others left on shore; and indeed, for these people life was never the same. Friends and family would forever feel the loss. Even to survive changes one's life. To relive the terror of the last moments of the *City of Rio de Janeiro* was a nightmare. For some of the living, like Pilot Frederick Jordan and Chief Engineer P. H. Herlihy, the stain of the sinking of the ship would hang over them for the remainder of their lives. Although he was not even on the vessel, Mark Ellingsen would have to carry with him the sounds of the ship's last moments.

At the center of this calamitous whirlpool were the fundamental errors of judgment that brought about the end of the *City of Rio de Janeiro.* Captain Ward was well aware of the danger of making the run through the narrows without adequate visibility, but he gave into the demands of his patron, Rounseville Wildman. Kate West recalled what Captain Ward said on the last night: "The *Rio* had better be late than on the rocks. If we attempt to enter the harbor in this fog we will be sure to go onto the rocks."[114] He was right.

CHAPTER 5

Clallam: The "Hoodoo" Ship

Nearly three years after the loss of the *City of Rio de Janeiro,* another supposedly jinxed ship met a tragic end. The loss of a new vessel, the *Clallam,* shocked the communities of the Pacific Northwest. "Countless thousands of tragedies could be told of the deep, restless ocean," wrote the *Seattle Daily Times* on January 10, 1904, "but one of the saddest springs out of the wreck of the steamship *Clallam.*"[1] The newspaper was responding to the bizarre series of incidents that resulted in the foundering of the Alaska Steamship Company's long-haul passenger ferry. While some people were to survive, the icy waters of the Strait of Juan de Fuca claimed many lives. From the moment of her launch, a dark cloud seemed to hang over her. According to many superstitious sailors, she was an unlucky ship likely to meet a tragic and untimely end.

After 1900, one of the last bastions for the construction of wooden-hulled ships was Puget Sound, the inlet connecting Seattle and other cities with the Strait of Juan de Fuca and eventually the open Pacific. A seemingly inexhaustible supply of Douglas fir permitted local ship-builders to construct a fleet of small boats and ships to sail the inland sea between Olympia, Washington, and the northern islands of the San Juan chain.

Shipwright Edward Heath, whose reputation as a builder of wooden vessels was unsurpassed, constructed the *Clallam.* Although relatively new to the Northwest, he had previously constructed many staunch ships for the Great Lakes. On Puget Sound, Heath had built the steamer *Majestic* and the ferry *West Seattle*.[2] In 1902, Heath had been given the commission to build the steamship *Clallam*. There was every reason to believe that this vessel would provide years of dependable service.

Launched in Tacoma, Washington, in the spring of 1903, for the Puget Sound Navigation Company (a subsidiary of the Alaska Steamship Company), the 673-ton ship was 168 feet long with a beam of 32 feet. One innovative feature was a promenade deck with saloon rooms and forty-four staterooms.[3] "Her fine, strong lines brought forth the opinions that she will be one of the finest steamers on Puget Sound," noted the *Tacoma Daily Ledger*.[4] She seemed a worthy addition to the company's expanding ferry fleet.

The vessel, though, was not ideal for the run between Seattle and Victoria. The propeller-driven ship was slow. Her eight-hundred-horsepower compound steam engine supposedly developed a cruising speed of only thirteen knots, but even this pace was probably optimistic.[5] While time was less important to the tourists enjoying Puget Sound scenery, commercial travelers were less impressed by the *Clallam*'s performance. She was scheduled for the Seattle-Victoria route only through the spring of 1904, after which time a faster vessel would take her place.[6]

FROM THE BEGINNING, the *Clallam* seemed destined for ill fortune. Named in honor of Clallam County in northwestern Washington, the *Clallam* was launched in a ceremony held on April 15, in Tacoma. After the speeches from dignitaries to the large crowd, the band struck up a tune. Then Hazel Beahan, elected by the people of Clallam County to christen the ship, took the bottle of champagne attached to the bow by a ribbon and prepared to smash it against the ship. However, the blocks holding back the hull were removed before she was ready, and the young woman swung widely and missed her mark. She quickly leaned forward, grasped the bottle, and tried again without success. The ship was picking up speed as it moved down the slipway. Miss Beahan had to reach far forward to take hold of the wildly swinging bottle, but it was becoming increasingly difficult to control, and again she missed. Finally, in frustration, she threw a hammer at the rapidly retreating bottle of wine still attached to the bow. "Several

Photograph of the SS *Clallam* shortly after her launch. (Puget Sound Maritime Historical Society)

old time shipping men in the big crowd that witnessed the launching could not refrain from saying that it was a bad sign . . . ," recalled the *Seattle Post-Intelligencer*.[7]

This was not the only ill omen that day, for when the ship, bedecked in bunting, reached the water, the Stars and Stripes had been raised so that it was flying upside down. This was the international signal of distress and, given the significance of the moment, a singularly unlucky event.[8] Even the launch of the *Clallam* broadside into the water—because the shipyard was on a narrow slough—was considered bad luck.[9] According to superstition, ships had to taste water stern first.

Not subscribing to sailors' superstitions, the principals of the Alaska Steamship Company were pleased with their new vessel. Indeed, while the *Clallam* carried collision and fire insurance, she had no coverage against wreckage.[10] The Alaska Steamship Company was begun in 1895—two years before thousands of gold seekers headed north, hoping to strike it rich in the Klondike—and had established a good, but by no means perfect, safety record on one of the Pacific's most difficult and dangerous coastal routes.[11] Perhaps it was the company's success on the wild waters of Alaska that led to its underestimation of the dangers of Puget Sound and Strait of Juan de Fuca. As it would emerge later, the *Clallam* failed to carry even distress rockets that could have alerted other ships or people on shore.

Captain of the vessel was fifty-three-year-old George Roberts, a veteran West Coast mariner.[12] Roberts was one of the founders of the Alaska Steamship Company and had a substantial interest in the enterprise. Roberts's career was not without mishap, for several years earlier he had wrecked his ship the *Dirigo* below Juneau. While the vessel was salvaged, it was so badly damaged that it had to be converted to a steam schooner hauling mainly freight.[13]

After the fitting out was completed, the *Clallam* was commissioned on July 3, 1903, with a license to carry 350 passengers.[14] Soon after, she began service on the Seattle-Victoria run, with a stop at Port Townsend, Washington. The vessel had a number of problems during her first months on the route. Not long after she began service, the *Clallam*'s rudder cracked and had to be replaced in late November. On her run to Victoria on December 19, before the ship reached Port Townsend, the *Clallam*'s engine suddenly stopped. While two tugs arrived to offer assistance, Captain Roberts apparently dismissed them. "The *Clallam* had a sail up at that time," reported passenger William Holden. "This was on a calm day but the boat was drifting towards the rocks."[15] A few minutes later the engine suddenly started and the vessel continued on to Port Townsend.

AT 8:30 A.M. on Friday, January 8, 1904, the *Clallam* had been in service less than six months when she was scheduled to leave Seattle for Victoria (Friday, according to sailors' superstition, was an unlucky day to begin a voyage). After a brief stop at Port Townsend, she was to reach Victoria sometime after 3 P.M.

During the off-season, when passenger traffic was reduced, the *Clallam* relied on freight to meet her expenses. On this trip, though, the ship was carrying little cargo. Since the vessel had no donkey engine by which to operate a winch, the stevedores wheeled on board 114 cases of tinned sausage, 16 cases of pickled pork, 10 cases of ham,

5 barrels of salted beef, 500 slabs of oil cake (a substance made from vegetable fats rendered into solid bars and used as animal feed), 24 bales of mattresses, 140 empty kegs, and a case of rubber packing. There were also a case of metal buttons, a case of copper rivets, a sack of assorted brass fixtures, and 2 boxes of armature coils destined for the British Columbia Electric Company's railway. Because Puget Sound rarely experienced the high seas common to the outer coast, little effort was made to properly stow her freight. Between Port Townsend and Victoria, though, the *Clallam* would leave her protected inland sea and face the dangerous waters of the Strait of Juan de Fuca.

At Seattle's Pier No. 1 at the foot of Yesler Way, the passengers walked up the *Clallam*'s gangway. Although it was not heavily overcast, the winds were gusting and there was a slight chop on the water as the lines were cast off and the ship began her slow voyage up Puget Sound. The passengers were a mixed group. Colonel Charles W. Thompson, president of the Washington Co-operative Mining Syndicate, was on his way to the community of Crofton on Vancouver Island. Thompson, fifty-three years old, had moved to Tacoma from North Dakota fifteen years earlier. With his wife in California, he took his young daughter Imogene to stay with friends in Seattle while he continued on to Victoria.

Thompson may have been in the company of Lenora Richards, part owner with her estranged husband of the valuable Richard III copper mine. In an age where women were expected to play little more than a supporting role in the world beyond the home, Richards was an exception. She had been the first woman to climb Mount Sicker on Vancouver Island. Before boarding the *Clallam*, she had made arrangements to sell her mining interests to a consortium and was traveling to Crofton to clear up the paperwork regarding the sale. As a major Northwest mining promoter who had interests in a smelter at Crofton, it seems likely that Thompson was acting for the buyers.

Jessie Galletly and her daughter Jeannie were returning home from the Green River Hot Springs in Washington State. The wife of Victoria bank manager A. J. C. Galletly, Jessie had been complaining of fatigue and hoped that the mineral waters at Green River would rejuvenate her.[16]

Mr. and Mrs. Samuel Bolton were from Leduc, Canada. After marrying in their hometown at the end of December, the couple decided to spend their honeymoon in the Northwest. They intended to return home via Victoria and had bought tickets for the Friday sailing of the *Clallam*.[17]

Twenty-year-old Louise Harris, a prominent Spokane socialite who had been visiting friends in Seattle, almost missed the *Clallam*'s departure. She arrived only moments before the vessel's lines were cast off. Harris was determined to take that particular sailing and would not be dissuaded. The young woman was traveling to Victoria to visit friends. Her father had been one of the original owners of the LeRoy Mine in Rossland, British Columbia, and Harris was heir to a fortune.[18] From entirely different circumstances was twenty-year-old waitress Minnie Murdock, who was also traveling to Victoria to visit friends.

Edward Lannen and Mary Reynolds were on their way to Victoria to marry. A widow, Mary moved with her daughter Laura from Missoula, Montana, to Seattle in late 1903. Mary had known Edward Lannen of Helena, Montana, since she was a child, and the two had recently become engaged.

Another Montana resident was probably the wealthiest passenger on the ship. He was millionaire railroad contractor Peter Larson.[19] Larson spent at least part of his winters on the West Coast, where the weather was milder.

Like Larson, other passengers found the rainy Pacific Coast climate an agreeable change from the more severe winters elsewhere. Egbert F. Ferris and his friend Rollo Case were from Michigan and had decided to take a winter vacation on the West Coast. After reaching Chicago, they enjoyed the train journey via Omaha to Portland, Oregon, and up to Seattle. There, they booked passage on the *Clallam* for Victoria.

Captain Thomas Lawrence was drawn to the north by the Klondike gold rush and had been for some years master of the Atlin Lake steamer *Scotia*. A well-known mariner in northwest waters, Lawrence had earlier commanded the tugs *Lorne* and *Pilot*. [20] Before freeze-up, he traveled to his home in Victoria and then took a business trip to Seattle. He was now returning home.

Albert K. Prince and Guy L. Daniels were vaudeville performers on their way to Victoria for a one-night engagement. The duo had whistled, sung, and strummed their way from coast to coast and were planning a tour of Alaska in the spring.[21] For Albert Prince, notoriety extended beyond the stage. In Kansas City on January 10, 1901, the musician's sister Lulu Prince Kennedy shot her husband. She received a ten-year sentence.[22] Prince was charged with complicity in the murder, but his case was dismissed.[23]

At a time when a train journey was regarded as dangerous, Prince and his partner had traveled by rail through almost every state in the nation. Both men had survived unscathed, and to Prince, his good luck seemed to show that he had a charmed life. Yet his future may have been cloudier than Prince liked to admit. During an earlier tour of British Columbia, a fortune-teller told him that death would suddenly find him while he was on the water. He seemed to place little stock in the prediction and mentioned it offhandedly in a letter to a sister living in Chicago.[24]

Many passengers like Charles G. Bennett of San Francisco and William H. Grimes of Redmond, Washington, were probably traveling to Victoria in search of work. Bennett had been to sea before, but on this journey he was a passenger. The reason why others like John Davis and Hale Baney were making a trip to Victoria on a blustery January day is not known.

A FEW MINUTES before noon, the *Clallam* slipped into her berth at Port Townsend, Washington. Most prominent among those boarding was Homer H. Swaney, forty-five, president of the Pacific Steel Company.[25] A lawyer and promoter originally from Pittsburgh, he had moved to Port Townsend several years earlier. He had bought up the assets of the Puget Sound Iron Company, which once operated a blast furnace at nearby Irondale, Washington. Swaney set about obtaining capital to restart the operation, and on December 15, 1901, the refurbished plant began production.[26]

Swaney was looking for new opportunities, and his ideas for the development of a Northwest iron and steel industry were limitless. Although intent on enlarging the Irondale operation, he recently had turned much of his attention to Seattle, where he and his family had moved two months earlier. His plan was to establish a large steel mill and rolling plant that would be the major consumer of Irondale pig iron. Only a few days before boarding the *Clallam* he had returned from the East, where he sought investment capital. After a visit to Irondale, he was on his way to Victoria to complete the purchase of British Columbia mining property to supply the raw material for his empire.[27]

With Swaney were Victoria land surveyor and mining promoter Livingston Thomas, and his business associate N. P. Shaw. Shaw was a wealthy former meat packer who had lately turned his hand to developing mining property on Vancouver Island.

Former Port Townsend resident Thomas Sullins had moved with his wife, Dellie, and their three young children to Mount Sicker, a mining camp near Crofton on Vancouver Island, where he had established a copper mine. For the holiday season the family had visited Dellie's niece in Seattle. Before returning home, Sullins and his family stopped off at Port Townsend, where they visited his father.

AT 12:10 P.M., the *Clallam* cast off her lines and steamed out of Port Townsend harbor. A storm warning was up and already the breeze was stiffening. As was often the case with West Coast sailings, the ship's manifest was inaccurate. Children who did not pay half fare were not included on the list. The names of some individuals known to be on board, such as Homer H. Swaney and Minnie Murdock, also did not appear on the manifest.

Shortly after the *Clallam* departed from Port Townsend, passenger Samuel Bolton noted that the wind had changed direction, but during the first minutes after leaving the wharf, the sea remained calm. For some time, he stood on deck looking out at the sea.

Crew member Harold Jensen came up to the promenade. "I looked out and saw a heavy squall coming down the straits. I called the attention of some of the crew to this. At the time there was no great sea but it was increasing."[28] Within a few minutes the storm would be upon them. Mountainous waves crashed over the *Clallam*'s decks.

When the sea rose and began pounding the ship, Bolton went inside and noticed that everyone, including his new bride, had become sick. "I believe I was the only one who was not so," he would later recall.[29] As yet, he didn't believe they were in danger.

This voyage was Montana native Edward Lannen's first trip by sea.[30] Until now his journey had been pleasant enough, for the ocean had not been particularly rough. A little more than an hour after leaving Port Townsend, Lannen began feeling seasick. He went downstairs to the main deck to relieve himself and was gone about fifteen minutes. When he returned, his fiancée, Mary Reynolds, was also severely affected by the rolling of the ship. Lannen sat with her and after a few minutes got up, found the purser, and rented a stateroom.

Saloon steward Archibald King had his first impression that something was wrong when he passed the engine room and noted that a "little water" covered the boiler room floor.[31] Puzzled, he looked on for some time before continuing to the dining room. Whatever the difficulty, he could reason that it was not his responsibility.

IN THE RISING SEA, Captain Roberts was having difficulty keeping the *Clallam*'s head into the wind. She tended to sag away to leeward. "The vessel became caught in the trough of the waves," oiler Edward Parker later remembered, "and the great seas pounded with such fury against the side that the vessel was shaken, and finally a port hole was broken in."[32] The heavy sea poured through the breach. Chief Engineer Scott DeLaunay called to Captain Roberts on the communication tube, telling him the vessel must be kept in the wind, but the *Clallam* would not come around. As the minutes passed, their situation worsened.

DeLaunay had been with Captain Roberts when the *Dirigo* was wrecked in Alaskan waters. He had experience dealing with emergencies at sea, and on this voyage he had much cause for concern. The porthole (properly called a scuttle) should have been protected by a deadlight, a metal hinged cover to seal the glass during heavy seas. The scuttle, which was normally about eighteen inches above the waterline, was often under the surface with the rolling of the ship. First Officer George Doney would later claim that the deadlight had been broken about a month and that DeLaunay had promised to repair it.[33] Using wood and nails, DeLaunay tried to stop the inflow, but with every new wave more water washed in.

After a few minutes, DeLaunay whistled up the tube again to tell the captain the situation. In response, Captain Roberts sent down First Officer Doney with a few seamen to assist the engineering crew. DeLaunay noted to his dismay that the circulating pump was not keeping up with the inflow of water.

Attempts to seal the scuttle continued. "We procured blankets, mattresses, oakum and every article possible to aid in stopping the flood," oiler Edward Parker reported. "For long hours we fought with the seas, and each few minutes saw the water gaining on us constantly."[34]

An increasingly desperate first engineer appeared on the main deck and told deck boy Harold Jensen to report to the captain and repeat the message to keep the vessel in the wind. "I reported this to the Captain and he replied he was doing so as much as he could," Jensen testified. "The wheel was hard over to starboard but the ship was not making much headway."[35]

Not long after the *Clallam* had cleared Port Townsend harbor, deckhand Richard S. Griffiths had gone to his bunk in the crew's quarters. A few minutes later, he was suddenly aware of a noise coming from somewhere above him. Climbing the companionway, he saw that the freight on the main deck had shifted to starboard.[36]

Griffiths returned to the crew's quarters and found some men to move the cargo back. As he quickly discovered, the task was not easy: "There was a carload of oil cake. . . . She was rolling so heavily that the oil cake shifted . . . and a quantity of coal that we had on the main deck shifted onto the oil cake. I started work to shift the oil cake back to port. We worked for about half an hour and then I saw the water washing about on the fire room."[37]

At the same time, several sailors were facing waves crashing over the forward deck as they attempted to seal the hatch leading to the main deck with tarpaulin. Trying to nail the wildly blowing canvas in place, Harold Jensen caught a glimpse through the damaged hatch of the crew shifting cargo on the deck below. A few minutes later, Jensen saw the chief engineer, now wet and dirty, pass up the companionway to the hurricane deck and then into the wheelhouse. After DeLaunay's conversation with the captain, Roberts ordered the jib set to aid the vessel in keeping her head into the wind. Even so, according to Jensen, "she . . . played off as far as the troughs of the sea and would go no further."[38]

Roberts came down from the hurricane deck and took the companionway below deck, where he ordered blankets be used to stop the leak. By now, though, it seemed impossible to plug the hole. Jensen proceeded down to the gantry above the two boilers. "I then saw water in the engine room. There would be from three to four feet on the floor."[39] Water began spilling into the fireboxes and extinguishing the flames. Adding to the problems, the leaking scuttle was now completely under water, making further attempts to contain the inflow hopeless. As would be revealed later, not all the water was coming through the deadlight. The amount was simply too great.

AT THE TIME, the passengers were unaware of their peril. John Davis was attempting to wait out the worst of the weather on deck when he met the watchman. "I was sitting at the aft of the steamship trying to feel well, while really I was getting pretty sick from the effects of the rough sea, when a man came out [on deck] by me with a life preserver on, and I began to laugh at him, because I thought he was geared without cause."[40] Another passenger who had been sitting near Davis also laughed at the crew member, but when they went up on the saloon deck the two were surprised to find other passengers already wearing life preservers.[41]

About 2:30 P.M., a seasick Hale Baney was in his cabin when Purser F. C. Freer, carrying a life preserver, came to his door. Freer gave it to Baney with instructions to put it on. When Baney reached the deck, it was apparent that the purser had good reason for distributing them. According to what was happening, there was seemingly every reason to believe that the ship would founder.

Saloon waiter Archibald King was also helping the stateroom passengers to put on their life preservers. To his surprise, he "found a little boy asleep in a lower berth."[42] The child may have been the son of Mr. and Mrs. Sullins, but if so it was strange that amid the obvious confusion his parents had not moved more quickly to retrieve their little boy. King wrapped him in an adult life preserver and took him on deck.

The vessel's list was increasing, and the water was level with the main deck abaft the engine room on the starboard side. Before moving to the passenger deck, Harold Jensen placed the plugs in the main deck scuppers to prevent the sea from rolling in even faster.[43] Moments later the ship's master ordered the lifeboats lowered. Captain Roberts, Jensen observed, "appeared to be very excited."[44]

This was an ill-considered move. First Officer George Doney, who would normally have been responsible for the boats, remained belowdecks attempting to reduce the inflow of water. Many of the seamen were also below. The captain remained on the hurricane deck. Purser F. C. Freer was ordered to fill the first boats. Freer, though, seemed interested only in making sure that the boats got away as quickly as possible, regardless of the circumstances.

Archibald King was one of the crew members sent to the hurricane deck to lower the lifeboats. The task was made even more troublesome due to the pounding the ship was taking from the wind-whipped waves. The craft were swung over the side on their davits and lowered as far as the railing of the passenger deck. Harold Jensen was by now on the promenade deck, attempting to calm the passengers, when he "heard the order given for the women and children to be put in the boats first."[45] Lifeboats No. 1 and No. 3 had been lowered to the promenade deck and were lashed to the rail.

A mishap occurred before the first boat was in the water. When the order to load women and children was given, passenger Jeannie Galletly quickly went to her cabin to obtain a few personal items. As she returned on deck, the *Clallam* suddenly lurched to starboard, throwing the young woman against the rail with such force that the left side of her face was crushed in.[46]

By now the engine had been silent for a few minutes and the only sounds were the wind and waves, as well as the uncertain voices of the men and women who had been mustered on deck. John Davis recalled that the lifeboats did not seem particularly inviting to the female passengers: "There was quite a few of the women [who] did not want to get in but the Captain and purser insisted. One woman especially [almost certainly Jeannie Galletly] did not want to go. She was bleeding from the mouth and nose. She was lifted into the boat."[47]

The boats were launched with such speed that the boat crews had no time to properly prepare them. Oars and rowlocks remained difficult to retrieve beneath their feet, and at least one craft was dropped into the sea without the drain plug in place. Lifeboat No. 1 was placed under the command of one of the passengers, Captain Thomas Lawrence. Although a longtime West Coast sailor, he had no experience with the type of lifeboats the *Clallam* carried on board.

An often-repeated story in the days following the disaster was that one of the boats capsized as a result of someone's foolhardy action. According to passenger Hale Baney: "I saw a man jump from the upper deck into one—either the first or second boat. I do not know who he was, but I think that it was the first boat and it appeared to turn the boat over, and I noted him strike and injure a woman as he fell in the boat."[48] The account was supported by passenger William King,[49] but many other survivors who had watched the launching of the first two boats failed to recall the incident. It may have been that in the confusion Baney and King were mistaken. First Officer George Doney returned to the deck about the time the first two boats were launched. He watched as "one boat went round the bow and the other around the stern."[50] Both craft were still filled with people.

Moments later, though, the boat under Lawrence's command capsized, spilling everyone on board into the sea. Deckhand Richard Griffiths, who was on deck, saw the captain and six or seven other people come to the surface. Griffiths later stated, "I threw a head line over to Captain Lawrence and hauled him up aboard to the forward rail but one of the other men that was in the water caught him by the foot."[51] Lawrence was dragged under.

The second boat, without the plug in place, began to fill while its passengers were immersed in the rapidly rising water. Griffiths recognized mess boy Alex Harvey as among those on board. The boat was eventually swept away in the heavy seas.

Awaiting launch, the occupants of the last starboard boat, No. 5, were unaware of what was happening. While he was unable to get his wife onto the first boat, Samuel Bolton succeeded in placing her on board lifeboat No. 3, the second boat launched. They said their final good-bye before Bolton left to take a seat on lifeboat No. 5, which by now had been lowered to the rail. Since all the women and children had been already loaded, the places on board this craft were for male passengers as well as crew to take the oars.

Bolton later testified: "I can remember as we were being lowered, someone saying, 'look that first boat is over already.' I looked for the second boat and saw her disappearing around the stern of the steamer."[52] A moment later Bolton's own fragile craft was hung up in its tackle, and as a wave struck, everyone was thrown into the dark ocean. "I then felt myself in the water and I saw people near me in the water. A wave then threw me up against the steamer and I caught a rope on the side of the steamer. A man then caught me by the feet and climbed up and also caught the side. I told him to move on to a window and he climbed up on deck. I just got on deck when I heard someone say that the second boat had capsized."[53]

Bolton gave an anguished cry when he heard that his wife's boat was also lost. He was so overwhelmed that he had to be held back from throwing himself into the sea. "I never witnessed a more harrowing thing than Bolton's grief," Purser F. C. Freer told a Seattle newspaper. "His suffering was something terrible to witness, and strong men shed tears at his plight."[54]

The first three boats were swamped, capsized, or hung up, throwing the occupants into the sea. From the ocean, few of the men and none of the women and children were rescued and returned to the deck. "Never as long as I live," passenger William King told a Seattle newspaper, "shall I forget the indescribable horror of the moments which followed the launching of the lifeboats. . . . the crying of the women and children, the shouting of the officers giving orders, the calling of farewells to loved ones left behind, and the waves dashing around the fated vessel."[55]

Passenger Charles G. Bennett was ordered to help in readying the port boats, but while they were placed over the side and lashed to the rail, none were launched. After witnessing what had happened with the starboard boats, few passengers or crew wished to trust their lives to the remaining craft.

Some passengers were unaware that the ship was being abandoned. Miner Thomas Morris had boarded the *Clallam* in Seattle. When the waves began to increase, Morris moved aft. "I think I must have been asleep and I heard some children cry and I looked up and saw some people with life belts on, and I looked out and saw a boat. She was about 200 yards away and had people in."[56]

Morris later testified: "I then went on deck and saw another boat with one end hanging from the davits and some men hanging on to the rope in the water. I tried to pull them up and when some help came we did get them up."[57] The launching had been a disaster. Not one woman or child remained alive.

Following the loss of the three boats, a crew member turned the ensign upside down and ran it to half-mast, an international signal of distress. When Captain Roberts noticed the flag he demanded that it be brought down. Despite the loss of many of the *Clallam*'s passengers and crew, Roberts apparently did not wish to face the seriousness of his situation.

Earlier the deck boy, Harold Jensen, recommended to Captain Roberts that the cargo be thrown overboard to lighten the ship, but received no reply. It was an indication of the crew's loss of confidence in the ship's master that after the lifeboat disaster they began to act without orders. Richard Griffiths and Harold Jensen were the first to unload the cargo. "We put over hams, mattresses, etc.," Griffiths recalled, "and the rest of the crew started throwing oil cake over; also the coal."[58]

AT 3:05 P.M., Victoria resident Herbert Taylor stood on top of Beacon Hill, overlooking the entrance to the city's harbor. As he looked out on the rough sea below him, he saw the *Clallam* in the distance. He trained his marine glasses on the vessel. As he told the Victoria inquest later: "She was about a mile off Trial Island and appeared to be in distress. I did not, however, see any signals of distress."[59] (Contrary to government regulations, the *Clallam* carried neither rockets or flares.)[60] As Taylor observed, "She had a small sail set and her bow gradually swung round until she was in the trough of the sea."[61]

A few minutes later, horse-drawn taxis were pulling up along Victoria's Wharf Street to await the arrival of the *Clallam*. Edward E. Blackwood, the Victoria agent for the Alaska Steamship Company, went to the roof of the Driard Hotel, which had a good view beyond the harbor entrance, where he could watch for the ship's arrival. He found her about ten miles out. According to Blackwood, "She did not appear to be moving and she did not appear to be 'just right.' "[62]

He could not see much, though, because he had not brought his pair of binoculars. Blackwood decided to take a hack to Clover Point, where he had a better view of the ship. There he borrowed a pair of heavy marine glasses and scanned the sea for the *Clallam*. "I could see then she was apparently in the same position and rolling heavily."[63]

The agent went to the nearest telephone and attempted to find in Victoria harbor a tug with steam up. Blackwood spent several hours in search of such a vessel, but none were available. A few small Victoria steamers did agree to brave the rough waters of the strait, but since they were not towboats the help they could offer was limited. In the meantime, Blackwood telegraphed Superintendent Frank Burns at the Seattle head office of the Alaska Steamship Company, who in turn arranged that two big tugs, the *Richard Holyoke* and the *Sea Lion,* be sent from Port Townsend. Much time had been wasted. It was 6 P.M. before the two towboats steamed out of Port Townsend harbor. Had a big tug been available at Victoria, the *Clallam* could have been quickly found and towed into harbor. (Later, the Canadian government would contract with the vessel *Salvor* to have steam up and be always ready at Victoria for such emergencies, but for the *Clallam* the agreement would come too late.)

THE LOSS OF the lifeboats had left the remaining passengers and crew with little hope of rescue. Without her engine, and by now with her jib ripped away by the wind, the *Clallam* was at the mercy of the storm. The ship, though, proved to be a more seaworthy vessel than many had supposed. As dusk settled in, she continued to take on the full force of the waves.

Although the bilge pump was normally steam operated, it was possible to work it by hand, and First Officer George Doney and deckhand Richard Griffiths set about to slow the steady rise of the water. The problem was that the line appeared to be blocked. Without other options, Griffiths suggested that they begin bailing brigades, and in a few minutes passengers and crew were put to work to fight against the water. Working in three crews from the engine room amidships, water was emptied bucket by bucket over the side. "I have no idea where the water was coming in," Archibald King stated, "but I know that it was coming from the stern some place."[64]

The task of the bucket brigades was made more difficult by the greasy film left by the oil cakes. The bars had been thrown over the side, but not before they had come in contact with seawater. Once moistened, a slippery residue remained on the main deck, causing men to slip and slide.[65]

By now the vessel was waterlogged and had taken on a severe list, but the brigades held their own against the inrush of the sea. The men, though, were becoming exhausted. It was clear that they could not continue on the water lines forever.

About 9:30 P.M., the lights of a tug were seen, much to the relief of everyone on board the *Clallam*. She was the *Richard Holyoke* from Port Townsend. By now the *Clallam* had drifted away from Victoria and was midway between Smith and San Juan Islands on the American side of the strait. According to Jensen, Captain Roberts "tried to hail her but could not make himself heard so he told the mate to hail the tow boat and ask for a tow. The tug Captain asked where to and Captain Roberts said wherever he could take us the quickest. I do not think either party understood each other very well."[66] Captain Robert Hall of the *Richard Holyoke* put a line on board the *Clallam* and began towing the vessel toward Port Townsend. Later it would appear that almost no one on board the *Clallam* believed she would remain afloat long enough to make port. Yet Captain Roberts failed to make the tug aware of the seriousness of his situation. There were a number of shallow locations along the shores of nearby islands where the ship could have been beached. He did not fulfill his responsibility to his passengers and crew. Roberts appeared more interested in saving his ship.

After the line from the tug was secured and the *Clallam* was in tow, the passengers and crew were ordered to return to bailing. While under tow, the ship was filling with water faster than ever. By now the water pressure had ruptured the deadlights in the galley and the sea poured in. Harold Jensen went aft to try to limit the inflow of water through the scuttles, but there was nothing to be done. The ship was now sinking quickly. "The Captain was told this," Jensen testified later, "and he ordered everyone to quit work and go on to the upper deck."[67]

About this time, the lights of another ship were seen. She was the tug *Sea Lion,* sent out from Port Townsend. As she approached, Captain Roberts hailed the boat and said the passengers and crew wanted to be taken off the *Clallam* and to tell the *Richard Holyoke* to stop the tow. With the *Clallam* almost submerged, it had been a mistake to send the *Sea Lion* away to the *Holyoke*. "The second tug by going after the first one," Richard S. Griffiths estimated, "lost twenty minutes or half an hour of valuable time before she could take us off."[68] This delay would cost lives. By now, as Harold Jensen recalled, "the *Clallam* was settling by the stern and was on an even keel and in 15 or 20 minutes she began to list to port. . . ."[69]

First Officer George Doney made his way to the hurricane deck, where he tried to free the life raft, which was still lashed to the top of the deckhouse. After a few minutes, Harold Jensen and a passenger arrived, and together the three men cut away the lashings and freed the craft. Passenger Egbert F. Ferris wrote later: "By this time she [*sic*] ship had careened over until her decks stood nearly perpendicular and her smokestack and mast lay nearly in the water. We had all climbed over the deck-rail as she turned over and were clinging to the side of the ship. Pretty soon she gave a lurch forward and the bow went under and I under with it."[70]

Minutes before the end, steward Chin Wing had gone to his bunk, retrieved his personal possessions, and secured them in a light white woolen blanket, which he rolled up and tied under his coat. After reaching the deck, he clung desperately to the starboard railing, but was soon washed away by a wave. When he finally surfaced he found himself near a wooden icebox, which he used to support himself. After the *Clallam* disappeared, one of the tugs moved into the debris field and picked up the crewman. Wrapped in his blanket, Chin noted that he was the only person on board the *Clallam* to escape with more than the clothes on his back.[71]

Railroad contractor Peter Larson was one of the survivors of the *Clallam* disaster. "We clung to the starboard rail until we were washed overboard. Next I found myself clinging to a door of the *Clallam* which had been washed into the sea."[72] Samuel Bolton, who was obviously suffering the effects of the loss of his wife and being tossed from a lifeboat into the cold Pacific waters, could only remember clinging to the *Clallam*'s mast as the ship went under. He could not recall the circumstances of his rescue.[73]

As he clung to her bow, deckhand Richard Griffiths was aware that the *Clallam* was literally disappearing under his feet: "I was at that time partially under water and as I could not make the people in front of me move up I passed over some of them and a sea broke over and washed everyone off the bow except myself. I then got into the rigging and went up as far as the mast head light. At this time the

Captain was hanging on to the side of the ship. I could see the people who had then washed off floating around and presently a sea came and took all those who were on the side of the ship."[74]

Passenger Charles G. Bennett of San Francisco had made his way up the side of the craft and into the ship's funnel when he noticed that the life raft had been lowered: "One man was on it. I made for the raft and when I got on it I noticed that it was the Chief officer. . . . Shortly afterward there were about ten or twelve people got on to it mostly crew. The Captain was on it and in about half an hour we were picked up by the *Sea Lion.*"[75]

Among the last survivors to leave the *Clallam* was William King, who had joined the vessel at Port Townsend: "As I saw the raft shove off I ran out on the mast and jumped off. . . . Fifty feet through such a sea was a long way to go, and it was all I could do to make it. Twice I was submerged in heavy rollers, but held my breath and didn't swallow any water. By the time I reached the raft the *Sea Lion* had a boat out. They brought us a line by which we pulled ourselves on board the *Sea Lion,* and the boat went on to pick up those left clinging to the wreckage."[76]

Oiler Ed Parker managed single-handedly to make his escape by using the last port lifeboat above the water. "I crawled to the upper part of the works and alone cut loose the third and last boat which had left the *Clallam.* Just before the ship went down I was forced to put off, as there was no one about me, and quickly I was carried away from the wreck."[77] Parker drifted in the boat all night and was picked up by the tug *Sea Lion* the next morning.

Passengers Edward Lannen, William Grimes, and Thomas Sullins were four of seven men who managed to gain a hold of the pilot-house, which had floated free. "One man," Grimes recalled, "whose name I did not learn saved his life by clinging onto Thomas Sullins' foot and leg. He hung on for dear life and was finally rescued along with the rest of us."[78] They remained holding on to the house for about half an hour before being picked up by the *Richard Holyoke.*

Peter Larson was rescued adrift on a ladder. "He was unconscious when we got him aboard," Captain C. C. Manter of the *Sea Lion* reported, "and I thought he was done for."[79] After a few minutes on board the tug, though, Larson revived, but he was in considerable pain.

Many of those who had endured until the end were sucked under as the ship disappeared below the surface.[80] Promoter Homer Swaney, who had made it as far as the raft, did not have the strength to hold on and was washed away before the survivors were taken on board the tug. When Swaney's body was eventually recovered floating in the waters off Port Angeles, Washington, on January 19, it was noted that pieces of gravel and wood chips were embedded in his clothing. Swaney had likely come ashore somewhere along the coast of Washington or British Columbia before being taken out to sea again by a high tide. Five days earlier, the body of rival promoter Charles W. Thompson was recovered floating near Trial Island.[81]

According to the pocket watches of the victims, the *Clallam* met her final end about 1:20 A.M. on January 9, 1904, the day after the ship left Seattle. The survivors had endured a twelve-hour nightmare.

After daylight, the tug *Bahada* was the first to pick up bodies near the scene of the disaster. The remains of one man were found lodged in part of the upper deck, which had separated from the *Clallam*'s hull and continued to float. The tug *Albion,* on a run from Victoria to Vancouver, picked up the body of Dellie Sullins. None of the bodies of the Sullinses' children were ever recovered, for there were no preservers small enough to fit them. It would be some years before vessels would be required to carry preservers in an assortment of sizes. One of the few adults not wearing a life preserver was musician Guy L. Daniels. His body was also never recovered.[82]

The body of Spokane socialite Louise Harris was later found at the bottom of a lifeboat. In death she retained her firm grip on the boat that had failed everyone on board.[83] The remains of Jeannie Galletly were found washed up at Clover Point on Vancouver Island, not far from where Edward Blackwood, the Alaska Steamship Company agent, had witnessed the *Clallam* in distress.

AFTER RESCUE, Captain Roberts, together with the remaining passengers and crew, were taken to Port Townsend where most were picked up the next day by the Alaska Steamship Company's vessel *Dirigo* and taken to Seattle. Ironically, this was the same ship that had been wrecked earlier under Roberts's command.

While few Northwest sailors would deny the severity of the storm the *Clallam* faced, the weather office at Victoria noted that the winds and sea were not beyond what would be expected during the winter months. The wind maximum did not exceed fifty-three miles per hour, far from the record set some years earlier.[84]

The *Clallam*'s wooden hull in the age of iron and steel ships seemed to many to be an anachronism. "She was a frail vessel at best," noted an editorial in the *San Francisco Chronicle.* "This was partly proved by the smashing of one of the deadlights set in her hull."[85]

The *Dirigo* had barely tied up at the company wharf when journalists besieged the passengers and crew of the *Clallam.* For many on board, the loss of the *Clallam* was the direct result of the actions of Captain Roberts. The decisions made by the ship's master during the *Clallam*'s last voyage left many questions. Hale Baney, whose legs remained severely swollen from exposure to the icy water, told reporters, "No one can make me believe that Captain Roberts used good judgment, either in sending the women and children away in the boats, when the seas were rolling mountains high, or after the tug *Holyoke* [took the ship in tow]. After we saw the boats swamped, and the women and children struggling in the water, there were mutterings on deck among the passengers."[86]

According to passenger Rollo Case, "The boats were launched fully ten hours before the sinking of the vessel, and it was only when the officers discovered that the boats could not possibly live in such a sea that the mistake of sending off the women and children was realized. Then, of course, it was too late."[87]

John Davis claimed to be one of a group of passengers who, during the last hour of the *Clallam,* had demanded that Captain Roberts signal the *Richard Holyoke* to take them off. According to Davis, he told the ship's master that the vessel was sinking fast, to which Roberts replied that he was in charge. Davis continued, "We asked him if he thought she could get to [Port] Townsend. He said yes she is good for three hours. She floated only about 20 minutes after this."[88]

IN THE COASTAL PORTS of the Northwest, flags flew at half-mast as relatives and friends of the victims questioned why the *Clallam,* a new vessel, came to such a tragic end. In Victoria, a coroner's inquiry was held over the bodies of twenty victims brought to that city. The Canadian inquest was typically thorough, with testimony from more than two dozen witnesses. One fact to emerge was that the ship's rudder had been defective and had to be replaced several months earlier. According to the testimony of deckhand Louis Meyer, there was no trouble with the replacement,[89] but Richard Griffiths disagreed.[90]

Even before the inquest, there was a general feeling in Victoria that Captain Roberts and the shipbuilder Edward Heath were responsible for the *Clallam* disaster. Heath came to Victoria and provided a detailed description of the solid construction that went into the vessel.[91] Threatened with arrest on the charge of criminal negligence, Captain Roberts failed to attend the Canadian inquest.

Although First Officer George Doney answered many of the questions that would have been otherwise put to Roberts, the officer was belowdecks attempting to stem the inflow of water when the order to lower lifeboats was given. Another important witness was Chief Engineer Scott DeLaunay, who testified that he believed the broken deadlight had brought about the loss of the ship. He pointed an accusing finger at Captain Roberts, whom he claimed failed to return to Port Townsend while there was still time.

The inquest heard from its final witness on February 19, 1904, and rendered its verdict several days later. The jury placed most of the blame on George Roberts, who was accused of what amounted to criminal negligence as a result of his handling of the disaster. He was not alone, for DeLaunay was also censured for his failure to operate the ship's pumps. Other charges were leveled against the Alaska Steamship Company's subsidiary, the Puget Sound Navigation Company, for its failure to keep the ship in good order.[92] It came out during testimony that the *Clallam* did not carry distress rockets as required by American law.

The coroner's jury had no power to issue an indictment against Roberts, but there is little doubt the verdict expressed the anger of not only the residents of Victoria, but also the people of cities along Puget Sound. Inquests are often imperfect means for finding the truth. Although many witnesses were interviewed, most jurors had little or no maritime experience. Much of the material was technical in nature, and it seems likely that the jury failed to grasp all the facts. While many of the passengers provided damning testimony against the master of the *Clallam*, Captain Robert Hall of the *Richard Holyoke* would later agree with Roberts's decision not to attempt to transfer passengers to the tug early on. At the time the sea was too high.[93]

The inquiry into the wreck of the *Clallam*, which began in Seattle on January 18, had a different complexion. The two U.S. marine inspectors, Bion Whitney and Robert Turner, were both experienced in their fields.[94] While it was certainly clear that Captain Roberts's behavior during the unfolding drama on the *Clallam* was in question, the captain had done nothing to bring about the rapid rise of water in the furnace room. Scott DeLaunay's explanation that the water came through the broken deadlight struck the inspectors as absurd, for the light was only eight inches in diameter. The opening was simply too small to admit enough water to threaten the vessel. After hearing witnesses, including some of the chief engineer's own crew, the inspectors made it clear that they believed the ship's circulating pump had been set wrongly and instead of removing water from the bilge, it instead entered through an open seacock.[95] For such an error, the chief engineer had to bear the responsibility. The inspectors also censured DeLaunay for his failure to immediately notify Captain Roberts that the ship was taking on water.

On February 14, Whitney and Turner revoked DeLaunay's license due to gross negligence. Captain Roberts, also judged guilty of gross negligence for his failure to run up a distress signal, received a one-year suspension of his license. DeLaunay would continue to regard himself as a scapegoat. He claimed that he had not carried out necessary repairs to the deadlight for fear of being fired, a defense regarded as "the merest twaddle" by the supervising marine inspector, John Birmingham.[96] The *Clallam* disaster ended the career of Captain George Roberts, who was so affected by the loss of his ship that he never returned to the sea. He died eleven years later.[97]

While willing to blame the chief engineer and captain, Whitney and Turner seemed less interested in uncovering evidence that may have implicated the ship's owners. For those who worked the waters of Puget Sound, this fact only confirmed their belief that the officials were too closely allied with the steamship companies. During the hearings, the inspectors received many letters concerning unseaworthy vessels. None were signed, for the writers probably had little doubt their names would be given to the companies involved.[98]

The Steamboat Inspection Service did nothing to investigate these complaints. However, the collector of customs put the revenue cutters *Grant* and *Arcata* to work inspecting the safety of Puget Sound vessels. While a number of operators were charged with breaches of safety, one of the most heavily fined was the owner of the *Clallam*.[99] The money the Alaska Steamship Company saved on a few basic safety devices had to be paid out many times over.

The horror associated with the loss of so many passengers and crew was not soon forgotten by the travelers. Taking advantage of the public's shaken faith in the Alaska Steamship Company's ships, the Canadian Pacific Railway (CPR) placed the 1,300-ton steamer *Princess Beatrice* on the Seattle–Victoria run.[100] For more than sixty years, CPR passenger vessels plied the waters between Seattle and Victoria. Ironically, although much larger than the *Clallam,* the CPR vessel was also a wooden vessel built on the West Coast.[101] Yet the Alaska Steamship Company was able to weather the adverse publicity and go on to establish large ferry fleets in Washington and British Columbia. The *Clallam* disaster was the only major exception to the company's excellent safety record.

The loss of the *Clallam* quickly brought an end to Homer H. Swaney's attempt to make Washington State a major steel producer. A week after Swaney's death the Pacific Steel Company was in receivership.[102] With Swaney ended the dreams of a large and successful blast furnace operation at Irondale, Washington. After the promoter's death, though, his plans were revealed to be long on promises and short on capital.[103] His steel bubble had been about to burst.

While the disaster eventually faded from the pages of the local newspapers, the survivors would never forget the events beginning on that stormy January afternoon in 1904. Of the ninety or so passengers and crew on board the *Clallam,* more than fifty died. Although not the worst Pacific disaster, the loss of the *Clallam* was one of the most horrific. For the survivors, there was nothing to do but go on with their lives. Passenger William H. Grimes, who had earlier been listed as among the lost, reflected the feeling of many of those who had been on board the *Clallam:* "I and every other survivor had a terrible time, but I'm alive and not dead, as reported, so I should be, and am, thankful."[104]

CHAPTER 6

Valencia: Appointment with Death

"In the history of marine disasters on the Pacific Coast," the *Seattle Post-Intelligencer* wrote in 1906, "the wreck of the steamer *Valencia* on Walla Walla reef on the night of January 21 [*sic*] offers no parallel."[1] While the ship actually struck the rocks a few minutes before midnight on Monday, January 22, the extent of the tragedy was no exaggeration. More people died when other Pacific Coast steamers went, but they sank relatively quickly and the passengers and crew did not endure terrible days and nights of suffering. The end of the *Valencia* was a theater of horror. Before dozens of dazed onlookers, disaster seemed to happen in slow motion.

SATURDAY, January 20, 1906, was a clear San Francisco morning. At Meiggs wharf, the last passengers quickly walked up the gangway onto the steamship *Valencia*. She was about to leave on her scheduled voyage north to Seattle via Victoria, British Columbia. A fresh breeze from the south had dissipated the morning low clouds and the green hills across the harbor were plainly visible.

The first hours on board were uneventful as she steamed through winter twilight. The weather continued clear under a canopy of stars shining against the backdrop of unfathomable blackness. About 5:30 A.M. the following day, the ship passed Cape Mendocino, almost two hundred miles north of San Francisco.[2] This was the last clear view Captain Oscar M. Johnson or his officers had of the coast. By about 3 P.M., a heavy southwest breeze had come up and in every direction only low cloud could be seen. Now and then, the captain was able to catch a glimpse of land through the swirling mist; but it disappeared again almost immediately, making it impossible to fix the *Valencia*'s position. Captain Johnson did not appear particularly worried. The weather was common for this time of year and the sea continued relatively calm.

THE PASSENGERS WERE the usual mix of midwinter travelers. Two men, Cornelius Allison and Fred Erickson, had been enjoying an off-season vacation through the western United States. Allison, who had always loved the sea, even though he now lived in St. Paul, Minnesota, had decided on the short ocean voyage to Seattle before taking the Great Northern Railroad to his home. Allison was a railroad conductor and Erickson an engineer.

For twenty-two-year-old Charles Samuels, passage on the *Valencia* was the end of an extended vacation in the Southwest; he was now returning to his job as fur cutter for the Simons Company of Seattle. An Austrian by birth, Samuels was among the many immigrants who came to America during the first decade of the twentieth century. He was unmarried and roomed in the home of his employer.[3]

Some passengers were leaving California to make a new life. On their way to Seattle to begin a business were second-class passenger F. J. Campbell, his wife, and his sixteen-year-old daughter. Until recently, the Metropolitan Life Insurance Company had employed Campbell as an agent, but he was restless. He had been born too late for the Australia and California gold rushes, but had traveled there, anyway. Now with a family, Campbell had resisted the siren song of the Klondike. Seattle, though, may have seemed the next best thing, for it was the gateway to the North. Also on board was his friend and business partner, G. P. Nordstrom, together with Nordstrom's wife and young daughter.[4]

Like Campbell and Nordstrom, passenger G. L. Willitts was lured by the booming Seattle economy. He was a skilled lathe operator and Seattle seemed the city of opportunity, so he had booked passage north on the *Valencia*. Once established, Willitts intended to send for his wife, who had remained in San Francisco.[5]

First-class passenger Frank F. Bunker, a former California high school principal, had recently been appointed Seattle's assistant school superintendent. He was on his way to take up his new post in the Puget Sound city. Bunker looked forward to the challenge before him, for Seattle seemed to offer opportunities not found in California's increasingly political school system. Traveling with him were his wife and two young children.[6]

On her way to Seattle was another first-class passenger, San Francisco socialite Laura Van Wyck. The Van Wycks were a well-known southern family who had moved to San Francisco some years earlier. Van Wyck was on her way to Seattle to visit her sister, who had married a prominent city attorney.[7]

While the ship would stop briefly in Victoria, most of the 154 passengers and crew were American. George H. Jesse was one of the dozen or so Canadians on board. A former clerk with the Hudson's Bay Company, Jesse was a muscular young man who had won a reputation as an outstanding oarsman. Jesse was returning home after visiting his brother Robert in San Francisco.[8]

BUILT IN PHILADELPHIA by William Cramp and Sons in 1882, the iron-hulled *Valencia* served on the East Coast until 1898, when she became part of the gold rush fleet, moving people and freight between San Francisco and Skagway, Alaska, for the Pacific Packing and Navigation Company.[9] At only 1,598 gross tons, the *Valencia* was one of the smaller vessels serving the North Pacific. She was 252 feet long, with a beam of 34 feet. She was a long, low vessel with a one-hundred-foot bow that gave, falsely, the appearance of speed.

The vessel had not been designed to ply the open waters of the North Pacific in winter. The long bow limited visibility from the bridge. In rough weather, the sound of the waves against the bow further hampered communication between the officers and the lookouts.

The *Valencia* carried six lifeboats and one workboat with a capacity of 181 occupants. In addition, the ship carried three life rafts that held 44 people. The boat deck of the *Valencia* was actually two separate decks divided by the aft mast. The forward quarter, known as the fiddler's deck, had four lifeboats, while two more were on the larger after quarter, called the hurricane deck. Another craft, No. 7, stored on the hurricane deck, was actually a working boat that doubled as a lifeboat. Two of the forward boats were wooden, while the remainder

Photograph of the *Valencia*. (Puget Sound Maritime Historical Society)

were metal of a self-righting design. The three rafts were also stowed on the hurricane deck.[10]

Almost all the ship's 386 life preservers were filled with tule,[11] a material that continued to be regarded by mariners as inferior to cork. They believed that tule became waterlogged quickly and would not keep a person afloat for long.

The *Valencia*'s brief history on the Pacific Coast was troubled. In 1901, on the Alaska run, her purser was arrested and charged with overselling tickets and pocketing the additional funds. He claimed that he was the scapegoat for others, including almost certainly the captain, who were benefiting from the scheme.[12] The *Valencia* was eventually fined almost $9,000 for carrying more passengers than her license permitted. Soon after she was sold to the Pacific Coast Steamship Company. In 1902, the steamer *Georgia* struck her in Seattle harbor. The *Valencia*, which was returning from a voyage to Valdez, Alaska, had one of her hull plates pierced above the water line. It was noted at the time that if the damage had been lower, the *Valencia* might have sunk.[13]

In 1906, now bound for Seattle via Victoria, she carried far less than her licensed capacity of 286 passengers. Many of the thirty-nine first-class staterooms were empty, and no one had trouble finding a seat in the smoking and social rooms. Those familiar with the passenger vessels of the Pacific Coast regarded her as a second-class ship, for she was small, all too open to the elements, slow—averaging only eleven knots an hour—and showing her age. Indeed, during the winter months, she usually served only as a backup to other ships of the Pacific Coast Steamship Company fleet.[14] It was in this role that the *Valencia* was put into service on the San Francisco–Puget Sound route when the company's regular vessel, *City of Puebla,* broke her tail shaft and required extensive repairs. On January 5, 1906, the *Valencia,* under the command of Captain T. H. Cann, was pressed into service.[15] Before she was scheduled to sail on her second voyage to the Pacific Northwest, Captain Cann was transferred to another company vessel, the *City of Topeka.*

Captain Johnson had been a master with the Pacific Coast Steamship Company less than two years, and not surprisingly was given command of one of the company's lesser vessels. His first commission on the *Valencia* had been during the summer of 1905, when she was placed on the San Francisco–Nome, Alaska, run. The voyage had not been without its problems, for on his return he had taken his ship hard aground. Although she was refloated, it had been necessary to jettison some of the *Valencia*'s cargo.[16]

The Pacific Coast Steamship Company apparently had not lost confidence in its new captain, for he continued to hold his commission. He was a longtime employee and had worked his way up from quartermaster to the command of his own ship. Johnson, who was married with one daughter, was known as a steady and dependable family man. Coming from a seafaring background—his brother Adolph was first officer on the steam schooner *Rival*—he made his home in San Francisco.[17]

Like Johnson, most of the crew lived in the San Francisco area. While many had worked for the Pacific Coast Steamship Company for some years, the firm did not guarantee crew members permanent positions on board specific ships. If employees wished to remain on the ship for the next voyage, they added their names to a list posted on the ship. Since the *Valencia* was used almost entirely as a relief vessel, she spent much of her time tied up at the company's berth in San Francisco. Therefore, many of the crew who served on board her were unfamiliar with the ship.

Captain Johnson had never commanded a ship on the Puget Sound run during the winter months, but he seemed unconcerned about what lay ahead. (He had not even gone to the trouble of obtaining the most recent charts of the coast.) From October to April, banks of low clouds often reduced visibility to such an extent that it was impossible to fix the ship's celestial position. Under such circumstances, navigators relied on dead reckoning—a theoretical position worked out by computing the compass heading with the ship's speed through the water—to determine a vessel's location. Since the vessel's progress was relative to the ocean current in which she sailed, this made plotting difficult. The navigator could not accurately calculate the speed of this stream, which made a significant difference in locating the ship's position.

On the Puget Sound run, it was important that the navigator have an accurate fix on the ship's location, for to miss the entrance to the Strait of Juan de Fuca could mean disaster. Through the mist, the sudden appearance of towering breakers on the shore of southern Vancouver Island surprised many an unwary mariner. At least thirty-three vessels had been lost there since the mid-1860s. For this reason, coastal steamers usually set a course for the *Umatilla* lightship, anchored fourteen miles south of Cape Flattery, Washington, at the entrance to the strait.[18]

If heavy weather prevented observation of the lightship, soundings—measurements of the depth of the ocean floor, made with a lead weight attached to a line with a float—were taken. Because the continental shelf suddenly drops off to 120 fathoms or more at the Strait of Juan de Fuca's entrance, mariners would use such readings as a point of departure for setting a course through the strait.

Through early Sunday afternoon, the ship continued on while passengers sat quietly reading in their staterooms or playing cards in the social room. Few ventured out on deck, for the northerly wind seemed to cut through even the heaviest winter coat. Also, at either the port or starboard rails, there was nothing to see but dark ocean swells fading into gray mist.

At 5:30 P.M., Johnson noted in the log that the *Valencia* had passed Cape Blanco, off southern Oregon, but according to Second Officer

P. E. Pettersen, no one on the bridge actually saw the lighthouse beacon. Her position was guesswork based on dead reckoning. Although the Pacific Coast Steamship Company would claim that Captain Johnson had an excellent reputation as a navigator, this skill was absent during his fateful last voyage.

Late Sunday afternoon the wind, which had been blowing lightly down the coast, switched to a southeasterly direction and freshened. During the winter months, winds from the southeast usually arrived in advance of a change in the weather. The ship's northward course would take her in the direction of the fronts moving down the coast from the Gulf of Alaska.

On the afternoon of Monday, January 22, the low cloud began to drop closer to the surface of the water and visibility was further reduced. Johnson did not believe he was near the entrance to the Strait of Juan de Fuca. He was convinced that the patent log—the device towed behind the ship that indicated the vessel's speed—overran by 6 percent. In this way, the distance the *Valencia* traveled was less than would be calculated without allowing for the correction. In fact, the opposite was true. During winter, most mariners were aware of the northerly moving Davidson Current, which frequently appeared off the Pacific Coast. Because of the erratic nature of the flow, it was impossible to calculate its influence on a ship's speed.

Not until 6 P.M. did Johnson order soundings, under the supervision of First Officer W. Holmes. The line was dropped every fifteen or twenty minutes and a reading obtained. The accuracy of soundings, though, depended on a reasonable notion of the ship's position, and Captain Johnson had had no accurate fix on that since the *Valencia* passed Cape Mendocino early Sunday morning.

Johnson had calculated that the *Valencia* would reach Victoria by about three the next morning. At 9 P.M., he ordered the course changed to north-northeast, where he hoped to find a unique line of soundings that led north to the *Umatilla* lightship.[19]

The vessel remained on this course until 10:45 P.M., when he ordered the new heading of north-northwest. By now, he had ordered the use of the sounding machine, which, unlike simply throwing the lead weight, gave an accurate reading of depth. Although the only proof of his position was his own dead reckoning, Johnson seems to have had no doubt that he was near the *Umatilla* lightship. The

Valencia was actually more than fifteen miles farther north, approaching the rocky west coast of Vancouver Island.

That night other ships had anchored to wait for better weather rather than risk a blind approach to the Strait of Juan de Fuca, but the master of the *Valencia* continued on. Given his earlier difficulty on the Nome run, it is probable that Captain Johnson did not wish to be behind schedule.

As the vessel proceeded, Second Officer Pettersen hoped to catch the whistle of the steam foghorn off Cape Flattery, but the only sound was the crashing of waves over the *Valencia*'s bow and the chug-chug-chug of the ship's engines. By now, Captain Johnson was becoming apprehensive. As the ship groped through the fog, he ordered the speed reduced to one-half. A few minutes later the depth was marked at sixty fathoms, then, minutes later, twenty-four fathoms. Something was wrong. The ocean bottom was shallower than it should have been if the ship was indeed off Cape Flattery. He signaled dead slow to the engine room. The quartermaster was ordered to take the ship hard to starboard.

As the ship began to come about she suddenly shuddered. At four minutes before midnight on Monday, January 22, 1906, within a few hundred feet of land, the *Valencia* struck a submerged outcropping of rock. The lookout, cold and tired from his six-hour watch in the freezing air, had seen nothing. Nor had the officers on the bridge.

"By God! Where are we?" cried Johnson.[20]

Immediately Captain Johnson ordered hard starboard. Firemen William Doherty and John Cigalos were on watch in the firerooms when the ship struck. The vessel shook from bow to stern. Her hull, though, seemed to be intact, for no water entered. A few moments later there was another jar, and water began pouring in, forcing the two firemen to scramble up the ladder to safety. "Some time after the ship got her death blow the whistle was blown," Doherty recalled, "and it was one of the most mournful sounds the ear of any mortal ever heard."[21]

In order to beach the stricken vessel, Captain Johnson then ordered full speed astern. Her propeller, though, made only a few revolutions before the vessel stopped with her bow now already underwater. The *Valencia* pivoted around until she faced broadside to the coast. Before he followed the firemen topside, First Assistant Engineer Thomas F. Carrick sounded the bilges and calculated they were filling at a rate of one foot per minute.[22] By the time the men reached the saloon deck, breakers were crashing over the hull.

Passenger G. L. Willitts had earlier braved the weather and was on deck to enjoy a late-night cigar. As he stood at the rail, the ship lurched to a grinding stop. "The command to back her off was given and she went astern at full speed but it was too late," he recalled. "The water was pouring in like a mill race."[23]

Another passenger on the deck was Charles Samuels, who had been in his cabin with three friends when he heard a rumor that a lighthouse could be seen from the deck (a story that proved untrue). He reached the saloon deck just as the ship struck the rocks amidships, the force of which almost threw him over the rail.[24]

Fate could not have picked a worse place for a shipwreck. The *Valencia* had gone aground on the rugged and sparsely populated west coast of Vancouver Island about twenty-two miles north of Cape Flattery. Above the vessel, like dark, looming, hunchbacked giants, were the great sandstone cliffs of the Pachena escarpment. Below, luminescent in the darkness, were the ghostly white breakers dashing over the ship and up onto the rocks closer to shore. The *Valencia* was fewer than a hundred feet from land, but that would be of no consolation. For anyone knowing the ocean, the roar of the surf as it crashed against the ship was the sound of death. No vessel could long withstand such a pounding.

Freight clerk Frank Lehm was on deck shortly after the ship struck. "Never have I seen such waves. They appeared to be as high as the mast head." Instantly all was pandemonium. "The screams of men, women and children mingled in awful chorus with the shriek of the wind, the dash of the rain and the roar of the breakers,"[25] he said later. None of those on board doubted that the *Valencia* was finished. Men and women half clad or still in night attire poured onto the deck and pushed and shoved to get near the lifeboat stations. None of the passengers knew where they should be, for no boat drill had been called since the ship left San Francisco. Many of the crew did not know where their stations were, for they had not read their assignment card posted at the beginning of the voyage.

George Harraden, a first-class passenger who had taken the *Valencia* from San Francisco, retired to his cabin early that evening. He was jarred awake by a shock running through the ship. Still not fully awake, he had begun to dress when a sailor knocked on his cabin door and told him to put on his life preserver. He reached the deck in time to hear someone say, "Lower the boats to the saloon rail."[26]

In the confusion following the wreck, husbands had become separated from wives, parents from children. George Harraden searched for his mother among the frightened passengers on the saloon deck; to his relief, he eventually found her in the social hall. After a few minutes, one member of the crew called out for the women and children to make their way to the boats. Many of the women hesitated, unwilling to leave the apparent safety of the ship. Harraden urged his mother to take her place in a boat, and reluctantly she agreed. That was the last time he saw her.[27]

It was said later that one of the passengers, J. B. Graham, who had made a fortune in Alaska, offered a bag of gold to anyone able to take him off the ship. For those whose own lives were in jeopardy, the gold meant nothing. As men and women scurried about the deck, the sack containing the precious mineral was trampled underfoot.[28]

Boatswain Tim McCarthy was one of the more experienced seamen on board. He had sailed on the *Valencia* under Captain Cann earlier that month and was at least familiar with the ship. He was below when she struck, and made his way up in response to the order for all hands on deck. "The Captain," McCarthy claimed, "had already given orders not to lower the boats below the saloon deck."[29] The command was ignored, though, and the craft were swung out into the water.

John Cigalos saw at least ten people jump overboard and attempt to swim to shore. He would have followed them if a friend had not restrained him. In the darkness, it was unclear what they faced beyond the confines of the deck.

Pettersen, the second officer, left the bridge and was making his way to his lifeboat station aft. The impact of the collision had torn open the cargo stored on deck and thousands of cabbages were now rolling underfoot. On his way down the companionway he slipped on the soggy green leaves and was knocked unconscious.[30]

Passenger F. J. Campbell, with his wife and daughter, reached lifeboat station No. 2, on the port side of the fiddler's deck, and saw the crew stand by and watch male passengers crowd into the craft. Despite the order to enter the lifeboats, most women remained in the social hall and the crew did not attempt to ensure a place for them. Only because of the intervention of a mess boy, who physically removed some of the men from the boat, was there room made for the Campbell family.[31]

Lifeboat No. 2 had one late arrival. Passenger Charles Samuels jumped into the boat as it was being lowered. Before the craft had reached the water, a wave smashed it into the side of the *Valencia*, panicking those on board. Eventually, though, the boat with its cargo of seventeen people began drifting away from the vessel. Captain Johnson had the searchlight turned on the men and women on board the small craft.

There were no officers on board lifeboat No. 2, and the crew was unfamiliar with working the craft. The oars were tied together, and took time to separate. Once they were in place, the wooden oarlocks snapped as soon as pressure was applied. Water was pouring in through the drain, and no one on board could find the plug. Alfred Willis, a sixteen-year-old naval seaman who was on his way to join his ship in Tacoma, did the first thing that came to mind: he jammed his finger in the hole. While no water poured in from the bilge, great waves continued breaking over the sides. Those on board were unable to keep the bow into the waves, and before reaching shore, five or six passengers were washed from the boat. As it neared shore, the craft was picked up by a giant breaker and hurled over the rocks to the base of the cliff. Willis, Samuels, and Campbell were among those who survived, but Campbell's wife and daughter were lost.

At lifeboat station No. 3, the ship's crew were also unable to deal with the panicked passengers that pressed around the boat. This craft, too, was launched without experienced sailors. The passengers on board included Frank Bunker, Seattle's new assistant superintendent of schools, together with his wife and two children. Eventually a wave pulled the boat away from the side of the larger vessel, and sent it sidelong into the rising surf.

Without sailors to handle the oars, the boat was picked up by a wave and capsized. Bunker was about to try to swim to the *Valencia* when the boat, which was now alongside him, righted itself, though it was now nearly filled with water. He turned back to find his wife clinging to the side of the craft. His four-year-old daughter had disappeared and his son lay limp in the half-submerged boat. Bunker dragged himself inside the craft, and with some effort resuscitated his son. The boy opened his eyes and began to cry. While holding his son's head above water, Bunker went to the aid of his wife, but he did not have the strength to pull her into the boat. At that moment another wave crashed over and capsized the craft. Something struck him on the head, leaving him dazed. In the terrifying minutes that followed, he was washed onto the rocky shore, only to be pulled back by the undertow. After three tries, he was finally able to take hold of a barnacle-encrusted rock and crawl beyond the breakers. There was no sign of his wife and children. The only other survivor from Bunker's boat was Frank Richley, a fireman who had crawled out of the surf. Together the two men struggled up the beach in an attempt to get out of the reach of the breakers.

Close by were Campbell, Samuels, and other survivors of lifeboat No. 2. Calling out to each other in the darkness, the nine men moved against the bluff as far away from the rising tide as possible. For the survivors on shore, this would be the worst experience of their lives. "We lost everything, hats, shoes," Samuels would later say, "and the rain was running down from the cliff down our necks."[32]

WHILE THE FIRST lifeboats launched were crowded, the last boats to reach the water were almost empty. All the remaining passengers were now aware that these fragile craft were an uncertain means of escape. Those crew members at the davits could see no more than a few feet, for the ship was in total darkness. At station No. 6, fireman William Doherty was lowering the portside boat when a great breaker crashed over the deck, carrying him into the sea. He had the good fortune to grab one of the lines over the ship's side and pull himself back on board.

First assistant engineer Tom Carrick was in charge of lifeboat No. 7, which was lowered over the side with five crewmen and only two passengers. Before the boat touched the surface, it was already partly filled with water. As it was being lowered, a frightened passenger cut away the aft tackle, and the lifeboat spilled its contents into the sea. Of those on board No. 7, only Carrick escaped a watery grave. Like Doherty, he caught hold of a line that rested against the side of the *Valencia* and was pulled back on board.

Frank Lehm watched helplessly as those on board lifeboat No. 7 were thrown into the water. "Like a shot the stern of the [life]boat fell to the water's edge, leaving the bow hanging high in the air. The occupants were spilled out like pebbles from a glass and fell with shrieks and groans into the boiling surf." Lehm stood transfixed. "The next wave swept them away, and where the glare of the searchlight played on the water we could see the white, terrified faces of the drowning people flash by with the look of deathly fear such as is seldom seen."[33]

After regaining consciousness, Second Officer Pettersen made his way to lifeboat No. 4. He later claimed to have attempted to fill the boat with more women, but almost all refused, saying they would rather go down with the ship. Of the eleven people in the lifeboat, only three were women. The action of the waves resulted in the boat pounding heavily against the side of the *Valencia,* so Pettersen climbed into the craft to attempt to steady it. He held onto the wire mesh rail while he tried to use his body to prevent the boat from swinging wildly. But before he could steady it, the boat fell out from under his feet, leaving him holding onto the sharp-edged wire mesh of the rail. Pettersen was about to release his hold when someone on deck noticed his plight and attempted to pull him back on board. Although the man tried, he could not pull the officer over the rail. Only when a second man came to his aid did Pettersen reach safety.

It had been only a few hours since the *Valencia* had run aground. With disastrous results, most of the lifeboats had been launched. Only lifeboat No. 5 was left on the aft port side. Two of the three rafts remained on the hurricane deck. (One of the rafts had earlier been washed away.) As the minutes passed, the steamer was gradually breaking up. Most of the forward quarter of the ship was now entirely submerged, and many of the men and women on board had climbed the foremast rigging. Others were either huddled on the hurricane deck or had taken to the rigging of the aft mast.

Throughout the night the wreck was illuminated in the light of the distress flares fired by Captain Johnson. According to Second Officer Pettersen, when one of the devices misfired, blowing off several of Johnson's fingers, the captain stoically remained on the bridge, which creaked and groaned with each incoming wave. Johnson faced the added difficulty of having no idea of his ship's location. He and First Officer W. Holmes were still convinced that they were twenty-five miles to the south, off the Washington coast. Thus, even if the remaining craft were able to land safely, no one had any idea where they could find help.

The distress flares seemed to bring order out of the chaos on deck. The passengers were given a brief glimpse of the rocks that stood between them and a safe landing. There was little to do but huddle against the cold and wait for daylight.

As the hours passed, the entire bridge and superstructure forward of the funnel was either underwater or had been washed away. Even the hurricane deck aft was no longer a safe refuge as waves broke over it. Clerk Frank Lehm recalled, "We were up to our waists in water almost all the time, and it was only by hard work that we succeeded in keeping hold of our support. The night seemed a year long."[34]

With the milky gray dawn of Tuesday, January 23, came a clear view of where the *Valencia* lay. The ship was only a few yards from shore, but it could have been a hundred miles distant. Great breakers smashed against the rocks, making the idea of a safe landing by boat or raft hopeless. The ship also was being ripped apart by the breakers. Along the jagged shore, the remains of those who were pulled from the deck, or drowned in the boats, washed against the rocky shore. Frank Lehm described the terrible scene: "The bodies of the drowned, which by that time, must have numbered fully sixty, were seen floating around the beach and dashing up against the iron-bound cliff, which loomed so close to us. The bodies were caught by the waves, thrown against the rocks and then caught by the undertow and drawn back."[35]

Shortly after daylight, Captain Johnson asked Boatswain Tim McCarthy to find a crew, take the last lifeboat, No. 5, and find a suitable landing place. McCarthy agreed, provided he could obtain men to crew the boat.

"By God, Tim," Johnson replied, "if you don't I will go with you myself."[36]

Johnson's last hope was the Lyle gun, a device that could fire ashore a rocket-powered projectile attached to a light line. The problem was that the line had to be thin to be carried by the rocket, and someone had to be on top of the bluff to haul up the heavier rope attached to the end. Once the rope was secured, a breeches buoy (a type of canvas harness) could be attached, and passengers and crew evacuated. McCarthy took the gun, attached it to the only part of the forward superstructure still above water, and rigged it with a new line. Then he left to prepare lifeboat No. 5 for its important journey.

At first McCarthy had difficulty finding crew members willing to take a chance on the last fragile boat, but when deckhand Charles Brown agreed, others also came forward. It was midmorning before McCarthy and his five-man crew were ready to leave. "The boat was lowered and cleared the ship," McCarthy said. "We worked her out to sea. The people cheered us. We rowed for quite a while along the shoreline. . . . We encountered several heavy seas before making land."[37]

Meanwhile, from the ship, First Engineer Thomas Carrick noted that one of the lines was dangling on the beach. If it was secured, Carrick observed, it might have been possible to evacuate the ship. "There was one man on the beach, how he got there I don't know, so we hollowed [sic] to him and pointed to him showing him which way to go and he walked about 50 feet forward. . . ." Unfortunately for everyone, "a big sea came and killed him along side the cliff."[38]

Frank Lehm and others still on board the *Valencia* watched another survivor who had been washed from the deck. About halfway between the wreck and the beach, he had managed to get a foothold on a large rock. As Lehm watched, "he tried several times to reach the shore, but was always driven back. The spray and waves washed over his little foothold, and at last he became exhausted."[39] After a valiant struggle lasting several hours he was washed away.

Later two half-naked, shivering men were seen clinging to a small depression in the cliff face. It was now low tide and it was obvious to everyone on board the *Valencia* that the small cave soon would be underwater. Eventually the two also realized their predicament and began a desperate climb away from the rising water. "When about half way to the summit," Lehm noted, "one was seen to stumble and lose his grip, and next minute both fell with a cry into the boiling surf. They were killed instantly."[40]

THAT SAME MORNING, Bunker, Campbell, Samuels, Richley, and five other survivors who had made shore began making their way up the cliff face. Young naval seaman Alfred Willis, who had stanched the flow of water into his lifeboat, had crushed his finger. Others were battered and bruised, while one man had a sprained ankle. All had little or nothing to eat since Monday evening and, with the cold, were losing their strength. Frank Bunker took charge of the sodden, dispirited group and led them slowly up the bluff. Once at the top, the party discovered a telegraph line that connected the lighthouse at Cape Beale with the Carmanah Point Lighthouse.

Bunker's group had no idea which way to turn. By taking the telegraph trail left rather than right, they walked away from the *Valencia*. They would be criticized later for callously disregarding the plight of the other survivors on board the ship. None of the survivors, though, knew anything about the Lyle gun or the aid they could have given to those left on board the vessel.

Bunker and his fellow survivors followed the trail for a short distance until they came to the Darling River, beyond Pachena Point. Although usually easy to ford, the river was now in flood stage. With remarkable courage, Bunker, with a rope tied around his waist, swam the river, but was almost swept over the falls at the edge of the cliff. Finally he succeeded in crossing the torrent and tying the rope securely on the other side. With this aid, the others in his party were able to make the river crossing. Many had no shoes and their feet were cut and bleeding. Others were too exhausted to walk further. To his relief, Bunker found a telephone in a hut used by telegraph linemen. The telephone connected the outpost with the Cape Beale Lighthouse, but to Bunker's frustration, he could not hear the person on the other end of the line. Thus, it was with mixed feelings that the few survivors of the wreck divided the few moldy biscuits found in the hut.[41]

AT CAPE BEALE LIGHTHOUSE, Minnie Paterson, wife of lighthouse keeper Tom Paterson, had taken the garbled call from the Darling River hut. While she eventually understood there had been a shipwreck, she was unable to grasp the gravity of the disaster. Since Bunker had no idea of his location, he was not in a position to give directions to the wreck site. Mrs. Paterson telephoned the transoceanic telegraph station at Bamfield and told them the little she knew. Bamfield was, in fact, even farther from the wreck than Cape Beale, but at least men would be there who could lend a hand.

Like the Bunker group, McCarthy and his sailors on board lifeboat No. 5 traveled northwest, in the direction of Cape Beale. McCarthy, believing that the vessel was off the northwestern tip of Washington State, looked for recognizable landmarks. The area did look familiar to him, and he believed he was not far from Tatoosh Island at the entrance to the Strait of Juan de Fuca.[42]

SOON AFTER McCarthy's boat disappeared from sight, Captain Johnson ordered that the Lyle gun be fired toward the top of the cliff. The first shot was unsuccessful, for the line rubbed against the side of the housing and broke. The second attempt was on target. The result gave the men and women clinging to the disintegrating vessel reason for hope. Once McCarthy's party reached the top of the cliff, they could be saved.

However, McCarthy and his men did not appear. In a giant arc, the line brushed the surface of the sea before rising up the cliff. With the line unsecured, it could not be pulled tight, and after some time the action of the waves frayed and parted the ship's thin contact with land.

Prompted by the failure of the Lyle gun, fireman John Cigalos decided on a desperate gamble. Tying a line around his waist, he waited for the crest of the next wave and dove into the cold Pacific water. In seconds, he was lost to his shipmates as a comber carried him forward. Immediately the line, which now disappeared under the great crush of water, paid out at terrific speed. A few minutes later Cigalos appeared on the slope of another huge wave. He fought the breakers for twenty minutes, his progress toward the beach eroded by the undertow. Cigalos jumped in repeatedly but had to be pulled back to the ship each time before reaching his objective: "I could breast the waves all right but the undertow was too strong for me. It was something terrible. It seemed to suck the life out of me, and time after time as I tried to make the shore I found myself getting weaker and weaker. When at last I was pulled back it took them some time to bring me back to life. . . ."[43] Cigalos's bravery seemed to rally the survivors.

IT WAS NOW AFTERNOON, and McCarthy and his men had been battling the wind and waves since the morning. Spotting a narrow channel to the northeast, McCarthy convinced himself that this was the relatively calm passage between Waddy and Tatoosh Islands off Cape Flattery. As the lifeboat neared the land, McCarthy realized that the waves were breaking against the rocks with a force far too great for this to be Tatoosh. Fortunately, the channel ended at a sandy beach, and with all the power his men could put into the remaining oars, the lifeboat rode in on the crest of a breaker. The force of the wave carried them as far as the trees beyond the beach.

It was now 3 P.M. and McCarthy and his men were exhausted. To their surprise, they found a white post that read, "Three miles to Cape Beale."[44] The sign came as a revelation, for they now knew that they had wrecked in Canadian waters. Cape Beale, though, was in the opposite direction from the *Valencia*. If help did not arrive soon it would be too late for the ship.

When McCarthy and his men finally reached the Cape Beale Lighthouse, it was 3:30 P.M. and the short hours of winter daylight were almost at an end. After a few minutes, Minnie Paterson had apologized for her inability to hear them on the telephone. It was the first time that McCarthy realized there must have been other survivors. Word of the disaster was immediately wired to Victoria and Seattle.

While McCarthy had secured a safe landing and alerted the world to the *Valencia* disaster, he had not succeeded in his original task. He and his men had not been there to retrieve the line fired from the Lyle gun.

ON THE AFTERNOON OF Tuesday, January 23, 1906, Captain James Gaudin, Victoria marine agent for the Federal Department of Marine and Fisheries, received a brief message from Cape Beale: "A steamer has been wrecked. About one hundred drowned. Nine have reached the telegraph hut. Will wire particulars later."[45]

The message did not identify the ship, but Gaudin knew the *Valencia* had been expected in Victoria and was overdue. Late arrivals, though, were common and he had not been unduly concerned. A second message a few minutes later from Tom Paterson, the lighthouse keeper at Cape Beale, revealed that the wrecked ship was the *Valencia*, which had probably gone aground near Pachena Point. Captain Gaudin contacted the ship *Salvor,* which, with her tender, the tug *Czar,* was under contract to the Canadian government to leave at a moment's notice for a shipwreck site. Nonetheless, it was many hours before she left her berth. Her captain later claimed he was unable to find a doctor willing to offer assistance. What seems more likely was that the *Salvor* did not have steam up, as was supposed to be the case. When she finally left, besides a doctor, she carried a complement of marine underwriters and coastal pilots. For whatever reason, the *Salvor* did not survey the wreck of the *Valencia,* but continued on to the little community of Bamfield.

Another vessel, *Queen,* had arrived in Victoria at 4:30 P.M. From his office in Seattle, J. E. Pharo, assistant manager of the Pacific Coast Steamship Company, ordered the passengers to hotels ashore, where they were accommodated at company expense, while medical staff, journalists, and company officials were taken on board. Some passengers remaining on board were American navy personnel bound for Seattle. The big steamer was in fact the first vessel to go in search of the missing *Valencia.*

In Seattle, many of the friends and families of the men and women on the *Valencia* laid siege to the company's docks, attempting to obtain information on the fate of their loved ones. From his office in San Francisco, W. E. Pearce, general manager of the Pacific Coast Steamship Company, issued no statement.

On the evening of January 23, another company vessel, the *City of Topeka,* was in Seattle loading a cargo of dynamite. It was Pharo's intention to send her to the stricken *Valencia.* The job of unloading the explosives and placing them aboard another ship, the *George K. Starr,* could not be rushed, however.[46]

In port, also, was the revenue cutter *Grant.* While such ships had been previously called upon to act as rescue vessels serving beyond the ocean boundaries of the United States, government regulations now limited a cutter's operation to American territorial waters. For those with friends and relatives on board the *Valencia,* though, it seemed that the shallow-draft ship would be well able to assist in the rescue. A prominent Seattle attorney, W. A. Peters, whose sister-in-law was on the ship, acted quickly to change this policy. After the intervention of Samuel Henry Piles, a U.S. senator from Washington, the somewhat bewildered captain of the *Grant* found himself heading for Canadian waters with orders to do all that was necessary to save the lives of those on board the *Valencia*.[47]

MEANWHILE, at Cape Beale, Minnie Paterson had contacted the Carmanah Point Lighthouse, twenty-five miles to the southwest, and informed them of the location of Bunker and his companions. Lineman David Logan, who lived nearby, Phil Daykin, the son of the lighthouse keeper at Carmanah Point, and trapper Joe Martin hurriedly organized a rescue party and left for the wreck site. Although the weak winter daylight would not last long, Logan was familiar with the trail and hoped to be at the scene of the wreck before midnight.

At Bamfield, thirteen miles to the north of the wreck, a party of operators employed at the telegraph station started off to aid the survivors. At Cape Beale, Mrs. Paterson continued to play an important role in the *Valencia* saga. In frail health, she nonetheless remained by the telephone for nearly three days, fielding questions from government officials, the press, and worried relatives.

At 10 P.M., the *City of Topeka* departed from the Seattle coal docks, rather than her usual berth at the company's wharf. The reason was to escape the crowd of relatives and friends waiting at the company's offices. The only relative permitted on board was W. A. Peters. Also on the ship were two nurses and a doctor, four reporters, and two marine underwriters, as well as the Pacific Coast Steamship Company's assistant manager, J. E. Pharo, and port captain, J. B. Patterson.

The Logan party, which had been expected to reach the site of the wreck first, found the going more difficult than had been imagined. Streams, usually so shallow they presented no problem, were now swollen and treacherous. After nightfall, the three men were held up near the mouth of the flooded Klanawa River. Logan attempted to negotiate with local Indians to take the three men across in canoes, but they were unwilling to trust their boats to the rampaging Klanawa. The three men had to spend the night on a high bank of the river as the water below them thundered seaward.

The telegraph operators from Bamfield had no difficult cataracts to cross, and arrived at the Darling River hut that night. The men prepared a fire for the nine survivors and gave them a proper meal.

Because most of the men were in no condition to carry on without assistance, the operators contacted Bamfield and were told that a rescue party from the steamer *Salvor,* together with a doctor, was on its way. The operators wished to push on to the wreck site, but the hut was on the opposite side of the Darling River and the rope across the water Bunker had used earlier had been washed away. One of the rescuers tied a telegraph line around his waist and attempted to ford the river, but was swept away and almost drowned. There was no choice but to remain where they were.

FOR THOSE ON BOARD the *Valencia,* the darkness was filled with foreboding, because even if a rescue craft arrived it would be unlikely to see them. During the night, some of the passengers surrendered articles of clothing that were dipped in kerosene, carried high into the mast, and set on fire. These signals, though, went unanswered. Many had given up all hope, surrendering to the rush of the waves that carried them to their death.

None of the rescue ships had a clear idea of the exact location of the wreck. Captain Norman E. Cousins of the *Queen* wasted valuable time anchored off Carmanah Lighthouse because of the mistaken belief that his sister ship had wrecked near there. Only after daylight, when he was able to read the signals posted by the lighthouse keeper, did he proceed to the *Valencia.*

Two of those in the *Valencia*'s foremast were George H. Jesse and Laura Van Wyck. In the face of the wind and rain, Van Wyck almost gave up, but Jesse moved to place his arms around her, giving the young woman words of encouragement.

By the early morning of Wednesday, January 24, the sea was exacting a terrible price. Without warning, the twenty or thirty people clinging to the foremast rigging were swept into the water as the spar gave way. Passenger Willitts recalled, "Their bodies were washed from the ship and we could see them dashed against the rocks."[48] Steward Frank Connors was one of the few who survived the plunge and found a hold on what was left of the superstructure. Still holding onto the remains of the foremast were Jesse and Van Wyck.

About 9 A.M., the *Queen* finally appeared on the horizon. While there were wild cheers from those on board the *Valencia,* it soon became apparent that the ship was not prepared to venture close enough to get a line on board. The arrival of the tug *Czar* a few minutes later renewed the hopes of the survivors. "Now we expected aid," freight clerk Frank Lehm recalled, "for a light draft vessel could have reached us. But she, too, kept away."[49]

Then, to the horror of the survivors, the *Queen* blew her whistle four times in a final salute, and made a sharp change in course and steamed into the distance. The *Czar* also steamed away, en route to Bamfield. For the men and women who had hung on in the face of freezing winds and icy water, the departure of the *Queen* and the *Czar* was a terrible blow. It was as if the world had written them off. There simply was no hope. Added to this, the last of the food and water that had been salvaged from the galley and passed out by the stewards was gone. In their desperate condition, some passengers still believed that the *Queen* would come back.

The survivors were unaware that another vessel had arrived from the south. The decision to send the *Queen* back to Victoria was made by Pharo and Patterson, the two company officials on board the *City of Topeka*. Communication between the two ships had been difficult at best and Captain Cann would later contend that he was not informed that there were still survivors on board the *Valencia*. (Captain Cousins, master of the *Queen*, would claim otherwise.)

At this point Captain Johnson urged the survivors to make use of the two remaining rafts. These offered the survivors their only chance of escape. Many, though, including the female passengers, decided to stay on what was left of the *Valencia*. Cornelius Allison and his friend Fred Erickson decided to take their chances on a raft. Erickson was right behind Allison, but as the raft pushed off the latter turned around and saw that his friend was gone. Allison was never sure whether Erickson had been washed away by one of the waves, or whether at the last minute he had changed his mind. In the end, eighteen men cleared the *Valencia* and paddled their pontooned craft out to the open sea. Allison would later conclude, "I don't know which was the worse experience—that on the ship or that on the raft. Both were terrible."[50]

The second raft attracted fewer than a dozen volunteers. Before he left, Frank Connors called up to Jesse to take a place on board with him. The young man, who was still tightly holding on to Laura Van

Wyck, said, "No, I have someone to look after here, and will stay and take my chances."[51] That was the last time Connors saw them.

The second raft also withstood the fury of the surf as those on board paddled away from the shore. The sea outside the line of breakers was less active, but the canvas boats offered little protection from the waves—water washed almost continuously over their occupants.

BACK AT THE Klanawa River, Logan's two companions found a damaged canoe on the riverbank, and the three men used it to cross the rain-swollen water. About 10 A.M. Logan and his party came upon a broken line lying across the trail. Through the thick bush, the three men followed the direction the line pointed until they came to the edge of the cliff. Below they saw what was left of the *Valencia.*

As Logan later recalled, he, Daykin, and Martin saw about a hundred souls clinging to what was left of the hurricane deck and aft mast rigging of the now almost completely submerged vessel. When the survivors saw the men at the top of the cliff, they cheered. According to one account, the last rocket from the Lyle gun was fired in the direction of the cliff top. While Phil Daykin was able to reach it, the line broke before he had a chance to haul it in. For the survivors aboard the *Valencia,* disappointment was palpable when it became clear that there was nothing Logan or his companions could do. With only one coil of rope among them, the three men were ill equipped for a major rescue. All they could do was watch as the *Valencia* was ripped to pieces.[52]

First, the starboard side of the deck was carried away, taking some of the rigging. Next, the funnel stays snapped, sending the stack tumbling into the water. The ship's funnel had been the last barrier against the onrushing sea. Now water washed over the entire ship, carrying away parts of the superstructure. Men and women wearing life preservers clung to pieces of floating debris bound toward the open sea. No ships were visible to pick up anyone surviving the final plunge into the frigid water. Finally, about noon, one huge wave crashed against the bluff and then washed back over the vessel. It carried away all but two of the survivors clinging to the aft mast. At that point, the three would-be rescuers turned their backs on the scene of this epic tragedy and continued on the trail toward the Darling River.[53]

• • •

THE *City of Topeka,* plying two miles off shore, could see almost nothing of the *Valencia.* Lawyer W. A. Peters, though, thought he spotted something on the crest of a wave. It was only a speck on the dark water. Company officials dismissed it as a log, but Peters was not convinced. Soon he attracted the interest of everyone except Pharo, Patterson, and Cann.

When the ship came about, to take another run along the coast, the nature of the small, dark shape became apparent: it was a raft. In the middle, supported by two other men, waving a shirt tied to an oar, was the indomitable Cornelius Allison, his white hair blowing in the wind. The *City of Topeka* lowered one of her boats with a six-man crew into seas still running high, and after a few minutes a towline was fastened to the raft. By this time, the raft was barely breaking the surface of the water, and as it neared the *City of Topeka*'s side, two survivors were washed overboard. Fortunately, both men were rescued before being carried away by the swell. Among those taken from the raft was John Cigalos, the fireman who had earlier braved the waves in a futile bid to secure a line to shore. When he was at last on the deck and offered spirits, Cigalos reportedly replied, "Give it to the others."[54] One of those survivors was G. L. Willitts, the lathe operator who was on his way to Seattle to look for work. Also rescued were Second Officer P. E. Pettersen and freight clerk Frank Lehm.[55] The *City of Topeka* spent several hours circling the area but found no other survivors.

The experience of the men on the second raft was even more grueling. Unable to attract the attention of the *City of Topeka,* the raft drifted past Cape Beale Lighthouse and into Barkley Sound. Some on board had already perished from exposure, and their bodies were consigned to the sea. With a lighter load, the raft floated a little higher in the water. About midnight, it drifted ashore at Turret Island. The sound of the breakers pushed Third Engineer W. Wilson beyond endurance. He jumped overboard and was battered to death on the rocks. Once on shore, a delirious Frank Connors believed he could see a lighthouse on the island and ran off into the bush. He was later discovered by a rescue party, quite insensible, sitting in a tree. Of the dozen or so men who had left on the second raft, only four survived.[56]

Crew from the *City of Topeka* towing a raft with eighteen *Valencia* survivors.
(Puget Sound Maritime Historical Society)

After receiving word of the disaster, the small British whaler *Orion* arrived at the scene. There, her captain took her into the breakers and within a hundred feet of the wreck. It was too late for everyone on board what was left of the vessel. All that remained of her crew and passengers were a few bodies lashed to the rigging, each grimly animated in a *danse macabre* to the rhythm of the waves crashing over the vessel.

On Friday, January 26, the *Salvor* rescue party finally reached Bamfield with the Darling River survivors. Frank Bunker, though, had not accompanied them. He had gone with some of the *Salvor* crew back to the wreck site in order to help identify the bodies—not an easy task since the action of the waves against the rocks quickly removed clothes and scraped away distinguishing features. As it would turn out, the sea would give up very few of its dead. Many of the bodies, including that of Captain Johnson, were never found.

Most of the survivors were taken to Seattle on board the U.S. revenue cutter *Grant*.

Not long after reaching Cape Beale, Bunker sent a telegram to the San Francisco school board, where its contents were released to the press. He put forward a number of questions including: Why were boatloads of passengers loaded into the water without sufficient crews or officers? Why was there so little discipline among those employed on the vessel? Why did the plugs not fit the drains on board the lifeboats? Why were the life preservers made of tule rather than cork?[57]

Although he did not respond to each point, W. E. Pearce, manager of the Pacific Coast Steamship Company, maintained, "Our equipment is open for inspection at any time by United States inspectors, or any person competent to make such inspections."[58] Since Pearce himself presumably defined "any person competent," the statement at best did nothing to reassure the public that Pacific Coast Steamship Company boats were safe.

Surviving crew members like Boatswain Tim McCarthy blamed the passengers for crowding the lifeboats, thus making the job of the crew more difficult. It became clear, though, that many of the crewmen had no idea where their rescue stations were, or what they were supposed to do in an emergency. Since leaving San Francisco, Captain Johnson had called no fire drills.[59]

THE FINAL DEATH TOLL was 117 passengers and crew. Only 37 people survived: 23 members of the crew and 14 male passengers. As was all too often the case during such disasters, not one woman or child made it to shore alive.[60]

For some, fate was kind. A few who had planned to sail on the *Valencia* had changed their minds at the last minute and were thus spared the agony of the sinking. Police captain Irving Ward was escorting a prisoner from San Francisco to Seattle to stand trial. Ward and his prisoner were standing in line in the Pacific Coast Steamship Company offices waiting to purchase tickets when the father of the accused came up to him and pleaded with the officer to take the train. It seemed that the elderly man wanted to accompany his son to Seattle, but was afraid to travel by water. Ward reluctantly relented, and purchased tickets for the train. A last-minute quarrel with Chief Steward J. Hoddinott kept waiter R. A. May from sailing. He angrily stormed off the *Valencia* a few minutes before the ship was scheduled to leave.[61]

Although he had a ticket, well-known semiprofessional baseball pitcher Gene T. Nonenbacher also missed the sailing. His trunk, along with many of his personal possessions, went to the bottom of the sea, however.

For some on board, fate played a particularly harsh hand. One of the passengers bound for his home was sixteen-year-old James Wright, who, while in Port Angeles, Washington, a year earlier, had been shanghaied on board a sailing vessel bound for Australia. The young man had worked his way to San Francisco and had taken second-class fare on the *Valencia* for Seattle, where his mother lived.[62]

Two teenage sisters, Mabel and Lulu Rowland, had run away from their Los Angeles home in the company of twenty-one-year-old Roy Hazard. All three traveled under assumed names, and it was some time before it was discovered that they had booked passage on the *Valencia*.[63]

By a strange quirk of fate, Donald Ross, one of the passengers who died on the *Valencia,* had lost his wife when the steamer *Clallam* sank in the Strait of Juan de Fuca two years earlier.[64] James Patterson, a cook on the *Valencia,* was making the voyage in place of a shipmate who was ill. Patterson needed the money as he had been aboard another company steamer, the *Queen of the Pacific,* on February 27, 1904, when it caught fire and was badly damaged off Tillamook Head, Oregon. While the ship had been refurbished and returned to service (newly renamed as the *Queen*), he still had not recovered. With a wife and six children, though, Patterson had no choice but to sign on.

Charles Flume, a baker on board the *Valencia,* seemed to be jinxed. He had been involved in four accidents at sea during the short time he had worked for the Pacific Coast Steamship Company. Flume, though, was not superstitious, so when his friend Frank Lipe told him of his premonition of disaster on board the *Valencia,* Flume laughed it off. As it turned out, the baker was not one of the survivors. Another man whose luck had run out was gambler Harold "Little Harry" Woodridge, who made his home in Helena, Montana. Woodridge had made and lost several fortunes during his lifetime and was a legendary figure throughout the West. He was on his way to Vancouver, British Columbia.[65]

WHILE THE CREW and passengers tended to view the disaster quite differently—each blaming the other for the lack of discipline—both groups agreed on the apparent failure of the *Queen* to aid the survivors on board the stricken ship. "We were working out a plan of rescue," said the embattled captain of the *Queen*, Norman E. Cousins. "Before anything had been done I was ordered to proceed on my trip."[66] The rescue attempt by the *Queen* was not supported by some of the contingent of U.S. navy personnel on the ship. "I was standing on the forward deck, and could plainly see the men and women on the *Valencia*," said Chief Boatswain's Mate C. P. Jorgenson, who was on his way to join the cruiser *Philadelphia* at Tacoma. "I volunteered to man a lifeboat with my men and attempt to rescue some of the imperiled ones. It was a life-and-death chance, but we all were willing to take it. The captain would not consent, and so we had to stand by and watch the signals of distress. After two hours, during which no attempt was made to launch a boat, the *Queen* put back to Victoria."[67] Cousins, for his part, denied the incident and blamed the captain of the shallow-draft tug *Czar* for deserting the *Valencia*.[68]

The Canadian government began a three-person commission under Captain James Gaudin on February 5, and its members examined a number of witnesses. The inquiry was not particularly probing, for the government did not wish to admit to its own portion of the blame in the *Valencia* incident. The government had not provided sufficient resources for West Coast maritime safety. When the findings were issued on March 20, 1906, the Canadian commission concluded that the ship had not been properly inspected in San Francisco before being returned to service to replace the *City of Puebla*. The lack of discipline among the crew and the failure of the rescue ship *Queen* to alert the other vessels that there were still survivors in the rigging were also noted as contributing to the disaster. The greatest blame, though, was placed on Captain Johnson for acting so recklessly: "We find it impossible to discover any justification for a prudent navigator to enter the Strait from the South in thick weather without definitely ascertaining his position in respect to that lightship."[69]

In the face of one of the worst maritime disasters on the Pacific Coast, the conclusions did not settle the question of who was responsible for the tragedy. During the following months, the press reported numerous charges and countercharges. One Vancouver newspaper reported that passengers on board the Canadian Pacific Railway Company vessel *Queen City* had been told by an *Orion* crewman that the captain of the whaler believed that the *Queen* and other rescue ships could have saved those on board the *Valencia.* The *Orion's* master allegedly told his crew that if he saw any of the captains responsible for mounting the rescue on the street, he would pass them by without speaking.[70] While the account was nothing more than hearsay, the story undoubtedly further increased growing public outrage over the handling of the *Valencia* incident.

Many of the *Valencia's* life preservers were made of tule rather than cork, which led Frank Bunker to charge that this material was not sufficiently buoyant to keep a person above the surface of the water. Government tests on the tule preservers revealed that they were effective in keeping bodies afloat. Still, not everyone was convinced. A few weeks after the wrecking of the *Valencia,* Frank Jackson, a passenger on the steamer *Multnomah* plying the waters between Olympia and Tacoma, took his pocketknife and slashed open about ten life preservers, then threw them overboard to see if they would float. Damaged, they quickly filled with water and sank. Jackson was arrested.[71]

A few days before the Canadian hearings had opened, an inquiry was begun in Seattle by two veteran steamship inspectors, Bion B. Whitney and Robert A. Turner. Before the first witness was called, questions regarding the condition of the ship that had been raised by Bunker increased the public's suspicion that the investigation would not be impartial. "ARE NOT MARINE INSPECTORS WHITNEY AND TURNER SITTING IN JUDGMENT ON THEIR OWN ACTS, HAVING ALREADY PASSED UPON THE *VALENCIA* AS SAFE AND HER EQUIPMENT IN ACCORDANCE WITH LAW?" wrote the *Seattle Star.* "This is even prohibited in courts of common law."[72]

The *Star* mounted a campaign critical of the close connection between the steamship companies, Senator George Perkins, who had a long association with the transportation interests on the West Coast, and federal agencies. One of the paper's editorials read:

> The powerful steamship corporations like the Pacific Coast Steam-
> ship Company, exert a hypnotic influence upon federal officials.
> It takes time to have proper boat drills on the ocean, and who
> ever would dare to stop a liner, or even a coasting boat, for proper
> drills when it would cost valuable time between ports and
> consequently some money?
>
> The steamship senator, he of the name of Perkins, of California,
> would see to it that such troublesome officials didn't hold office
> very long.[73]

Seattle residents had not forgotten the loss of the *Clallam*, which was in part brought about by the failure of the Revenue Service to ensure that vessels at sea were equipped and that safety drills were routinely held. President Theodore Roosevelt received many telegrams demanding an impartial inquiry into the *Valencia* disaster. Even the conservative Seattle Chamber of Commerce added its support for a broader investigation.

In response, President Roosevelt ordered the creation of a commission under Assistant Secretary of Commerce and Labor Lawrence B. Murray to investigate the *Valencia* tragedy. This panel opened in Seattle on February 14, 1906.[74] The result of the federal commission report was more far-reaching than its Canadian counterpart. Both Pacific Coast Steamship Company assistant manager J. E. Pharo and port captain J. B. Patterson were censured for sending the *Queen* back to Victoria at such a critical time. Implicitly, all ships involved in the rescue attempt were criticized for not doing enough to establish communication with the *Valencia,* including the Canadian tug *Czar* (whose relatively shallow draft should have allowed her closer access to the *Valencia*). "It was practically the unanimous opinion of a large number of witnesses," the report stated, "that ordinary lifeboats could have been safely taken in toward the wreck as long as they kept outside the line of breakers."[75]

Although most of the responsibility for the disaster was placed upon the shoulders of Captain Oscar M. Johnson, who had brought the ship upon the rocks, the commission noted that the great loss of life was the result of inadequate navigational and lifesaving aids on the Northwest coast.

While governments rarely act out of deeply felt humanitarian concerns, the *Valencia* tragedy was an embarrassment to the Canadian cabinet. Three months after the wreck of the *Valencia,* Chief Engineer William P. Anderson of the Department of Marine and Fisheries was sent to British Columbia to evaluate the means by which shipwrecks along the west coast of Vancouver Island could be diminished and a greater number of lives saved.[76]

The result was the establishment of more navigational and safety aids for southwestern Vancouver Island. Although these changes would go on to save other lives, they had come too late for the men and women who sailed on the *Valencia.*

Even before the federal commission was convened, Assistant Manager J. E. Pharo of the Pacific Coast Steamship Company submitted his resignation. "Pharo's action regarding the *Queen,*" the *Seattle Star* wrote, "can in no way be condoned. It was one of the most inexcusable proceedings connected with the whole lamentable affair."[77]

The Pacific Coast Steamship Company would face other disasters. In 1913, the *State of California,* on a run to Alaska, struck a shoal and went down, taking forty people with her.[78] On September 14, 1916, the line's recently purchased 8,000-ton flagship, *Congress,* under Captain Norman E. Cousins, caught fire off Coos Bay, Oregon. While all the passengers and crew were rescued, the vessel was completely gutted. (Ironically, Captain Cousins had been master of the *Queen of the Pacific* in 1904 when that ship caught fire off the Oregon Coast.) The remains of the *Congress* were sold to the China Mail Line.[79]

In early September 1916, plans were already underway to merge the Pacific Coast Steamship Company with the Admiral Line.[80] The fire on board the *Congress* may have hastened the implementation of the agreement.

Now, MORE THAN ninety years after the *Valencia* tragedy, the responsibility for that terrible wreck still haunts maritime historians. That many of the rescue vessels did not show the courage expected of mariners in times of crisis is entirely true. That neither the Canadian nor American governments did enough to ensure the safety of the ships plying the northern Pacific Coast is also correct. Yet the question of ultimate responsibility always comes back to the *Valencia*'s master. The captain could have waited for clearing weather as other masters did that night, but Johnson pushed blindly forward. As the *Portland Oregonian* observed, "Unstinted pity is the futile mead of those who perished in the 'dread sweep of the downstreaming seas,' when the good ship *Valencia* went to pieces . . . and censure is justly added to the man who took the chance which caused the catastrophe."[81]

CHAPTER 7

Columbia: Disaster off Shelter Cove

Summer fog along the Pacific Coast was a common cause of ship-wrecks at the beginning of the last century. From June until October, coastal ships moved blindly, relying on deep-throated fog whistles to warn them of approaching danger. When Captain Peter A. Doran of the steamer *Columbia* encountered the swirling mist, it was not his custom to reduce speed. The *Columbia* was part of the sea arm of the Union Pacific Railroad, and the company expected its vessels to run on schedule. However, ships were not trains, and the strict adherence to timetables was a routine instituted by men who knew little about the sea. On a July morning in 1907, Doran's blatant disregard of the gray danger was to have deadly consequences.

OVER A quarter century earlier, the newly launched *Columbia* was regarded as one of the staunchest steamers on the Pacific Coast. Built by John Roach and Son of Chester, Pennsylvania, for the Oregon Rail-way and Navigation Company, the vessel was completed in 1880. The ship was one of the first vessels to be fitted with electric lights operating from a dynamo.[1] The experimental system was a success, and soon other vessels were replacing their coal oil lamps with incandescent bulbs. After completing sea trials, she sailed around Cape Horn to San Francisco to take on her first cargo and passengers.

At a time when mechanical problems on West Coast steamers were common, reliability was highly regarded by the shipowners and the traveling public alike. There was a no more dependable passenger ship on the Pacific Coast than the *Columbia*. As one observer noted in

Early promotional drawing of the *Columbia*. (Courtesy of New Westminster Public Library)

1895, "The *Columbia*'s record on the Portland and San Francisco route is remarkable, as only once in fifteen years has she been longer than one night at sea on the down trip between the two cities."[2] At the time of her first major refit fifteen years after her launch, the *Columbia* had completed more than four hundred round-trips between the cities.[3]

The 2,721-ton vessel had a length of 309 feet and a beam of 38.5 feet with a capacity of 382 first-class and steerage passengers.[4] In keeping with maritime regulations, the vessel carried eight metal lifeboats and one wooden lifeboat. In addition, she had a wooden workboat that could be used in an emergency. She was also equipped with five life rafts and carried 537 life preservers.[5]

About the turn of the twentieth century, the Union Pacific Railroad took over the Oregon Railway and Navigation Company. In 1904, the subsidiary's name was changed to the San Francisco and Portland Steamship Company.[6] The *Columbia* apparently well served her new owners. The regular beat of the compound condensing engine, which was fed by four boilers, regularly propelled the single screw vessel on her north-south route.

New steam vessels, however, were exploiting state-of-the-art technologies, as lighter steel hulls were replacing the heavy iron plate construction of older ships. Modern liners relied on triple- or quadruple-expansion engines and forced draft boilers to gain both speed and economy. To keep them afloat longer after sustaining damage, recently

Columbia, capsized by the 1906 earthquake, Union Iron Works Yard.
(San Francisco Maritime National Historical Park, Herbert Meyers Photographic Collection [A4.271n])

launched vessels like the *Minnesota* were built with a dozen water-tight bulkheads. Breaching one of the bulkheads did not necessarily mean the loss of the ship. Few mariners would deny the *Columbia* was well past her prime.

When the great San Francisco earthquake struck on April 18, 1906, the *Columbia* was at the Union Iron Works dock undergoing a refit. The shock shifted her supports and the *Columbia* rolled onto her side, coming to rest against the dock. Her plates were punctured in nine places, partially filling her with water. It took two months before temporary patches could be made to the hull and the water pumped out.

Her owners planned to take her to the dock at Hunter's Point where extensive repairs to her hull could be completed, but on the way she encountered a rough sea that caused the ship to list heavily and one of her steampipes to burst. Fearing an explosion, her crew quickly abandoned ship, but the vessel was eventually towed to her dry dock and repairs were made.[7]

After her return to service in January 1907, the vessel spent four days locked in pack ice on the Columbia River. She escaped, however, seemingly undamaged, and was soon returned to the San Francisco–Portland run.[8]

• • •

WHEN THE *Columbia* cast off her lines a little before noon on the morning of Saturday, July 20, 1907, it was a pleasant summer day. The fog in the harbor, which was responsible for her sailing delay— she was almost an hour late leaving San Francisco's Spear Street wharf—had burned off, revealing a cloudless sky.

Many of the passengers on board were schoolteachers who had attended the National Educational Association convention in Los Angeles.[9] The trip on board the *Columbia* was an opportunity to enjoy the fresh ocean air before returning east. For Minneapolis schoolteacher Lulu Hanson, the first hours of the voyage had been pleasant. The weather remained fair and the wind that was blowing in from land was so light as to be almost imperceptible. Gradually, though, a swell began to develop after the vessel steamed beyond Point Reyes, and Hanson experienced a bout of seasickness. With her stomach churning, she retired early.[10]

Also on board were the usual mix of commercial travelers and tourists who were the mainstay of first-class passenger service on coastal vessels. Ottilia Liedelt, who taught music in San Francisco, had purchased a ticket on the *Columbia* for Portland, where she had planned to vacation. Before she left, her friends had joked that while the *Columbia* might sink, Liedelt would be unharmed for she would remain above the surface of the waves. The jest was to be closer to the truth than she or her friends had imagined.[11]

As EVENING APPROACHED, fog could be seen in the glow of the ship's lights. Night came and the *Columbia* continued on her course. By midnight, the vessel was a little more than a dozen miles southwest of Shelter Cove, at the southern extreme of the Mendocino coast. Quartermaster Paul Hinner, who had recently come on watch, was at the wheel, while Quartermaster J. Ellis was on the bridge with Captain Peter Doran and Second Officer Richard Agerup. "We were steaming along at full speed through a dense fog," Hinner recalled, "and our course was north by northeast."[12] The fog had kept Captain Doran on the bridge. At the beginning of the watch he had gone to his cabin, but as the evening fog thickened, he soon returned.

Lookout S. G. Peterson peered out into a night that was so thick he could see only about two ship lengths off either rail. The *Colum-*

bia's fog whistle blew regularly as she knifed through the water. Peterson had not been on watch long before he heard an answering sound somewhere off starboard. He reported what he had heard to the bridge, but Captain Doran did not reduce speed. The *Columbia* continued blindly through the thick night. Moments later, the captain and the second officer could hear the whistle of the other ship on the bridge, but Doran still did not order the engine room to reduce speed. The sound was repeated every sixty seconds for about fifteen minutes until Peterson saw a ship emerge through the gloom. She was about 150 feet away and was coming "square on" toward the *Columbia*.

Agerup saw a headlight about two points off the starboard bow. Doran ordered the second officer to blow two blasts on the whistle, the signal for passing. The ship looming out of the night answered once, which was followed by several short blasts signaling danger.[13]

COMING FROM SHORE was the 457-ton steam schooner *San Pedro*. The vessel was built in California in 1899 to carry lumber. On this run, her decks were piled high with cargo. The schooner was loaded with 390,000 feet of redwood destined for San Pedro, California.[14] She had left Eureka, California, about five o'clock Saturday afternoon and was steaming a southeast by south course at eight knots an hour.

On the *San Pedro*, First Officer Ben Hendricksen took charge of the watch from Second Officer A. L. Shaube at midnight. Sailor Ole Swanson was at the wheel and E. Soderberg was the lookout. About 12:15 A.M., Soderberg shouted out that he could hear a fog whistle off the port bow. On the bridge, Hendricksen did not hear the other ship, but ordered a change in course, taking the *San Pedro* farther out to sea. Like Doran, he did not signal the engine room to reduce speed. As the seconds passed, the sounds of the approaching ship were louder, until two blasts off the port bow seemed to come almost on top of the *San Pedro*.

Hendricksen saw the vessel looming ahead. "When I saw the lights on the *Columbia* I gave four rapid blasts of the whistle, that is the danger signal. The engine was stopped before I sounded the danger signal, because I gave the engineer two bells to stop before giving the four whistles. The *Columbia* was crossing the *San Pedro*'s bow."[15]

• • •

ON THE BRIDGE of the *Columbia,* Captain Doran had ordered full speed astern, but it was too late. The *San Pedro*'s momentum carried her forward, penetrating the larger ship's iron hull. The time by the clock on the *Columbia*'s bridge was 12:22 A.M.[16]

"What are you doing, man?" Doran shouted at the other vessel, and told her to stand by. The reverse thrust of the *Columbia*'s engine resulted in the two vessels drifting apart. Seconds after the collision, Richard Agerup recalled: "The captain whistled down to the engine-room but got no answer, so he sent me down to the engineer on watch to find out if the ship was making any water. I went down in the engine-room and asked the first assistant, M. Burpee, if there was any water there, but he said no. Returning on the bridge, I reported so to the captain, but just then the watchman came on the bridge and reported the water was streaming in forward."[17]

Passenger William L. Smith, the twenty-year-old son of an army contractor, was returning to Vancouver, Washington, after a visit with friends in San Francisco. On the evening of the disaster, Smith had been in the cabin of Chief Engineer John F. Jackson about midnight. After leaving Jackson, he made his way along the deck. It was a dark, chilly night with fog swirling beyond the deck lights. In his stateroom, Smith had prepared for bed when he suddenly became aware of the exchange of fog whistles. "Despite my scanty attire, I ran on deck and saw the *San Pedro* upon us. I was amidships and saw the lumber schooner strike. It was not a sharp compact, but a sort of long, soft grind. The collision was so light that I was not thrown down. The fog was so thick that when the *San Pedro* backed away I could not distinguish a man standing on the schooner six yards away."[18]

The wooden-hulled *San Pedro* was also badly damaged and taking on water, but of greater concern was the *Columbia*. The steam schooner's chief engineer, A. V. Williams, picked his way forward through the wreckage to glimpse the damage to the other vessel. He could see in her side a hole "large enough to put a hack through."[19] Captain Magnus Hanson also climbed forward. He described the opening in the *Columbia* as approximately six feet square. There was no doubt that the *Columbia* was finished. Hanson ordered that the schooner's three small boats be lowered to pick up survivors.

After watching the collision, *Columbia* passenger William Smith ran to the cabins and began kicking at the doors, attempting to rouse the sleeping occupants. "These passengers," Smith noted, "scarcely had a chance for their lives. They had but three or four minutes in which to get out."[20]

On the bridge, First Officer W. P. Whitney had arrived and was given command while Captain Doran went forward to inspect the damage. Before leaving, he ordered Agerup to uncover the lifeboats and prepare them for launch.

Chief Engineer Jackson was in his berth when he felt a shock strong enough to awaken him. He dressed quickly and went to the engine room, which he found to be still dry. After warning First Assistant Engineer M. C. Burpee, who was in charge of the watch, not to be caught below deck, he decided to go to the bridge to find out how badly the ship was damaged. Before he reached the hurricane deck, though, the captain ordered, "Everyone to the boats!"[21]

Fireman John Swift was in the boiler room. "The shock was something terrific, and it did not take me long to learn that a big hole had been knocked in the side of the *Columbia,* and that she was doomed. I remained on duty a few minutes, however, and then, with orders made a rush for the deck. Time seemed pretty valuable all at once."[22]

LIKE LULU HANSON, Ottilia Liedelt had found the first few hours out of port agreeable, but eventually the rolling waves, half-hidden by the fog, left the young woman restless and vaguely apprehensive. Early in the evening, she returned to her stateroom on the portside upper deck, undressed, and slipped into bed. Sleep, though, eluded her, and she lay in her berth as the ship rose and fell on a moderate sea. Unlike other cabin passengers, some of whom slept through the collision, Liedelt later described the impact as severe. She claimed that she knew from the moment of impact that the blow to the *Columbia* was fatal.

Liedelt quickly arose, put on a skirt and blouse, and made her way on deck. She saw a scene of total confusion. Men moved around as though in a daze while the crew tried to prevent them from returning to their staterooms, climbing the stanchions to the hurricane deck, or jumping into the lifeboats before the craft had been launched.[23]

William Harding Lucas of Seattle was in bed when the two ships struck. The jar of the collision was hardly noticeable, but the grinding noise that followed was enough to fully awaken him. He was sure the ship had struck a shoal, for the scraping noise seemed to be the sound of metal striking rock. "For a few seconds I heard no other sounds," he recalled later, "and decided to await developments or information."[24]

News was not long in coming. A few seconds later he heard one of the crew calling for all hands on deck. Still he did not dress, assuming that the order was for the crew. He moved only after he heard someone call, "Everybody on deck: she's struck."[25]

Imagining the chaos above decks, Lucas decided that he would not be part of the rush to the lifeboats. After dressing completely and putting on his life preserver, he made his way toward the deck. "As I climbed the stairs the vessel lurched considerably to one side, and I quickly felt the seriousness of the situation."[26]

As Lucas made his way up the companionway, he passed several women unable to find their life preservers. In the panic following the collision, passengers had forgotten that they were stowed under their bunks. "As I passed along, I noticed a boat filled with people and others were trying to clamber into it. Those inside were pleading that no more should get in, because the boat would surely sink, so I left them and climbed over the ship's rail. . . ."[27]

After pounding on the cabin doors, William Smith did his best to assist his fellow passengers. Many of the men and women in their staterooms were so seasick that they had no interest in saving themselves. Others fumbled with life preservers, unable to adjust them. "I assisted one family consisting of a father, mother and three small children. The last I saw of them they were standing in the cabin holding hands. All were lost."[28]

Lulu Hanson also recalled the chaos on deck. "I looked up and above me I saw the captain," she said. "He was the only cool one in the whole ship. He tried his best to calm people, shouting: 'This is the captain speaking. Obey me and you will all be safe.' I was thinking how I was to save myself."[29]

After hearing the order to go to the boats, Chief Engineer Jackson quickly returned to his cabin to pick up his life preserver. It was missing, though, for he had left his door open and someone had taken it. He returned to the engine room and called down into the darkness, but received no reply. "I immediately went up on deck and made for my boat, which was No. 4, and proceeded to cut it adrift with my knife. At that time the steamer was gradually going over to starboard. . . .

She was also sinking forward at the same time. She careened over so quickly that our boat commenced to float without lowering it into the water."[30]

The settling of the ship took under many of the people who were on the starboard side of the top deck. As the forward quarter sank, the stern rose correspondingly and Otillia Liedelt found she was suddenly farther above the waves. A little more than seven minutes had passed since she had first heard the disquieting noise in her cabin. It was obvious the *Columbia* had little time left.

For Liedelt, her escape from the ship was a matter of good fortune:

> As I stood at the rail I saw a raft directly below me in the water, and instinctively I mounted the rail and leaped down upon it, suffering some injury to my hip, but luckily landing safely enough under the circumstances. It was dark there on the raft, and wet and cold. I was almost instantly lonesome, but I was not to be alone more than a few moments. Some poor woman who had evidently seen me jump, leaped after me, but missed the raft and plunged to her death in the black waves right alongside of me. I would have saved her, but could do nothing more than look for her to come close. And my own position on the raft was not too secure.[31]

Second Officer Agerup was on the hurricane deck abaft the funnel cutting away the life rafts. "While doing this I heard the whistle blow, and looking around saw the bridge nearly under water. I saw there was no time to spare, so I threw a life-buoy overboard and jumped over the stern." He struck the water with such force that he injured his leg. A moment later, the *"Columbia* disappeared and the suction brought me down with it."[32]

First Assistant Engineer Burpee had waited too long to order his men topside, and fireman John Swift almost did not escape.

> I had got only as far as the door of the fire-room when the *Columbia* went down. How in the world I ever got out from below decks and to the surface is something I can hardly realize now, or figure out, but I know this, that as I was fairly bursting down below there, under the water, a piece of wreckage with a protruding nail, took me to the surface, this nail catching in my flannel shirt

and fixing itself firmly. . . . That board, or whatever it was, and that nail, helped me mightily to get up where I could strike out for myself.[33]

Some of the passengers found themselves in desperate circumstances. Although the *San Pedro* was only about seventy-five yards off, the distance seemed overwhelming.[34] By the time commercial traveler A. S. Biegel reached the deck, the ship was all but under. "I had to wade through water to the rail and knew there was no time to be lost. I had on a preserver and started climbing over the rail when the ship reared, gave a quick plunge and I was thrown clear of the rail. An instant later I felt myself being drawn down with fearful force. It was a horrible sensation. But fortunately some force must have counteracted the suction from the sinking ship, and before I lost my breath I was at the surface again."[35]

Stella Cannon, her contractor brother, Louis, and her mother were on their way to visit Mrs. Cannon's other son, who lived in Portland. After the collision, Stella and Louis had helped Mrs. Cannon with her preserver, and the older woman sat on a bench at the stern of the ship and waited for the end. It was only seconds before the *Columbia* seemed to slip away under them. Many passengers were pulled down underwater violently and then propelled upward by what appeared to be an explosion. When Stella was able to draw a breath, she was suddenly aware of great pain. Her thumb and two ribs had been fractured.[36]

At the time, it was assumed that the ship's boilers had exploded, but such an event would have likely killed many people near the sinking ship. "I am quite positive that the boilers did not explode," noted Chief Engineer Jackson. "I would have known it if any one did, as I stood directly above them when the ship pitched head foremost into the sea."[37] A more likely explanation was that a force of air that had been compressed below deck was suddenly released with considerable force. The result would counteract the downward suction of the ship and push some people to the surface.

Liedelt was no longer alone in her raft. Passengers and crew jumped from the ship or crawled on. "I saw men trying to reach rafts, and know that some of them failed, and I saw others wearing life preservers, and clinging to small pieces of wreckage that had been thrown overboard. And then the plunge of the *Columbia* as she went down! Terrible it was! Words cannot express the awfulness of it all."[38]

The raft had been close to the *Columbia* when the vessel went down and Liedelt watched Captain Doran on the bridge. "He had tied down the whistle cord and stood in the center of the bridge as the steamer's bow went down and [he] braced himself against the rail." During the final moments, "he extended both of his hands and appeared to say good-by. He went down as he stood, and the boiling waters closed over him and the ship. Even the whistle . . . seemed to die out in a last farewell."[39]

Not more than two minutes earlier, Chief Engineer John Jackson, Third Officer Robert Hawse, and four other crew members pushed off in a lifeboat from the *Columbia*. Purser J. E. Byrnes and several passengers were taken off the last few feet of the top deck still above water, and a few more passengers were picked up from the sea. "Then I sung out to the third officer to pull away from the ship," Jackson said, "for fear we would be drawn in with the vessel, as she was going down fast."[40]

Stella Cannon was one of the survivors picked up in the water and moments later she thought she heard her brother's voice somewhere in the darkness. Despite her pleas, Jackson would not attempt to find the man; the chief engineer claimed that floating debris might have damaged the boat.[41] Later Louis was rescued by another boat, but Stella's elderly mother died in the frigid waters.

Lifeboat No. 4, under Chief Engineer Jackson, reached the *San Pedro* and discharged the passengers. He then sent the boat back under Third Officer Hawse to find more survivors.[42] Jackson later would be criticized for not taking more people from the water. There were seventeen people in lifeboat No. 4, which was rated to carry twenty passengers.[43]

Although she was badly damaged, the *San Pedro*'s cargo of lumber kept her above water and the vessel immediately launched three of her boats to aid the *Columbia*'s lifeboats in picking up victims. Soon this small fleet began to ferry survivors from the wreck site to the *San Pedro*.

Wearing a life preserver, William Harding Lucas had immediately attempted to distance himself from the *Columbia*, which was clearly about to go down. A few seconds after she disappeared, the sea suddenly roiled as pieces of the vessel came to the surface. Lucas clambered on board an empty raft, but without paddles or a rope he could not aid others in the water. "After the noise of the sinking vessel subsided I heard a most heart-rendering wailing, mingled with piercing screams of those in their last struggles, and some of these were shrieking the names of friends from whom they had been separated. . . . To be a witness of such distress is indeed a frightful experience, especially when one cannot possibly render assistance."[44]

In the chaos on deck, Lulu Hanson looked for a lifeboat, but the only one nearby was still covered, and none of the crew appeared to be coming to cut it loose. Then suddenly the *Columbia* seemed to plunge down into the sea. "I found myself floating about, buoyed up by a life preserver which I had fortunately put on before leaving my stateroom. I don't know how long I was in the water before I was picked up by a lifeboat, of which Third Officer [Hawse] was in charge."[45]

William Smith saved himself by swimming toward the *San Pedro*'s mast light, visible in the darkness. Smith, who had a reputation for strength, survived the numbingly cold water that took so many lives. On the surface, the fog had dissipated somewhat, but a breeze had arisen. "The water was bitter cold," Smith recalled, "and the wind was cutting so that the survivors were numbed and exhausted."[46]

The life raft containing Otillia Liedelt reached the *San Pedro*, and she and other victims of the disaster were taken on board. Lying low in the water, the lumber schooner was hardly more secure than the canvas-and-tule craft that had taken Liedelt from the side of the *Columbia*. At any moment, the *San Pedro* appeared about to capsize.

Although in shock, commercial traveler A. S. Biegel found one of the *Columbia*'s life rafts and pulled himself on board. Later, he, too, would join the growing number of survivors on board the *San Pedro*.[47]

When the *Columbia* sank, Maybelle Watson, the sixteen-year-old daughter of a prominent Berkeley, California, family was on her way to visit her brother in Portland, Oregon. After putting on her life preserver, Watson boarded one of the lifeboats launched from the starboard side of the vessel. The small craft was filled beyond capacity and, as the ship went down, it was sucked into the *Columbia*'s vortex.[48]

After a few minutes, Watson came to the surface. She found she was not alone, for a number of men and women were in the water around her. One young woman, whom Watson later discovered was Cleveland schoolteacher Emma Griese, had apparently strapped her life preserver on backward and her head was thrust forward into the water. Hearing Griese calling for help, Watson looked in the woman's direction. As she later told a reporter: "There were many men nearby and I called to them to help her. I felt pity for the miserable creatures for what they did, for they refused to help her one bit. 'For God's sake it's all I can do to save myself,' was the reply from them."[49]

Watson swam over to Griese's side and attempted to force the woman's head out of the water. Because the exposure was draining Watson's strength, the task was not easy, but Watson kept Griese's head out of the water until they were picked up by the *Columbia*'s No. 4 boat under Third Officer Robert Hawse. "To my mind," Hawse would later say, "there is but one heroine in the catastrophe which befell the *Columbia.* That is Miss Maybelle Watson of Berkeley."[50]

ABOUT 5:30 A.M., the small coastal vessel *George W. Elder* reached the wreck site.[51] Soon after came the steamer *Roanoke.* The *San Pedro,* with her bow missing, had a bad list.[52] The survivors were unloaded from the *San Pedro;* some of the victims were taken to Eureka, while others went on to Astoria and Portland. One boat with eighteen passengers and crew under quartermaster Paul Hinner managed to reach Shelter Cove unaided. There local residents aided them until help arrived.[53]

Once on land, Robert Hawse blamed Captain Magnus Hanson of the *San Pedro* for refusing to accept a second boatload of survivors. The No. 4 boat had been forced to stay at sea, waiting for daylight. "If the *San Pedro* had taken these passengers I could have saved many more lives. I could take no more, as my boat was fully loaded."[54]

The third officer seemed to enjoy press attention, and even wrote his own account of the disaster for the *San Francisco Examiner.* "If there had been a rush for the boats on deck," Hawse claimed, "I would have taken my revolver and shot down the passengers until it was stopped."[55]

Hawse was no less forgiving of anyone whom he regarded as a coward. As he later recounted: "I was unfortunate enough to pick up two big heavy men that lay in the thwarts of the boat, groaning and more comfortable. One of the women was delirious and had on nothing but an undershirt. The others were nearly naked. Neither of the men would move. . . . I would have shot them if I had had a .45."[56]

His cavalier attitude left the public concerned. On other ships, pistols had been used only as a last resort to control panicked passengers. Hawse, however, seemed to look with relish on the prospect of disposing of a few of the ill-disciplined rabble. As his comments were published in the newspapers, his role in the *Columbia* rescue became increasingly controversial.

When the shock of the ordeal lessened, some passengers refuted Hawse's accusations. William Koldt of Seattle indignantly disputed what he claimed were the third officer's malicious stories.[57] H. H. Decker, described by the press as a cripple from Telsa, California, was traveling with his wife to Portland. Floating on his preserver, Decker was picked up by Hawse's boat. Once he was on board, Hawse ordered him to crouch down in the craft, an impossible challenge for the handicapped man. Decker recalled: "I didn't crouch low enough for the man in charge, whom I later saw was the third officer [Hawse], and he yelled out, 'Knock him on the head and throw him overboard.' I tried to get away from him. . . . Then [Hawse] said, 'I had no business picking you up, anyway. I ought to have let you drown.'"[58]

Many other survivors who had shared his boat regarded Hawse's behavior as reprehensible. Schoolteacher Lulu Hanson recalled that Hawse was first concerned with his own comfort.

> The sailors and others who had managed to escape from the *Columbia* with a goodly share of clothes and some few passengers who had managed to save some of their personal belongings acted beyond criticism. As half-drowned men and women were pulled into the boat wet and shivering, piece by piece the men distributed their clothing among them, favoring the women, and giving them as much protection as they could. Men were crouching in the bottom of that life boat with but one garment on, some a pair of trousers, others with a single shirt. And all this time Third Officer sat in the stern of the boat fully dressed, with a tarpaulin over his shoulders. I don't think he had as much as his feet damp, shouting his orders to everyone on the boat.[59]

J. Grant Kline was one of the passengers rescued during No. 4 boat's first trip to the *San Pedro*. One victim taken from the water was a heavy woman, suffering from exhaustion and exposure. When the boat finally pulled alongside the lumber carrier, Hawse became angry when the woman could not climb the rope ladder fast enough to suit him. When Kline refused to leave her to the last, Hawse became angry and threatened to toss the man overboard.[60] Later some of the survivors signed statements repudiating the charges Third Officer Hawse had made against the *San Pedro*'s captain.[61]

Hawse's crew were also critical of his behavior. Quartermaster W. Curran, one of the lifeboat crew, leveled charges against Hawse. It was clear that Curran heartily disliked the third officer.[62] Conditions were difficult in a rising sea, but Hawse seemed to have no idea of the problems the men pulling the oars were facing.

Other victims supported the conduct of Hawse. Alma Osterberg, a Cleveland, Ohio, schoolteacher, had secured a place in one of the lifeboats. Before the tether could be cut, the ship suddenly disappeared from the surface, taking the boat and its passengers down. She alternately floated and swam for about three hours, losing the scant clothing she was wearing in the water. After she was picked up by Hawse's boat, she was given a jacket by one of the crew.

When Maybelle Watson, holding the head of an unconscious Emma Griese above water, was found, Hawse had them carefully brought on board the boat. As Osterberg told the inquiry: "Miss Griese was unconscious when picked up out of the water and Hawse cared for her tenderly, keeping her well covered. One of the men in our boat who was rough and selfish in his treatment of women received severe condemnation from Hawse, who sternly but justly threatened to throw him out if he was not more considerate."[63] Maybelle Watson also was prepared to testify in support of Hawse's conduct in the lifeboat.[64] Hawse, though, had more detractors than supporters.

The third officer's criticism of Captain Hanson and the crew of the *San Pedro* was not shared by most people who were taken on board the schooner. Hanson had loaded between seventy and eighty survivors on his ship—so many that they had to hold on to each other to avoid being washed overboard every time a wave crashed over the vessel.

As the condition of the *San Pedro* worsened, Hanson recognized that the people in the lifeboats and life rafts were more fortunate than the passengers on board his ship. Already the deck cargo had brought down the mainmast, which swept away four of the people crammed aboard the vessel.[65] The lumber, which now floated free, also threatened to damage approaching boats.

WHEN THE *Columbia* went down she took with her the clothing and personal possessions of the passengers and crew. "I do not know where my supper is coming from tonight," said passenger Joseph Rumley after reaching Astoria. "I haven't a cent left in the world."[66] At the same city, P. E. Goslinski left the *George W. Elder* wearing a rough canvas sailor suit. With the exception of his overcoat and watch, he had lost everything. Others also suffered. Many of the schoolteachers on board were from the East or the Midwest and knew no one locally.

Although the loss of the vessel had created considerable hardship, the San Francisco and Portland Steamship Company was of little assistance to its fare-paying customers. "What should our feeling be toward the owners of the *Columbia?*" passenger J. Grant Kline asked a week after the loss of the ship. "They have never contributed one cent toward allaying the suffering pangs of hunger and distress of the survivors. They have even refused to refund to us the full return value of our tickets, asking us to discount it $2.50."[67]

THE *Columbia*'s crew received little criticism and much praise in the press. Captain Doran's death on the bridge seemed to atone for the fact that he recklessly ran his vessel at full speed through a heavy coastal fog. The San Francisco newspapers carried stories attesting to the captain's bravery and skill. Risking death, many sailors worked on freeing the rafts and boats until the moment the *Columbia* sank.

The surviving passengers praised the actions of the captain and crew of the *Columbia*. Under difficult conditions, they had displayed discipline and courage. The only exception was Third Officer Robert Hawse. Rumors among the passengers on the rescue ship *George W. Elder* that Hawse was a "morphine fiend" were noted in the *San*

Francisco Chronicle. An interview with Dr. S. B. Foster at the U.S. Marine Hospital revealed that following the disaster, his patient Hawse had made at least three requests for the drug.[68] After his release, he was given a room in Second Officer Richard Agerup's San Francisco home.

On July 29, 1907, Hawse was taken to the Mission Street police station and then to the detention ward of Central Emergency Hospital.[69] He was held, noted the *San Francisco Chronicle,* "pending an investigation into his mental condition." According to the newspaper, "Hawse was very excited when first taken to the [police] station, cringing and acting as though he were in fear of others. He had the newspaper clippings in which passengers and members of the *Columbia*'s crew had given interviews reflecting on his conduct."[70]

EIGHT MONTHS BEFORE the *Columbia* sank, the local inspector of hulls, O. F. Bolles, and a boiler inspector, John K. Bulger, visited the vessel and certified her as seaworthy. With their reputations at risk, it is not surprising that after she went down, both men immediately defended the structural integrity of the vessel. Bolles had a long connection with the *Columbia;* he had stepped on board in 1880 as the ship's first master and taken her around Cape Horn to San Francisco. He had spent more than fifteen years as her captain. Although she was twenty-seven years old, he claimed that the *Columbia* was "in the best of condition."[71]

Inspector Bulger similarly maintained that the steamship "was practically a new boat." After the earthquake, the *Columbia* had been completely refitted. "She had four water-tight bulkheads," he noted in a statement to reporters. "The law requires three in a boat of her size."[72]

However, he would imply that watertight bulkheads were frequently useless. "In the event that one compartment is filled with water through a hole made by collision, the rapid settling of the injured ship would bring the water up to the level of the top of the bulkhead and would then flow into the other water-tight compartments and the ship would go down like a piece of lead."[73]

Bulger's assessment was not wrong. However, the compartments served another purpose. While they did not necessarily prevent the loss of a ship, in most cases they at least slowed the rate at which the vessel filled with water.

The wreck of the *Columbia*, together with the loss of the *City of Rio de Janeiro*, the *Clallam*, and the *Valencia*, had undermined confidence in both the shipping lines and the steamboat inspectors. A suspicious public no longer accepted claims that major refits resulted in older ships being "as good as new." The *Columbia* was a ship built using old technologies, and was now regarded as "something of a tub."[74] In explaining the sinking, the *San Francisco Examiner* wrote, "The *Columbia*, an iron vessel, bore the brunt of the impact, and her iron plates—brittle with age—cracked and the gash, seven feet across the forward hatch, allowed the water free ingress."[75]

The result was that the *Columbia* went down like a stone. Between eight and nine minutes after the collision, the ship was on her way to the bottom.[76] Of 251 people on board, 88 passengers and crew died.[77]

The close connections between the local inspectors and the steamship companies seemed even more apparent when R. P. Schwerin, the new president of the San Francisco and Portland Steamship Company, was issuing a similar statement to Bulger's press release at about the same time. "It is an impossibility to build an unsinkable vessel for practical use," Schwerin claimed. "Put in as many water-tight bulkheads as you please. Have as many water-tight compartments as you like."[78]

The next day, Bulger retracted part of his statement, noting that a vessel would not necessarily sink as the result of the flooding of one compartment. He claimed, though, that two compartments filled with water increased significantly the likelihood of the vessel going down.[79]

In the *Columbia*'s case, it is unlikely that any of the watertight bulkheads delayed the inflow of water. However, the speed with which the vessel went down was astonishing. The press was increasingly critical of regulations that permitted unsafe vessels to carry passengers and demanded answers. As the *San Francisco Bulletin* noted in an editorial: "Seagoing passenger vessels should be provided with compartments and all other known devices to secure safety, and no matter how sound a vessel may be, she should be taken out of the passenger service when she becomes out of date with reference to safety. A vessel which was safe ten years ago may be comparatively unsafe today, in view of the improvements in the construction of ships."[80]

SOMEBODY BLUNDERED

Following the loss
of the *Columbia,* the
Portland Oregonian
published this cartoon
on July 23, 1907,
depicting Pacific Coast
maritime disasters.

While the investigation of such disasters was usually the responsibility of steamship officials Bolles and Bulger, two days after their statements to the newspapers, the two men found themselves on a ship
bound for Hawaii to inspect a vessel there. As a result, Chief Inspector John Birmingham was to take charge of the *Columbia* inquiry.[81]
Given their statements following the disaster, it would be difficult to
accept the inspectors as impartial evaluators of the evidence.

Since its inception, the Steamboat Inspection Service had been
closely associated with the interests of the large West Coast shipping
companies; but in the case of the loss of the *Columbia,* the inspectors
had gone too far. It was clear that they had made up their minds before hearing one piece of evidence. The public expected a fair hearing.

Chief Inspector Birmingham heard testimony from both passengers and crew. In the end, he concluded, "a water-tight bulkhead
extending up to her main deck and 50 feet abaft her collision bulkhead would have saved the ship and all aboard."[82] While he noted

that the *Columbia* complied with existing regulations, he stated that the law should be changed. In effect, although Birmingham argued that the San Francisco and Portland Steamship Company was not responsible for the disaster under maritime law, the vessel was unseaworthy in relation to modern construction standards.

The responsibility for the accident was placed on Captain Doran of the *Columbia* and First Officer Ben Hendricksen of the *San Pedro*. Both men had proceeded blindly at excessive speed through the fog. In going down with his ship, Doran had paid the ultimate price for his actions.

Birmingham's report stated that at the sight of the *Columbia*, Hendricksen made the mistake of porting his helm, which guaranteed a collision. Hendricksen's license as a steamship master was subsequently revoked for five years.[83]

Captain Magnus Hanson carried a degree of responsibility, for he did not come to the *San Pedro*'s bridge though he had been told of the fog. He also failed to issue written orders to his officers. His license was revoked for one year.[84]

A FREQUENT AFTERMATH of maritime disasters is revelations of the strange twists of fate that determine whether individuals die or survive. Rowena and Ruby Cooper of Fayette, Missouri, were schoolteachers touring the Pacific Coast. After visiting their cousin in Sacramento, the sisters planned to go on to Portland, but Ruby had a mild fear of train travel and the two decided to go by ship. Following the sinking of the *Columbia*, Ruby Cooper was rescued while Rowena drowned.[85] "If my sister sank," Cooper said, "I wanted to sink with her. If one of us was to die I thought that it was better that we should die together."[86]

An Oakland restaurant worker, Rose Anderson, had planned a trip to Seattle via Portland, but when she arrived at the wharf she agreed to exchange her ticket with a stranger. The woman, Anderson believed, was probably a schoolteacher from the East who had attended the Los Angeles educational conference. This person was unable to get passage on the *Columbia*, and had to wait for a later ship. Anderson did not object to waiting, so she agreed to trade tickets at the last minute.

She had no time to discover the woman's name and thus never knew if this simple exchange cost the traveler her life.[87]

At the time he wrote his exams for the San Francisco Fire Department, Al Robertson had served for about a year as second assistant engineer on board the *Columbia*. When he received word of his acceptance by the fire department, Robertson was about to sail with the *Columbia*. He tried to have the department postpone his starting date, but it would not, and on the day the *Columbia* was to sail, he moved his belongings from the ship to the fire station.[88] Engineer Max Claus, who took Robertson's place, was lost with the ship.

The deaths of Louis Malkus and Inez Ellzey on the *Columbia* put an end to the mystery concerning the whereabouts of the couple. The former labor commissioner for the state of Louisiana, Malkus was already married and had one child when he eloped with Ellzey. With him apparently was $5,000, which was part of a trust fund held for the construction of a Louisiana Odd Fellows' home for widows and orphans.[89]

When Grace and Effie Kellar of Decatur, Illinois, reached the Spear Street wharf a few minutes after 11 A.M. on July 20, they were sure they had missed the *Columbia*'s sailing. They were supposed to meet their mother, Mrs. G. A. Kellar, and their sister Alma on the wharf, but the two women were late. The vessel had been delayed, though, and the two were the last passengers to walk up the gangway, where they met their mother and sister. All four died.[90]

After the *Columbia* sank, there were so many reported premonitions of disaster that the *Portland Oregonian* believed that the evidence supported foreknowledge of the future: "The women who foresaw the wreck of the *Columbia* could not have told why they felt as they did. So far as they knew, there was no reason for apprehension. The vessel was seaworthy, the crew competent, the captain experienced and able. And yet they predicted disaster and their prediction came true."[91]

The loss of the *Columbia* was a severe blow to the city of Portland, which always regarded itself as badly served by the San Francisco shipping companies. It was inconvenient for steamers on the San Francisco–Seattle run to sail over a hundred miles inland to Portland. Such an excursion would add more than a day to the passage. The San Francisco and Portland Steamship Company soon leased the steamer

City of Panama as a temporary replacement until a more appropriate vessel could be found.

Early in the morning of August 8, 1907, the small steam schooner *Alliance*, bound from Coos Bay to Portland, ran aground at the confluence of the Willamette and Columbia Rivers. Unaware that the channel was partially blocked, the *City of Panama* ran her bow into the stern of the schooner. The crash was heard three miles away. "The *City of Panama* arrived at Alnaworth dock at 7:10 o'clock this morning, and bears marks of her encounter with the smaller craft. Only the fact that the *Alliance* is a wooden hull saved the *City of Panama* from having her bow doubled up."[92] Coincidentally, the officer of the watch on the *City of Panama* was Second Officer Richard Agerup, who had been on the bridge of the *Columbia* when she collided with the *San Pedro* only seventeen days earlier.

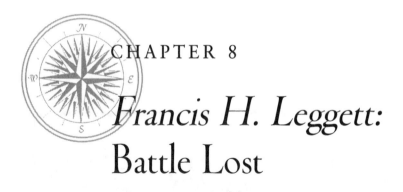

CHAPTER 8

Francis H. Leggett:
Battle Lost

In terms of the number of dead, the sinking of the steamer *Francis H. Leggett* off the coast in 1914 is Oregon's greatest maritime disaster. Yet at the time, West Coast newspapers devoted limited space to the tragedy. One reason was the ship was a steam schooner rather than a passenger liner, and the press was often less interested in the loss of working vessels. The distinction between the two types of ships is not always clear, for passenger vessels also carried cargo and coastal freighters often carried passengers. At the time of her sinking, the *Francis H. Leggett* had on board about forty passengers and thirty crew members. Other events on a grander scale pushed the loss of the *Francis H. Leggett* into the background.

IN MID-SEPTEMBER 1914, an early storm off the coast of Washington and Oregon would be remembered as one of the worst of the season. After leaving Puget Sound on her trip to San Francisco, the new liner *Admiral Schley* ran head-on into a sixty-miles-an-hour gale. Waves towered above the ship, crashed over the bow, and swept along the main deck. The steamship was making slow progress, and her wireless operator contacted the Marconi Company's Columbia station that she would be arriving late at San Francisco. This was an inauspicious beginning to the career of a prestigious new liner on her first voyage.[1]

Another ship, the *Francis H. Leggett,* bound for San Francisco, would be caught in the same storm. Unlike the *Admiral Schley,* the *Francis H. Leggett* was not one of the most luxurious of the coastal vessels, but she had a reputation as a stout working ship. Originally

Photograph of the freighter *Francis H. Leggett*. The vessel took sixty-five passengers and crew to their deaths. (San Francisco Maritime National Historical Park, P. M. Holmway Steam Co. Photographic Collection [P78-084a.087n])

built at Newport News, Virginia, in 1903, the 1,606-ton freighter was 241.5 feet long with a beam of 41.2 feet. She was principally a lumber carrier that also accommodated up to sixty passengers. The ship was owned by Hicks Hauptman Transportation Company of San Francisco and leased the previous year by the Charles R. McCormick Company.[2] The sturdy steel-hulled *Francis H. Leggett* had been among the largest carriers on the San Francisco run, but new ships able to carry up to almost twice as much lumber were now competing with the eleven-year-old vessel.

IN GRAY'S HARBOR, along Washington's southern coast, the sea was deceptively calm. After taking on lumber and railroad ties from two large Hoquiam, Washington, sawmills, the *Francis H. Leggett* steamed toward the harbor entrance. By the time the ship was under way on Wednesday, September 16, 1914, daylight was beginning to fade. In addition to cargo, the ship had taken on twenty passengers who had arrived by train from Seattle. Most had recently arrived from Alaska and little was known about them. Of those from Seattle, the most prominent was C. A. Rohrabacher, who was city agent for the Union

Mutual Life Insurance Company. After his arrival in Seattle about 1902, he had started a publishing business. His best-known book, produced in 1907, was *The Seattle Spirit,* which recounted the history and described the resources of the city. Rohrabacher, seventy-six, was traveling to El Paso, Texas, to visit his daughter. Other passengers included Homer D. Snedjker, his wife, and his twelve-year-old son; they were on their way to see Mrs. Snedjker's sister, who lived in San Francisco. Snedjker was employed by a Seattle department store.[3] Another traveler, Nellie Lee, of Tacoma, had left her husband and booked passage under her former name, Gomez. He was unaware that she was sailing on the *Francis H. Leggett.*

About twenty people from the communities on Gray's Harbor had taken passage on the ship. Among them were Nellie Anderson and her twelve-year-old daughter Helen, who lived in Aberdeen, Washington.[4] They were on their way to San Francisco, where Mrs. Anderson intended to meet her sea captain husband. He was taking a cargo to Callao, Peru, and would return to the California city, where he and his family planned to spend the winter.

Local residents who lived in the small ports found the *Francis H. Leggett* convenient transportation to the larger cities along the West Coast, but the lumber schooner also attracted passengers who wanted an inexpensive conveyance. The lumber carrier had its drawbacks: in exchange for the reduced fare, the passenger had to endure a slow and plodding trip. Even in ideal conditions, the carrier under a full cargo probably made no more than ten knots an hour.

One of the passengers was Sacramento native James A. Farrell, a steam shovel operator who had probably come to the Northwest in search of employment. In 1914, however, there were few jobs for people who operated big earthmoving machines; with the completion of the Panama Canal, most of the skilled workers employed on the project flooded the American market.

George Poelman of St. Cloud, Alberta, was an agricultural laborer looking for better opportunities in the cities of the West Coast. Before taking passage on the *Francis H. Leggett* for San Francisco, he had worked on a farm on Whidbey Island, Washington. He was traveling with a friend.

Captain Charles Maro did not seem particularly concerned about the formalities of a passenger manifest, and no purser was on the ship to ensure an accurate record was made.[5] In addition, at the last moment the *Francis H. Leggett* took on five or six additional crewmen, but did not forward their names to the company.

Although less than forty years old, Maro was a veteran sailor. He had served aboard the *Cascade,* the *Yellowstone,* the *Yosemite,* and the *Multnomah* before taking command of the *Francis H. Leggett.* He had a reputation of being an able commander and an outstanding navigator. Maro had recently married and lived with his wife in Long Beach, California.[6]

The crossing over the Gray's Harbor bar at 8:30 P.M. was uneventful, but as soon as the *Francis H. Leggett* reached open water, she felt the full impact of a southeast gale. Not a fast ship even in good weather, the vessel made slow progress down the coast. The fury of the storm grew as the ship was buffeted by lofty waves. On the first day, most of the passengers were seasick and spent time in their cabins.

A passenger who watched the storm with an experienced eye was Captain Jens Jensen, the former master of the wooden schooner *Nokomis.* In the spring of that year, he had piled his vessel on a reef seven hundred miles off the Mexican coast. Although everyone on board had survived, conditions on the reef were difficult and the master and crew were reduced to a diet of fish and seagulls. The *Nokomis* survivors were rescued after Captain Jensen and three crew members sailed one of the ship's boats as far as Acapulco on the mainland to seek help. The ill-fated seafarers returned to the United States in July 1914. After completing business in the Northwest, Jensen was on his way to San Francisco, where he was to meet his wife and children.[7] He had boarded the ship in Aberdeen, Washington.

When Harry Hafford, a second cook, had arrived at the Portland berth of the *Francis H. Leggett* on September 12, 1914, he discovered she had sailed for Hoquiam. Hafford considered taking a train to catch up with the vessel, but believed the job was not worth the expense of a rail ticket. This decision probably saved his life. Less than a week later, the ship would be at the bottom of the Pacific.[8]

Wednesday night passed and Thursday brought no letup in the gale. Facing a severe headwind, the ship had made less than fifty miles in twenty-four hours. At eight o'clock on Thursday evening, either Charles J. Fleming, the seventeen-year-old chief wireless operator, or his assistant, H. F. Otto, contacted the Marconi station near Astoria, Oregon, and informed them that the *Francis H. Leggett* was off the mouth of the Columbia River. The report did not mention that the ship was in difficulty, which was not surprising, for during her years on the coast she had weathered greater storms. However, this trip may have been different. The ship was heavily laden with lumber, possibly beyond her capacity.[9]

BY EARLY FRIDAY AFTERNOON, it was clear that all was not well on board the *Francis H. Leggett*. The deck cargo had begun to shift, causing the ship to cant sharply. Captain Maro ordered the passengers to their cabins while the crew cut loose the railroad ties that had been lashed to the deck. It was, however, already too late. The *Francis H. Leggett* had been weakened by almost two days of steady pounding. A towering wave broke over the bow and carried away a hatch cover, allowing a hold to fill with water. As successive waves spilled over the hatch, the ship listed to starboard.[10]

The watertight bulkheads kept the engine room dry and the pumps continued to work, but they were no match for the inrush of the sea. It was only a matter of time before the *Francis H. Leggett* sank. The wireless operators began to send a distress call giving the name of their ship and her location. There was no response. The *Francis H. Leggett*'s Marconi transmitter had a limited range and none of the land-based stations were able to pick up the signal. About three o'clock that afternoon, the *Francis H. Leggett* sent a final message: she was sinking.

The passengers were ordered to put on their life preservers and to come on deck. While Captain Maro remained on the bridge, Captain Jensen took charge of the passengers. "When it was seen that there was no hope for the vessel," passenger James Farrell stated, "Captain Jensen ordered a lifeboat launched. . . . He commanded the men to wait until the women were in and threatened to shoot the first man that attempted to disobey his orders."[11]

Passenger George Poelman stood at the rail. "I saw men attempt to launch the lifeboat and they told me to get in. I got in and they started to lower the boat, but it was so rough that they pulled it back again and I got out."[12]

A few minutes later, filled with about thirty people, the boat was lowered again. Despite Captain Jensen's urgings, only two women elected to take their chances in the fragile craft. While the fate of the ship was certain—she was going to the bottom—the lifeboat did not seem a better risk. It did not take an experienced eye to see that the odds against a boat living on this turbulent sea were poor. To remain on the *Francis H. Leggett,* it appeared, at least delayed the inevitable.

James Farrell watched as the craft was lowered by its falls. "As soon as the lifeboat struck the water it capsized and all the occupants were thrown into the water and I think they were drowned immediately. It was an awful sight. I could see the men and women were clinging frantically to any piece of lumber that had been washed overboard from the *Leggett.*"[13]

Not long after the first disaster, a second boat was readied and lowered over the side. "It was almost certain death," Farrell recalled, "and only a few boarded it."[14] The craft met the same fate as its predecessor, spilling its occupants into the ocean.

More than half of those on board the doomed ship had been lost in the two boats. The remainder of the passengers and crew crowded onto the small boat deck abaft the bridge. "Captain Maro was near me then on the deck near the wheel," Poelman said later. "He seemed dazed and stood looking at the deck."[15] Few believed anyone would live.

The end of the *Francis H. Leggett* came suddenly. "I was among the last to leave the ship and was on the bridge helping to launch a lifeboat," James A. Farrell recollected. "I leaped as the ship rolled over and I know she turned turtle because I saw her keel the full length."[16]

As Farrell struggled, the ship began sinking immediately. "I went down with the suction, how far I cannot say, but it was a long way, and, as I came to the surface, I saw the vessel's bow stick out of the water and then gradually sink. Fortunately, I was able to grab a floating tie and I clung to it, drifting about and chilled to the bone by the ice-cold water."[17] It was about 3:15 P.M. when the ship went down.

Passenger George Poelman recalled his last moments on the ship: "I was holding to the rail then when, all at once, the boat seemed to drop out from under me, but I held on as long as I could and went clear under water with it before I lost my hold. When I came up I grabbed hold of two ties and hung on. I looked around me and saw lots of men holding to the ties."[18]

The time between the breaching of the hatch cover and the capsizing of the ship was only a few minutes. (It seems likely that under the shifting deck cargo, water had already gained entry to the ship's holds.) Yet in those minutes, so much happened.

Many of the railroad ties, which were last to escape the sinking ship, shot to the surface like missiles, striking, injuring, and probably killing some of those who had survived the sinking. "One man held up his hand to me," George Poelman said, "and I saw one of his fingers had been cut off and his hand was all bloody."[19]

Farrell, like other survivors, had been severely battered by railroad ties and his face was badly bruised. On the surface, he "saw Mrs. Anderson and her 12-year-old daughter floating near, also one or two other women. There were six women, including two Mexican women, on board. I could not hear many cries, but saw people in the water."[20]

That afternoon, the sun remained hidden behind heavy clouds while the southwest wind buffeted the few figures still clinging to railroad ties. Breaking waves sent people under a mountain of water, to surface gasping for air. The daylight gloom deepened into the dimness of early evening. No lights appeared on the horizon. No rescue ship came.

The *Francis H. Leggett*'s transmitter was not state of the art and the vessel was out of reach of the Marconi land station at the mouth of the Columbia. However, just within range of the lumber schooner's distress signal was the Japanese cruiser *Idzumi*.[21] Two months earlier, as one of the Allied powers, Japan had declared war on Germany and the warships of both nations had stalked each other in the Pacific. With the United States still neutral, the German armored cruiser *Nürnberg* had been allowed to visited Honolulu. There were also other German naval vessels rumored to be in the area.[22] While it would be expected that the *Idzumi* would have gone to the aid of an American ship, the warship was probably wary that the SOS was a German trap.

About 4 P.M. on Friday, September 19, the Associated Oil Company tanker *Frank H. Buck* heard the Japanese cruiser radio the Marconi station near Astoria with news that the *Francis H. Leggett* had sunk off Cape Meares, Oregon. The *Idzumi* did not identify herself, but the same messages were sent by code to her consulates in Seattle and Vancouver, where they were then forwarded to Portland.

Further attempts to contact the warship were fruitless. The location where the steamer was supposed to have sank was vague, but Captain B. H. Macdonald of the *Frank H. Buck* changed course and headed for the scene, arriving in the general vicinity about 11 P.M. After beginning a search, the ship found a debris field spread over a wide area.

Captain Edward Mason of the 4,500-ton liner *Beaver* was on his way to Portland from San Francisco when he received the distress call relayed by the *Frank H. Buck*. He also changed course and headed for the area.

IT IS OFTEN the case that survivors count not the wind, the waves, or even the numbing cold as their greatest enemy, but loneliness. Death is an antagonist far more formidable when faced alone. With every hour, the number of survivors was decreasing. George Poelman heard someone shout, but was unable to comprehend what was said. "It was awfully cold and the people near me drifted away, all but one man, and I could see him until it got dark, then I was all alone for a long time."[23]

For James Farrell, the night would also find him alone. By evening every one had died or drifted away from him. "Until dark I saw the wireless operator floating about on a tie. After dark I called, but could not get any answer."[24] Farrell's hold on reality was at times tenuous. "I kinda lost my head twice, but the waves dashing into my face brought me back."[25] Farrell estimated that at least two dozen people survived the sinking of the *Francis H. Leggett*.

George Poelman watched as the murky light of late evening faded into a starless night. Poelman now clung to a piece of wreckage, which still rose and fell on a heavy swell, but the worst of the storm seemed to have passed. The wind had died down slightly. "Then I saw the lights of the *Buck* and I shouted as loud as I could. They were not far away and I shouted again, but they went right past me and I thought it was awful."[26]

• • •

ABOUT MIDNIGHT, Captain B. H. Macdonald of the *Frank H. Buck* was in his stateroom when he received word that someone had been calling in the dark night beyond the ship. "I rushed to the bridge to confirm it, and, believe me, it was a call for help from a pair of powerful human lungs and charged with all the terror one human voice could carry."[27]

Ordering his ship to be brought about, Macdonald heard the voice growing louder. Finally, the head and torso of a man wearing a life preserver was captured in the beam of the bridge searchlight. With the seas still running high, Macdonald did not consider it wise to launch a boat, but took the ship as close to the survivor as possible. Then holding on to a lifeline, Quartermaster Lars Eskildson jumped overboard and swam to the man in the water. After reaching the exhausted man, Eskildson tied the line around him as both were hauled up on board the tanker. "Lars Eskildson did what I consider to be one of the best attempts at rescue work I have ever seen," Macdonald said.[28]

Poelman had expended what remained of his energy on his last cries for help, and was semiconscious when pulled on board the tanker. Eventually, under the care of the ship's crew, his condition improved. "These men on the *Buck* were good to me," he recalled after reaching shore, "and I am glad I am alive."[29]

A little more than an hour after Poelman had been taken on board, the *Frank H. Buck*'s searchlight revealed another man clinging to a rail tie. Captain Macdonald decided it was safer to launch a rescue boat, and a craft was lowered to the water. "In launching the boat," Captain Macdonald recalled, "one of the lifesavers was washed overboard but was quickly picked up."[30] In the mountainous waves, the crew on board the boat lost the man, but after a long search, James Farrell was finally found. Because of the difficult conditions, the rescuers chose to transfer the survivor to the passenger ship *Beaver*, which had recently arrived at the search location, rather than attempting to take him all the way back to the *Frank H. Buck*.

Both vessels covered the area, but no other survivors or bodies were found. Although other ships later recovered a few remains of nine passengers and crew, most of the victims either went down with the *Francis H. Leggett* or floated further out to sea. One of the bodies recovered was that of Nellie Lee. She was later identified by her jewelry and diamond tattoos on her right arm. Apparently fearful of being robbed, Lee had taken the precaution of tying her wallet containing her money around her right ankle, which was then concealed by her long dress.[31]

IN THE WAKE OF prejudices generated by World War II, some observers have looked back on the *Francis H. Leggett* incident and found the actions of the captain of the Japanese warship to be callous. The *Idzumi* sent a partially unintelligible wireless message that gave only a vague location of where the ship sank. In 1914, though, many people were less critical of the conduct of the cruiser's captain. As the *Portland Oregonian* observed:

> Shipping men, commenting on the loss of the *Leggett* yesterday, spoke warmly of the action of the commander of the Japanese cruiser *Idzumi* in sending out a wireless message telling of the wreck, because, while his mission on the coast is to protect shipping of the allies and to watch for German vessels, his act in using the wireless made known his whereabouts in a general way, which had been kept secret. . . . Had the Japanese not paid attention to the 'S. O. S.' call of the *Leggett,* probably no one on the coast would have been notified of the wreck.[32]

Some later writers have argued that the *Idzumi* could have been first at the site of the disaster and picked up more survivors, and that she could have immediately broadcast accurate coordinates for the location of the sinking. It should be remembered, though, that the Japanese cruiser was a warship operating in a war zone with enemy vessels believed to be nearby.

The *Idzumi,* of course, did not bring about the loss of the *Francis H. Leggett.* Captain Charles Maro chose to leave the protection of harbor and face a severe storm. For that reason, he must be held accountable. It was also Captain Maro who had ultimate responsibility for overburdening his ship, which led to the disaster. Yet his vessel was facing increasing pressure from a new generation of steam schooners able to carry greater cargoes less expensively. Even though he was aware that the *Francis H. Leggett* would be soon facing a severe storm, Maro may have felt pressured to load his ship beyond the level of safety. Soon after the loss of the lumber carrier, the *Astoria Astorian* noted "the imperative need of an American 'Plimsoll-Mark' on every floating-freighter operating on our coasts and under our flag."[33]

IN THE CASE OF the *Francis H. Leggett* disaster, West Coast newspapers gave the event only limited coverage. In the wake of the war, world affairs dominated the headlines and filled the pages.

It was also true that although the loss of a passenger steamer caught the public's attention, there was little interest in the loss of freight vessels. Most people regarded the sinking of cargo carriers like the *Francis H. Leggett* as inevitable. Such events were simply the price of maintaining coastal commerce. (This, of course, was not the case. Lax safety standards cost the lives of many sailors.)

Moreover, with few exceptions, the passengers on board the vessel were not the kind of people who booked the more expensive cabins on passenger liners, and with whom most newspaper readers readily identified. The schooner was simply an ordinary working vessel carrying ordinary men and women. However, as it happened, the last voyage of the *Francis H. Leggett* was anything but ordinary.

CHAPTER 9

Princess Sophia:
A Grave Error

Like the sinking of the *Francis H. Leggett* off the coast of Oregon four years earlier, the loss of the *Princess Sophia* in the frigid waters of Alaska was overshadowed by world events. World War I, which cost the lives of so many soldiers on both sides, was at last coming to an end. At the same time, as if to rival the atrocities of war, a deadly influenza strain was rapidly spreading. No other epidemic in recorded history has killed so many people so quickly. Rather than taking the most vulnerable—the very young or very old—the "Spanish Lady," as it was called, claimed people in their most productive years, the same generation that had made such great sacrifices in the trenches of Europe.

This, then, was the backdrop to the catastrophic loss of the *Princess Sophia*. While it pales when compared to the deaths caused by war and disease, the sinking of the *Princess Sophia* was nonetheless a significant tragedy. When judged by the lives lost, the foundering of the Canadian Pacific Railway vessel on October 25, 1918, is the worst maritime disaster in the history of the West Coast. In all, an estimated 353 people died. No one survived.

THE STEAMSHIP SERVICES of railroad companies had a reputation for reaching their destinations on time. While independent lines may have made allowances for fog or storm, railroad-owned vessels pushed on, often at full speed, to reach their destinations. Such a practice was not surprising since the parent companies were greatly concerned with meeting timetables. While memos from the operation managers frequently instructed captains to consider safety over schedules, there is no doubt that the railroads' concern with time affected the way captains ran their ships.

In 1914, the Canadian Pacific Railway (CPR) was the largest and most profitable transportation enterprise in Canada. It had completed Canada's transcontinental rail line almost thirty years earlier. In 1891, the company had begun to assemble a transoceanic Pacific fleet connecting Vancouver with Asia and later Australia.[1] The CPR next turned its attention to the Pacific Coast.

After taking control in 1901 of the independent Canadian Pacific Navigation Company, the railroad expanded operations in Washington State, British Columbia, and Alaska. The CPR was soon to know the hazards of coastal shipping on the North Pacific when its Glasgow-built, 1,500-ton vessel *Islander* struck an iceberg off Douglas Island, Alaska, and sank within twenty minutes. The ship had been steaming at full speed along Lynn Canal, a fjord that cuts a deep swath into the Alaska Panhandle. Over forty people died as a result of the disaster, including the ship's master, Captain Hamilton Foote.[2]

In the late spring of 1902, the company ordered a replacement for the *Islander,* the 1,942-ton *Princess Victoria.* The ship had a reputation for speed—in her sea trials, she reached nineteen knots. Because speed was more important on the shorter runs, she was placed on the Vancouver-Victoria-Seattle route. The *Princess Victoria* also had a reputation for running on time despite the weather, which on one occasion had fatal consequences when she rammed and sank the liner *Admiral Sampson.*[3]

THE LOSS OF the *Islander* was only a small setback for the Canadian Pacific's coastal service operations in the far North. There was much money to be made carrying people and freight on the Northern route between the boomtowns of Skagway and Dyea, Alaska, and the rapidly growing coastal city of Vancouver. From Vancouver, other CPR ferries took passengers on to Seattle, the city that was the major southern benefactor of the Alaska gold rush.

In 1907, the company began to modernize its operations, and by the outbreak of World War I, nine new vessels had been added to the

Princess Sophia. (National Archives of Canada)

railroad's West Coast fleet. One of the new ships was the 2,320-ton *Princess Sophia,* which was completed in Scotland in 1912.[4]

ALTHOUGH THE northern gold rush was over, new mining companies had arrived using steam dredges and hydraulic pumps to take out the gold that had been too difficult for independent miners to obtain. Gold was no longer the product of individual enterprise, but of industrial organization. Yet many of the early gold seekers remained in the far North, anticipating the discovery of a rich new vein of the precious metal that would finally make their fortunes. By 1918, though, many inhabitants of Alaska and the Klondike were forced to admit that the chances of discovering another fabulous strike to rival Rabbit and Eldorado Creeks in the Yukon Territory or Anvil Creek near Nome were increasingly remote.[5]

As with the California rush, the Klondike stampede had depended on the sea to carry passengers and supplies from distant cities to Dyea and Skagway, the gateway ports leading to the goldfields. For ships, though, the voyage from the southern cities to Alaska was filled with danger. Writing in 1955, James A. Gibbs observed: "Alaska has a wicked coastline, broken and battered with bold outlying ridges, and inside passages bristling with sharp turns, narrow defiles and jagged headlands. . . . The most violent storms sweep Alaska's outer reaches, born there, in fact, in its northern seas."[6] Even after the introduction of radar, vessels continued to meet destruction along the coast. As recently as 1952, the CPR's *Princess Kathleen* ran aground in Lynn Canal. Fortunately, all the passengers and crew escaped, but the ship was a total loss.[7]

While other opportunistic companies had gone out of business when the rush ended, the CPR saw the far North as a source of long-term profits.[8] Captain James W. Troup, manager of the CPR's British Columbia Coast Service, was a man of vision. Early on, he saw the summer tourist trade as becoming an important source of revenue for his ships on the Alaska run. In 1918, though, local passengers and freight traveling to and from Alaskan ports generated most of the northern revenue.

Despite the loss of the *Islander* and other mishaps, the traveling public came to regard the CPR as a safe carrier that operated a fleet of well-maintained vessels with competent crews. Troup expected no less from the crews of his coastal steamers than the men and women who served on the company's prestigious Empress fleet crossing the Atlantic and Pacific Oceans.

THE *Princess Sophia* had been designed for the northern run. A single-screw steamship with a maximum speed of less than fourteen knots, she was functional rather than luxurious, which seemed to appeal to the people of the North. Troup had planned that the vessel would serve a dual purpose. During the summer, she would operate between the southern coast of British Columbia and Alaska. After freeze-up, the ship would be put on the Vancouver-Victoria run.[9]

The vessel was equipped with eight steel lifeboats, one wooden workboat, and six life rafts. In addition, she carried 548 life preservers, including 20 in children's sizes.[10] Although her capacity was 250 passengers, more could be accommodated if additional life rafts were added.

An early photograph of Captain Leonard P. Locke, master of the *Princess Sophia*. (Courtesy of New Westminster Public Library)

In the fall of 1918, her captain was sixty-six-year-old Leonard P. Locke, who had served on ships since he was sixteen. He had come to Victoria in 1891 and took command of the tug *Lorne*. After joining the CPR coast service, he was master of the *Joan,* which ran a regular route between Vancouver and Victoria. During his career on the West Coast, he had sailed on many vessels in the coast service fleet.[11] He had been given command of the *Princess Sophia* two years earlier. Captain Troup regarded Captain Locke as one of the most experienced navigators in his employ.[12]

The master of the *Princess Sophia* had a reputation as a disciplinarian who ran a "tight ship." There was also another side to Locke: he enjoyed reading and writing poetry. The captain was particularly impressed with the works of Robert Service and wrote many pieces in the poet's characteristic style. When not at sea, he lived with his wife in Victoria.[13]

First Officer Jerry Shaw had advanced from quartermaster, and now held a master's certificate. A veteran on the northern run, Shaw was an experienced pilot. Six months earlier, however, Shaw received a mark against his record when the *Tees,* the 689-ton salvage vessel he commanded, went aground on a reef on southeastern Vancouver Island. The ship was refloated and later chartered to the B. C. Salvage Company. The first officer of the *Princess Sophia* was usually "Chubby" Harrison, who was on leave, and Shaw was filling in.[14]

With its head office in Victoria, most of the *Princess Sophia*'s crew were from that city. However, some of the crew, like Wireless Operator David M. Robinson and stewardess H. Browning, were from Vancouver.[15]

ABOUT THREE DAYS' sailing north of Vancouver is Lynn Canal. At its northern end, ninety miles from the entrance, is the port of Skagway. At the time the *Princess Sophia* sailed, the city was the terminus of the White Pass and Yukon Railway, and the gateway to the goldfields of the northern interior. The railroad extended only as far as Whitehorse in Yukon Territory, but a subsidiary, the British Yukon Navigation Company, operated a fleet of paddle steamers along the lakes and rivers that served as the main route into the interior of Alaska, the Yukon, and northern British Columbia. At the beginning of the short northern spring, passengers arrived by ship at Skagway, on their way to the interior. As the northern winter approached, it was at Skagway that many of the residents arrived by river and rail. From there ships left for Seattle, Vancouver, and San Francisco. By 1918, it had become a familiar cycle.

IN THE FALL OF 1918, Captain James Troup was a worried man. On October 13, the big CPR ship *Princess Adelaide,* on her run between Vancouver and Victoria, had gone aground on Mayne Island. Although there were no injuries, the ship was damaged and would be in dry dock for some time. The *Princess Mary* was then placed on the run, but this meant that there were no additional passenger vessels to call upon if there were any other difficulties on company routes. "For God's sake, keep out of trouble this winter," Troup warned Locke before the *Princess Sophia* departed on her last northern run of the year.[16]

The *Princess Sophia* left Vancouver on Saturday, October 19, 1918, and was scheduled to make brief stops at the communities of Alert

Bay and Prince Rupert, British Columbia. When the *Princess Sophia* reached her first port of call, she received an SOS from the 3,709-ton liner *Alaska,* which had struck a reef near Swanson Bay on the central coast of British Columbia. The Alaska Steamship Company vessel was southbound from Skagway headed for Seattle. After steaming to Swanson Bay, the *Princess Sophia* found that the *Alaska* had worked herself free, but that she was extensively damaged and had to unload her passengers at Prince Rupert, the nearest port. Describing the incident, W. C. Dibble, a fireman on the *Princess Sophia,* wrote his wife: "She had 300 passengers aboard. They will land in the morning [at Prince Rupert], but I do not know what they will do except to have to wait for another ship, as we will be more than full from Skagway, and we have fixed up beds in every corner of the boat; as there are over 800 people waiting to come down."[17]

The influenza epidemic had reached Vancouver two weeks earlier, and was spreading rapidly through the city. On October 21, crew member Joseph Woosnam became ill while the ship was docked at Prince Rupert and was admitted to the hospital. On October 28, the young steward had recovered sufficiently to telegraph his father that he was all right.[18] Ironically, the disease that would take between 15 and 25 million people worldwide[19] saved Woosnam's life.

After leaving Prince Rupert, the *Princess Sophia* arrived at Juneau late on October 22, where she unloaded passengers and freight. The liner reached Skagway the next afternoon and discharged the remainder of her cargo and passengers. The *Princess Sophia* was not the only vessel making a last trip to Skagway before freeze-up. About midnight on October 21, the Grand Trunk Railway's 3,379-ton *Prince Rupert* had boarded 327 passengers for Vancouver.[20] As the men and women who crowded Skagway knew, winter was not far away. Already the water that filled the puddles along the town's muddy streets was freezing over.[21]

The *Princess Sophia* was scheduled to leave at seven o'clock on the evening of the twenty-third, but the loading of passengers and freight took longer than expected. She did not leave until a few minutes after 10 P.M.[22] At the dock, a hundred people remained behind as the *Princess Sophia* pulled up her gangway.[23] The *Admiral Watson,* which had been hurriedly pressed into service, was on her way from Seattle to Skagway to pick up those northerners still waiting for a ship.[24]

Of those leaving on the *Princess Sophia,* most were going to the United States. More than half of the 278 passengers on board were holding transfer tickets to Seattle. Among them was Oscar Poppert, who, with his twin Walter, had hoped to strike it rich in the Alaskan interior. In 1918, as winter approached, the twins had enough money to spend the winter in the South. When they reached Skagway, Walter booked passage on the *Prince Rupert,* but Oscar had already obtained a ticket for the *Princess Sophia* and did not want to give up his first-class cabin. As a result, the twins were separated. After reaching Seattle, Walter took a room in the Diller Hotel and waited for his brother.[25]

Florence Beaton was said to be the first European woman to arrive in the Iditarod district of Alaska in 1909. Her husband, John, and his partner, W. A. Dickerman, had made a major gold strike there in 1908. While Beaton remained at the site, his wife and their two children booked passage on the *Princess Sophia.*[26]

Merchant Sam Henry, a native of Lincoln, Nebraska, had prospered in the Klondike. He and his wife Josephine arrived in 1896 and raised a family in Dawson.[27] The Henrys were well known in northern social circles. He was a member of the Masons and the Eagles; she was a member of the Order of the Eastern Star.[28] They rarely left the North, and Josephine had only been south once since 1898. However, in 1918, the couple planned a visit to Seattle to see a married daughter. The Henrys booked a first-class cabin on the *Princess Sophia.*

Probably the wealthiest man to board the *Princess Sophia* was William Scouse, credited with taking the first bucket of gold from the gravel of fabulously rich Eldorado Creek.[29] In 1896, Scouse was living in Nanaimo, British Columbia, when he, his brothers, and several friends decided to take a hunting trip to Alaska and boarded a small vessel going north. Once there, they heard about the strike at Rabbit Creek and trekked into the Klondike, where they staked nearby Eldorado Creek. According to author Pierre Berton, Scouse, his brothers, and one of the original members of his party took out a fortune in gold.[30] The hunting had been better than the Nanaimo residents had supposed. After making his fortune, Scouse divided his time between the Klondike and his home in Seattle.

A well-known traveler on the *Princess Sophia* was U.S. collector of customs John Fraser Pugh of Juneau, whose job frequently took him to ports along the Alaska coast. Pugh had been born and raised in Washington State and attended school at Port Townsend. He came to Alaska about the turn of the century, and had joined the customs service as an inspector. He quickly rose through the ranks to become collector. When he boarded the *Princess Sophia,* he was returning to his wife and family in Juneau.[31]

Some passengers were bound for Vancouver. James Alexander, who had spent ten years developing the Engineer Mine, seventy miles from the community of Atlin in the far north of British Columbia, was planning on selling what was claimed to be the world's richest gold mine. All that remained was for the engineer employed by the prospective purchasers to confirm the value of the mine. Alexander was a flamboyant figure who was said to possess uncommon physical strength. One tale claimed that Alexander, to win a bet, swam a quarter of a mile through frigid waters.[32] Traveling south with him was his wife, Louise; Clarence S. Verrill, a mining engineer; C. E. Watson, of the Mining Corporation of Canada; and George Randolph, a Toronto mining expert.[33]

Another familiar passenger was William O'Brien of Dawson. He was a member of the city council and held a seat in the Yukon Territorial Legislature, as well. Bound for Vancouver, he boarded the vessel with his wife and five children.[34]

Of those boarding the *Princess Sophia,* eighty-seven passengers were employees of the White Pass and Yukon Railway and its steamboat subsidiary.[35] With the coming of freeze-up, workers were returning to their homes in the United States and Canada. Captain C. J. Bloomquist of the stern-wheeler *Dawson* held a transfer ticket to Victoria. He had come outside for the winter to his home on Shawnigan Lake, Vancouver Island. James Bowker, first engineer on the steamer *Yukon,* had spent many summers in the North. As freeze-up approached, he took passage with a transfer to Seattle, where he and his wife lived.[36]

With the gradual decline in the gold economy, many were not planning to return in the spring. The hold of the vessel was filled with the household goods of passengers. There was approximately $140,000 in the ship's two safes and mailbags kept in the chart room.[37] At least one passenger, Lulu Mae Eads, did not trust her valuables to the purser. She secreted her jewelry in her stateroom.[38] According to one source, Eads had been the inspiration for "the lady that's known as Lou," recalled in the famous Robert Service poem "The Shooting of Dan McGrew."[39]

Before leaving port, Captain Locke telegraphed Captain Troup in Victoria: "*Sophia* south, 10 P.M., 23rd; 268 passengers, 24 horses, 5 tons freight."[40] The few people who remained at the wharf watched the ship slip out of the harbor and toward the main channel. Already a cold north wind was blowing down from the mountains. The departure of the *Princess Sophia* on her final trip of the season was like the last leaf falling from a tree. The men and women who planned to stay behind faced a long, cold winter. Many of the well-wishers who crowded the wharf probably envied their friends and relatives who were escaping to the warmer weather "outside." Those who were coming back would not return until after the spring breakup.

As THE *Princess Sophia* entered the main channel, snow began to swirl around the ship. Visibility was reduced, but there is no indication that the vessel slowed to a safer four or five knots. Captain Locke had been three hours late leaving Skagway, and unless he made up the time, he would reach Vancouver behind schedule.

There is little evidence about what took place on the *Princess Sophia*'s bridge after she left Skagway. Either the captain or the first officer would have plotted a course along the west side of Lynn Canal and fixed their position at the Eldred Rock Light, between Sullivan Island and the west shore. Following this course, the ship would pass close to Point Sherman, about eight miles down the canal. The headland was used by mariners as the point of departure for a new course to the channel west of unlighted Vanderbilt Reef, about sixteen miles farther on.[41] Under unfavorable conditions, it seems likely that either Captain Locke or his first officer, Jerry Shaw, made a navigation error, taking the *Princess Sophia* on a mid-channel course that ended abruptly at 2:10 A.M. on Vanderbilt Reef. The *Princess Sophia* was in the center of the canal, more than a mile off course.[42]

A rocky outcropping rising about fifteen feet above the water at low tide, Vanderbilt Reef's flat surface is submerged under high tides or heavy swells. The only warning of the hazard then was a buoy placed on the south end of the rock. Many regular travelers along

Windward side of *Princess Sophia,* stranded on Vanderbilt Reef, October 24, 1918. This photograph was taken from a rescue ship. (National Archives of Canada, William Kaye Lamb Collection)

Lynn Canal had petitioned authorities for a lighted buoy, but their requests had been ignored.[43]

The *Princess Sophia* struck with such force that some of the passengers were thrown from their berths. Alarmed, women still dressed in their nightclothes rushed on deck. According to a letter written aboard the ship and later found on the body of a victim, the captain ordered the lifeboats readied and swung out over the side in preparation for launch, but it was clear that no one would live in the stormy sea.[44]

At the same time, twenty-year-old Wireless Operator David M. Robinson was sending out a distress signal. At Juneau, the message was received and forwarded to Frank Lowle, the CPR agent in that city. Within minutes, Lowle was contacting the captains of harbor boats. In little more than an hour, the first vessel in what would become a small flotilla of rescue craft left Juneau for Vanderbilt Reef.

Soon after receiving a call from Lowle, the sixty-five-foot gasoline launch *Estebeth* had cast off her lines and was making her way toward the stricken ship. On board was Captain James P. Davis and his six-member crew.[45] The vessel left so hurriedly that she did not take on such essential provisions as sugar and coffee.[46]

About 8 A.M., the 140-ton fishing boat *King and Winge* was tied up at the Juneau dock unloading fish when Lowle approached Captain James J. Miller and asked him to go to the *Princess Sophia,* which had grounded on Vanderbilt Reef. Miller finished unloading his cargo and got under way at 10:10 A.M. Once beyond shelter of the harbor, the sea began to rise.

AT 2:15 A.M., ten minutes after the ship struck the reef, Captain Locke had no doubt about the seriousness of the *Princess Sophia*'s plight. The vessel had struck the northeast end of Vanderbilt Reef and was wedged firmly in the rocks. The *Princess Sophia*'s transmitter was incapable of reaching the southern coast, so it was necessary to relay a message via the Juneau cable office to CPR coast service headquarters. (It was difficult for the ship's telegraph operator to send a message as far as Juneau, only twenty-seven miles away. The mountainous terrain was a formidable obstacle to the signal.) Locke waited until after 9 A.M. before forwarding word of the grounding to Troup: "The *Princess Sophia* ran on Vanderbilt Reef, Lynn Canal at 3 o'clock [two o'clock Alaska time]; ship not taking any water; unable to back off at high water; fresh northerly wind; ship pounded; assistance on way from Juneau."[47]

When the *Estebeth* reached the scene about 11 A.M., the tide had receded and cook Christ Dimitri could see that the vessel was suspended on the reef with her bottom about nine feet above the surface of the water. The snow had stopped and although the sea continued rough, it was not so heavy that a lifeboat would not have survived.[48]

Captain Davis rowed his workboat to within fifty feet of the *Princess Sophia* and hailed Captain Locke, asking him if he was going to abandon the vessel. The captain replied that he had inspected the hull and determined that it was securely wedged in a crevice in the reef; the ship was in no danger. Davis believed it would have been possible to lower the ship's metal lifeboats and launch them from the reef. The task would not have been easy, for each craft weighed more than a ton. Davis, though, believed that with the aid of the stronger members of the crew and passengers, it could be readily accomplished.[49] When the *Amy,* a ship of similar size to the *Estebeth,* arrived, Locke also told Captain Edward McDougall that he did not intend to take off the passengers.[50]

Other small ships arrived, but by late afternoon, the weather had deteriorated and many craft had made their way to the limited shelter available in the canal. The *Estebeth* and the *Amy* stood by, although all they could do was reassure everyone on board the *Princess Sophia* that they were not alone. As the afternoon wore on, Locke hailed the two vessels, telling them that the *Princess Sophia* was in no danger and to seek out a safe anchorage for the night.[51]

At 3 P.M., the 1,341-ton lighthouse tender *Cedar* was anchored 72 miles southeast of Juneau when Captain John W. Ledbetter received a message that the *Princess Sophia* was on the rocks. Ledbetter sent a wireless message to Locke offering his assistance. The captain of the stricken ship immediately accepted.[52]

As the *Cedar* steamed toward Vanderbilt Reef, Captain Ledbetter contacted the *Princess Sophia* at 4:30 P.M. and asked if it were possible to remove passengers that night. Locke replied: "Impossible to get passengers off tonight. Sea running too strong. May get off tomorrow; strong tide."[53]

At 6:20 P.M., when the big gasoline fishing boat *King and Winge* arrived, the weather had deteriorated further. The fishing vessel managed to get within nine hundred yards of the *Princess Sophia,* but it was impossible to contact her because Captain Miller had no wireless. The crew on board the fishing craft could see people moving about the deck of the *Princess Sophia.* With the storm raging, Miller realized the help he could offer was limited.[54]

Only the *Cedar* was equipped with wireless and was able to communicate without great difficulty with the wrecked ship. Alone, the *Cedar* had the capacity to take on four hundred people, more than the number on board the *Princess Sophia.*[55] However, the weather was continuing to worsen, as the snow that had been falling steadily since the afternoon increased to a blizzard. At high tide, a severe wind swept down from the northeast. Its force virtually drove the *Princess Sophia* further on the reef.

Feeling there was nothing further he could do, Captain Ledbetter withdrew to the protection of the lee side of Benjamin Island, about four miles from the reef. As the hours passed, conditions on the *Princess Sophia* continued to deteriorate. At 8:30 P.M., the lights went out and the heating failed when one of the main pipes from the boiler ruptured.[56] Despite these problems, Captain Locke felt the integrity of the ship was not threatened.

According to the testimony of the *Cedar*'s wireless operator, Elwood M. Miller, later given to the Canadian maritime inquiry, the steampipe was repaired at 11:00 A.M. the next day, October 25.[57] Passengers again enjoyed heat and light, but more importantly, the *Princess Sophia*'s wireless was fully operational. The emergency batteries that had allowed the liner's wireless operator, David Robinson, to signal to the *Cedar* were now recharged.

Despite the worsening weather and rough seas, the *King and Winge* managed to approach within two hundred yards of the *Princess Sophia*, but unless the people on board were ready to take their chances in the icy water by leaping overboard, there was no way of helping them. (Captain Miller estimated he could rescue no more than 10 or 20 percent of those who would have taken such a chance.) About 1:30 P.M., Miller took his vessel to the lee side of Benjamin Island, where the *Cedar* was at anchor. He spoke with Captain Ledbetter, who told him that he had been in touch with the liner and she was seemingly not in difficulty. Exhausted by the pounding he and his crew had endured, Captain Miller anchored the *King and Winge* beside the big lighthouse tender.

CAPTAIN JAMES TROUP had ordered the 3,100-ton liner *Princess Alice* to be made ready the previous day to pick up the passengers from the *Princess Sophia*. She steamed out of Vancouver harbor on the evening of October 24. With the damage to the *Princess Adelaide* earlier, the coast service had no replacement for the Vancouver-Victoria-Seattle run and the night sailing was canceled.[58]

The CPR now chartered the *Tees*, which the company had recently leased to B. C. Salvage. She first took on a load of coal and provisions—then, that evening, Captain Hewison steamed out of Victoria harbor on a thousand-mile journey to Vanderbilt Reef. On board was a salvage expert representing Lloyd's of London, the vessel's insurer, and two deep-sea divers. Despite optimistic reports in the newspapers that the *Princess Sophia* was in no immediate danger, the CPR had serious concerns.

For Troup, a thousand miles from the scene of the wreck, and with no direct communication with his liner, the hours of waiting must have been intolerable. He received his final message from Locke in the early morning hours of Friday, October 25. It read: "Steamer *Cedar* and three gas boats standing by, unable to take off passengers account strong northerly gale and big sea running; ship hard and fast with bottom badly damaged but not making water. Unable to back off reef; main steam pipe broken; disposition of passengers normal."[59]

ALL DAY the storm continued to rage. At two o'clock, Elwood Miller, the wireless operator on board the *Cedar*, had been at his post more than twenty-four hours. When the power on the *Princess Sophia* failed again about that time, it was an opportunity to receive some much needed rest because David Robinson, his counterpart on the liner, would have to conserve his batteries. Both men were extremely tired. Before resting, they promised to make contact at 4 P.M. Elwood Miller lay with his headset on in the event there was an emergency call from the *Princess Sophia*.

As agreed, he attempted to contact Robinson at four o'clock, but received no reply. Miller would have thought that Robinson likely slept through his signal. At 4:50 P.M., his headphones came alive with an SOS reporting that the *Princess Sophia* was sinking. Miller answered that the *Cedar* was on her way. Robinson's batteries were so low that at times it was impossible to hear his signal. At 5:20 P.M., Miller heard the faint call: "For God's sake, hurry. Water is coming into my room."

Miller answered: "We are coming; save your batteries."

Robinson responded: "All right, but keep talking to me so we will know you are coming."[60] This was the last message Elwood Miller received from the *Princess Sophia*.

• • •

THE *King and Winge* was at anchor at 5:20 P.M. when Captain James Miller "heard two whistles from the *Cedar,* which meant that she was getting up her anchor to get away."[61] The *Cedar* approached Miller's vessel and Captain Ledbetter hailed him, saying that the *Princess Sophia* had gone down and that he was on his way to Vanderbilt Reef. Miller recalled: "We were anchored about 200 yards off-shore, but we could not see the land because it was snowing so heavily. A northwest wind was blowing. The *Cedar* said she would go out, and if the snow stopped for us to come out to assist."[62] Miller said he would wait an hour before joining the *Cedar.*

About forty minutes later Miller heard the whistle of the *Cedar.* Like many captains, Ledbetter used the time between the whistle and the echo to judge his nearness to land. The *King and Winge* responded by blowing her whistle so that the lighthouse tender could find her way back. The snow was so thick that the captain of the *Cedar* got within twenty-five feet of the fishing vessel before he saw her stern. Miller later said, "I asked what they had found out, and he replied that it was blowing a gale of wind with a blinding snow storm, and thought himself lucky to get back."[63]

The weather had moderated somewhat by 7:20 A.M. the next day, October 26, and the *Cedar* and *King and Winge* weighed anchor for Vanderbilt Reef. All that was visible above the water was the *Princess Sophia*'s foremast. No bodies, no pieces of wreckage could be seen. The two ships began a search off Shelter Island, and three overturned lifeboats were spotted. The *Cedar* found a piece of skylight and a life raft beached on the north end of Shelter Island, but it was too rough to attempt a landing. At 12:45 P.M. the U.S. Army transport vessel *Peterson* arrived and aided in the search. As the weather moderated slightly, other smaller vessels reached the scene.[64]

With the improvement in the weather, twelve bodies were recovered and taken to Juneau, and many more were seen along the shore. Conditions, though, worsened the next day, October 27, and it was impossible to continue the grim task.

On October 28, Captain Robert Griswald of the boat *Monaghan* and Deputy Marshal Harry Morton left Juneau. They arrived at Vanderbilt Reef at low tide and climbed up the exposed rock. The surface of the reef had been worn smooth. Noting the foremast above the water, the two men observed that the ship was facing opposite to the way she had struck the reef. [65]

Due to the extent of the scouring of the rock surface, it was generally concluded that at high tide the wind pushed the vessel along the reef, causing it to pivot on its bow. The action tore open the ship's bottom, and when the *Princess Sophia* was pushed off the reef into deeper water, she quickly sank.

The wind had diminished and more than 150 bodies were recovered from the rocks along the shore and from the water on October 28. Most of the remains were covered with a thick layer of oil from the *Princess Sophia*'s bunkers. They were taken on board the search craft and brought to Juneau.[66] With a shortage of coffins in Vancouver as a result of the influenza epidemic, 225 adult and 25 children's caskets were ordered from Seattle. They were shipped to Juneau on board the steamship *City of Seattle*. Accompanying the coffins were three embalmers.[67]

Because most of the victims were wearing life preservers, the body count quickly climbed to almost 250 by October 30. One body, tentatively identified as Lulu Mae Eads, was brought in with an estimated $5,000 in jewelry hidden on her remains.[68]

In Juneau, the bodies were carried to a warehouse that served as a temporary morgue. Covered in thick sludge, the corpses first had to be washed in gasoline before embalming. The grim task of scrubbing fell to the citizens of Juneau. The bodies were later dressed and placed in coffins. While the victims from Alaska were readily identified, many from the Yukon were unknown. As more remains were recovered, they were brought into the small Alaska port, where the process of cleaning, preparing, and identifying the dead continued.[69] With the exception of those whose relatives wished them to be buried in Juneau, all of the bodies recovered were taken on board the *Princess Alice*.

THE *Princess Alice* left Juneau on November 9, carrying 156 dead. On November 11, 1918, Armistice Day, marking the end to a bloody and senseless four-year war, she reached Vancouver, her first port of call, and delivered 62 bodies.[70] With characteristic efficiency, the CPR had laid out plans for the temporary accommodation of the *Princess*

Sophia's former passengers and crew. H. W. Brodie, the company's passenger ticket agent, had earlier announced: "Arrangements are being made to reserve suitable space on the outer end of Pier D, where all the caskets will be placed in proper order, so that identification may be readily proceeded with. Undertakers will be present to assist. All the caskets are suitably marked. If any unidentified bodies remain they will be removed to the morgue, where they will be kept for further enquiry and identification."[71]

The CPR undertook shipping cost for bodies outside Vancouver, and wherever the final burial place of the victim, the company also paid "all reasonable funeral expenses."[72] The cost of the tickets for the *Princess Sophia* was refunded to the next of kin.

In Victoria, the *Princess Alice* unloaded her remaining cargo. The bodies destined for Seattle and other cities were loaded on ships. While the *Princess Alice* would serve in the CPR coastal fleet until 1949, taking many vacationers on the scenic Inside Passage run to Alaska, she was never able to quite overcome the epithet "Ship of Sorrow."

WITHOUT A SINGLE human survivor, the sinking of the *Princess Sophia* left many questions unanswered. Why, for example, was the vessel so far off course when she struck the reef? Shortly after the incident, a former pilot, R. E. Davis of Controller Bay, Alaska, told the press that it was well understood that Vanderbilt Reef was the most hazardous obstacle on Lynn Canal. "Every captain on the run knows the reef and could avoid it in calm weather," he said, "but if a strong northeast wind were sweeping down the canal the ship would be blown directly against the reef."[73] Yet it is difficult to believe that the *Princess Sophia,* which normally would have passed no closer than a mile to Vanderbilt Reef, could have been so far off course. Although the weather was difficult at the time, the vessel was not yet facing a severe gale. It must be wondered why a master of Locke's experience did not take conditions that were common in Lynn Canal into account. Also, First Officer Jerry Shaw had spent many years in the North Pacific and acted as pilot.

Captain Locke's reluctance to disembark the passengers at a time when it was seemingly safe to do so may have been explained by a rising barometer, which gave the false impression that the worst weather had passed. (On the afternoon of Thursday, October 24, the day the ship struck, Captain Ledbetter of the *Cedar* had noted the rising barometric pressure. As an experienced mariner, Captain Locke would have been watching closely his own glass.)[74] An evacuation would have been difficult because of the weight of the lifeboats, but would have saved the lives of many on board. The ship was hard aground and there was no guarantee that the *Princess Sophia* would float free at high tide. Locke's first duty was to his passengers, and in this he failed.

ON NOVEMBER 5, the weather was calm enough to send two divers from the vessel *Tees* down to the sunken ship. They located the express locker containing $100,000 in bullion, which was returned to the safekeeping of the salvager. They also discovered the body of passenger George Paddock, who had been caught between decks.[75] Before the ship could be searched completely, squalls buffeted the *Tees* and work had to be suspended.[76]

Salvage operations by local divers would continue into the new year. Al Winchell, the husband of one of the victims, hired Juneau diver S. Jacobson. Despite several attempts in January, Jacobson was unable to reach Cabin 35, which was supposedly occupied by Mrs. Winchell.[77] Winchell then hired Seattle diver J. J. Donovan, whose search showed that there were many more bodies on the vessel. In the end, the CPR undertook another search of the wreckage and recovered eighty-six more victims. In July, the body of Winchell's wife was finally recovered.[78]

SOME INDIVIDUALS were more fortunate than others. Captain Harry C. Baughman was master of the stern-wheeler *Whitehorse,* on which he had served for thirteen years. He had booked passage on the *Princess Sophia,* but decided to leave earlier on the ancient steamer *Humboldt.* Baughman relinquished his tickets to his second engineer, Richard Haws. Baughman returned to his family in Lewiston, Idaho. Haws never left Alaska alive.[79]

The engineer's son, Richard Haws Jr., was more fortunate. As he recalled more than forty years later: "I was on the way out to join the crowd about to sail on the *Princess Sophia* but on the way up the river

I was in a poker game, and I owed the cook on the boat some money. I was second engineer on the *Whitehorse.* I went up to the office at Whitehorse to cash my check and pay my debt to the cook, and while there ran into a friend Paul Bourne who persuaded me to come out with him on the *Prince Rupert.* "[80]

Like steward Joseph Woosnam, the Spanish Lady saved the life of First Engineer Archibald Alexander. Two of his children contracted influenza, and he received permission to return to Victoria before the ship sailed. Engineer Charles Wallace, who had served on another company ship, replaced him. As far as is known, Alexander's children both recovered.

ON OCTOBER 27, the news of the sinking of the *Princess Sophia* was the lead story in the *Seattle Post-Intelligencer.* "Not One on Board Ship Saved When She Goes on Vanderbilt Reef in Gale,"[81] the newspaper announced. The *Princess Sophia* disaster shared the front page with Allied advances in France and other war stories.

The spread of influenza continued to be a topic of public concern. Seattle's health commissioner, Dr. J. S. McBride, urged residents to stay home to avoid spreading the disease. On the previous day, 19 flu-related deaths and 494 new cases were reported.[82]

In Vancouver, Mayor Robert Gale had already issued an urgent call for persons to act as nurses. "Vancouver people are actually dying in considerable numbers," the mayor's press release stated, "and without the care that even the meanest stranger within our gates is entitled to receive at our hands . . ."[83] On the same day that the loss of the *Princess Sophia* was announced in the *Vancouver Daily Sun,* the newspaper noted the need for volunteer telephone operators, as almost half the regular staff were off ill.[84] As the days passed, stories about the Alaska tragedy were pushed to the inside pages of the West Coast newspapers.

THE CANADIAN GOVERNMENT'S commission into the sinking of the *Princess Sophia,* under Judge Auley Morrison and British Columbia's wreck commissioner John D. Macpherson, began in Victoria on January 10, 1919. Hearings were also held in Vancouver and, with the agreement of the American government, Juneau. Many of the captains and crews of the rescue vessels were called as witnesses. The verdict was released on April 24, 1919:

> From the evidence adduced, the conclusion arrived at . . . is that the ship was lost through peril of the seas. As to why passengers were not landed is a matter of conjecture, but . . . from the evidence of all the surrounding circumstances, such as the ship being staunch and well officered, other craft being in the vicinity and other ships approaching, the inhospitable shores and the lack of shelter sufficiently near, the time of year and the weather conditions, [we] were prepared to find that it was not unreasonable for Captain Locke not to land his passengers.[85]

Not surprisingly, the outcome displeased many of the relatives and friends of the victims. Since the disaster occurred in American waters, it had been the decision of most of the relatives to take on Canadian Pacific in a U.S. court. Yet there was a long history of such claims against passenger carriers, and only rarely were shipping companies held responsible. The litigation begun by relatives of the deceased went on for years. In 1932, after fourteen years of court battles, the U.S. Circuit Court of Appeals awarded the estates of 227 passengers only $643.[86] Excluding legal fees, each claimant was thus entitled to $2.83.

WHEN THE *Princess Sophia* went down, she created a vortex that carried down forever the stories of the final days and hours on board the ship. Concluded the *Victoria Daily Times*: "The last heart-rending chapter never will be written, for there remains nobody to write it."[87]

CHAPTER 10

San Juan: End of an Era

On August 29, 1929, a tragic event befell another veteran of the Pacific Coast passenger fleet. "The *San Juan,* which had been in service for forty-seven years and is said to have been the oldest ship in passenger service sailing Pacific waters, finished its career as the victim of one of the most horrifying tragedies in Pacific history . . . ," the *Los Angeles Times* wrote.[1] This was no overstatement, for the old ship became an iron crypt for scores of people trapped below deck.

By its nature, the *San Juan* disaster was reminiscent of another tragedy, the loss of the *Columbia* in 1907. Both the *San Juan* and the *Columbia* were vessels with iron hulls, built in the early 1880s at Chester, Pennsylvania. The accidents occurred about midnight, and the ships were proceeding in reduced visibility. Other vessels struck them, and they went down rapidly with heavy loss of life. On the West Coast, the *San Juan* holds the unenviable record of departing the surface faster than any other similar ship. It took her only three minutes to go down after her collision with the oil tanker *S. C. T. Dodd.*[2]

THE FINANCIAL DIFFICULTIES of the Pacific Mail Steamship Company, the old line that had played such an important part in the California gold rush, led to the purchase in 1925 of the firm's entire fleet by W. R. Grace and Company of New York. The company's newer and better vessels were placed in the service of the new owners. The others were quickly sold. The *San Juan,* one of the oldest ships, was disposed of immediately. The buyer was the White Flyer Line, which operated a cut-rate service between San Francisco and Los Angeles.[3]

However, within two years, creditors besieged the company. The *San Juan* and her sister ship on this route, the *Humboldt,* became the property of the Los Angeles and San Francisco Navigation Company. The *San Juan*'s outmoded two-cycle compound engine developed only 1,250 horsepower.[4] Unlike other lines, the company did not advertise its ships as fast or luxurious, but a ticket in steerage on the *San Juan* or the *Humboldt* sold for as little as $8.

It would be wrong to assume, though, that these ships appealed only to the poor. Many middle-class journeyers found a ticket on the *San Juan* less a strain on their finances. When travel was necessary, businesses with a sharp eye on their balance sheets sent their staff on the *San Juan* or the *Humboldt.*

The *San Juan* carried six lifeboats, with a capacity of 132 persons, and 110 adult life preservers, as well as 17 for children. She also had two luminous buoys that would be visible to rescue ships at night. In case she grounded on a reef, she was equipped with a Lyle gun.[5]

THE LOS ANGELES and San Francisco Navigation Company was a small operation and its two vessels usually attracted residents from the San Francisco and Los Angeles areas, rather than tourists visiting from other states. The *San Juan* had not been the first choice of San Francisco resident Harry Wade, a marine engineer, and his friend L. B. Heatley of Manila. Wade was perhaps more aware of the potential dangers of traveling on the *San Juan.* For almost five decades her bow had ploughed the waters off the West Coast. For years she had been regarded as a third-class ship with the Pacific Mail Company fleet. Still, it was impossible on short notice to book fare on any other liner bound for Los Angeles.[6]

Theater manager and Hollywood resident Charles M. Welstead had bought a round-trip ticket to San Francisco. He had boarded the *San Juan* with the intention of visiting his friend A. L. McMeans in San Francisco. However, when he arrived unannounced on Thursday, August 28, at McMeans's office, he discovered his friend was out of town. Impetuously, Welstead decided to take the Thursday evening sailing back to Los Angeles, and boarded the *San Juan* just minutes before she sailed.[7]

The *San Juan,* built in 1882 by W. Roach and Son of Chester, Pennsylvania.
(San Francisco History Center, San Francisco Public Library)

San Francisco–trained nurse Max Wilkes had accepted a short-term job in Los Angeles and packed only what he thought he would need during the time he would be away. A few moments before boarding, he told friends, "Gee! In a way I feel like not going."[8] Wilkes did not heed his intuition about sailing on the *San Juan,* though.

When they walked up the gangway, retired Mountain View, California, merchant Theodore Granstedt and his wife Emma were leaving to pay a surprise visit on their daughter Greta. Greta Granstedt had moved to Los Angeles a few years earlier with the intention of becoming an actor.[9] Although her name was not widely known, Greta had played supporting roles in a number of silent pictures, including *Close Harmony* in 1929. (She was to have a long motion picture career that continued until 1970.)

In the 1920s, the notion that the United States was a land of limitless opportunities was still held firmly in the minds of many Europeans. The start-and-stop economy of the 1920s did not provide the kind of skilled jobs some immigrants had hoped to find.

Danish architect Martin Hanson, his wife, and his two young children had recently immigrated to the United States and settled in San

Francisco. However, he had not been able to find a job suitable to his qualifications, and the family decided to move on to Los Angeles. They withdrew all their money from the bank, packed up their few personal possessions, and purchased tickets on the *San Juan*.[10]

Los Angeles interior decorator R. O. Gorman had taken the *Humboldt* to San Francisco, where he completed a job. His return passage was booked on the *San Juan*, but before he was to leave, he received an urgent telegram from his firm to return as soon as possible. He then managed to book passage on the *Harvard*, one of the fastest liners on the West Coast, and sold his ticket on the August 29 sailing of the *San Juan* to Willis Barton, a twenty-year-old Los Angeles soda fountain clerk who had been visiting in San Francisco.[11]

Harry Kidder, a forty-six-year-old sales representative from Los Angeles, was on a visit north to see his sister, Mrs. A. C. Pearson. After leaving her home in Stockton, California, he journeyed back to San Francisco, where he boarded the *San Juan*.[12]

Maudie Dansby, twenty, had walked up the gangway of the *San Juan* at Pier 17 a few minutes before five o'clock. Several days earlier she had decided to take a few days off work to visit her fifteen-month-old child, who lived in Los Angeles with her parents and sister. "It just happened that I took the *San Juan* for the trip," she wrote later," but I was fond of the sea and ships. . . ."[13]

Insurance broker George Houghton was returning to his home in Los Angeles. He was booked in stateroom No. 9 on the upper deck, which he shared with an elderly man. His cabin mate apparently spoke no English and Houghton was unable to learn his name.[14]

Compared with Los Angeles temperatures, San Francisco's summer was refreshingly cool, and it may have been for that reason that Marjorie Pifer had traveled north to visit her mother during the hot season. As September approached, Pifer booked passage for herself and her son on the *San Juan*. Returning with her for a visit in Los Angeles was her sister Betty Simons.[15]

Two hours late, the lines of the *San Juan* were finally cast off and she began to come about slowly. Already fog was beginning to hang above the water like dirty cotton. With her lookouts peering into fading light, the ship proceeded under a slow bell along the south channel. She passed beyond Point Lobos and then proceeded on a south-southwest course. Because of the late departure, the passengers dined as the ship was leaving the harbor.

After dinner, Maudie Dansby joined three others for a game of bridge. About 9:30 P.M., she accompanied Purser Jack Cleveland to his office to arrange a change of staterooms. As they stepped out on deck, Dansby was suddenly aware of the heavy shroud that had been cast over the ship. As she recalled: "Standing in the midst of the fog it seemed to suffocate me and, while I am not really superstitious, I felt a shudder of dread as though something terrible were imminent. Perhaps there is something to woman's intuition, after all. Fog had never before inspired any especial emotion in me. I really believe I had a premonition."[16]

On the bridge was Captain Adolf F. Asplund, who had agreed to take command of the *San Juan* while her regular master was on leave. (It was rumored that the leave was permanent, for the former captain had resigned.) It was claimed that sixty-five-year-old Asplund took the post as a favor to the new owners.[17] The captain's record, however, was hardly unblemished. In 1915, the Board of Steamboat Inspectors took his license for sixty days when his ship, the *Graywood*, struck the motor launch *Helen H.* in the Oakland estuary, killing its operator. Eight years later, Asplund lost his license for a year after beaching his steamer a few miles south of Punta Gorda, California.[18]

Captain Asplund was no stranger to the *San Juan*. This was his third round-trip passage on the ship since taking command. He had apparently also served as its relief captain earlier that year.[19]

The shipping line's practice of selling tickets on board the ship ensured that no accurate passenger manifest remained on shore. The company also failed to keep a reliable account of its own employees, noting that there were supposed to be forty-seven crew members on board. There may have been more or less, the Los Angeles and San Francisco Navigation Company admitted.[20]

OTTO V. SAUNDERS was on the bridge of the Standard Oil Company tanker *S. C. T. Dodd*. Still relatively new, the 7,054-ton oil carrier had been built in 1920 at Oakland, California. Unlike the *San Juan*'s wrought-iron plates, the 425-foot tanker had a steel hull.[21]

Although serving for only eight months as third mate of the *S. C. T. Dodd,* Saunders had been on the West Coast a dozen years and was regarded as an experienced mariner. The journey up the coast seemed to be routine: "The weather was clear when I came on the bridge at 8 o'clock. We were then abreast of the Point Sur lighthouse. At 11:34 the Santa Cruz light was abeam, and I could see the loom of the Point Pigeon lighthouse fourteen miles away. Visibility was then fairly clear, with a short, choppy sea."[22] However, a few minutes later, fog was beginning to close in on the ship, and he reached up and put his hand on the whistle.

Shortly after 11:45 P.M., Captain Hugo Oscar Bleumchen was asleep in his cabin when he was called by Saunders, who reported that fog was closing in. Bleumchen ordered the sounding of the fog whistle: "I got up and got into a robe, and just then I heard the engine-room bells ring 'Stop.' I came onto the bridge and saw the *San Juan* bearing across our starboard bow, perhaps a quarter of a mile away."[23]

Charles J. Tulee, first officer of the *San Juan,* who was off duty, recalled: "I was in my room on the bridge deck. . . . The blowing of the fog whistle kept me awake. When I heard the *San Juan* and a nearby steamer [the *Dodd*] each blow three blasts I ran on deck, knowing that a collision might occur, as that was the signal to reverse full speed. When I got on deck I saw the tanker approaching. The collision seemed inevitable and I returned to my stateroom for my trousers."[24]

Tulee returned to the bridge in enough time to witness the collision. "The *Dodd* seemed to strike us a glancing blow," he said.[25] The gash in the *San Juan*'s port side allowed water to pour into the engine room, which quickly disabled the generator. Water continued to fill the hull at a rapid rate.

AT ELEVEN O'CLOCK, Harry Wade and his friend L. B. Heatley went down to the former's cabin. Heatley, who was used to the warm Philippine weather, shivered. Complaining that the room was cold, he rang for the steward, who brought him several blankets. Bundled in the blankets, he sat on the settee and talked with his friend. A few minutes passed before Heatley commented that the fog whistle was blowing almost continuously. "The steam is going through the right place instead of through the [cabin] radiator," marine engineer Wade observed.[26]

Moments later the two men were jolted by a violent crash. Wade wrote:

> I leaped from my berth . . . and opened the door. We were in Cabin 20 on the main deck on the port side opening into the saloon.
>
> The lights went out. We groped our way through the dining saloon.
>
> Someone struck a match and that was our salvation. We saw the staircase leading from the saloon to the upper deck and the two of us dashed up this—not a moment too soon, as the water was on the floor under the dining tables.[27]

About 11:45 P.M., the twenty-two-year-old chief wireless operator, Clifford Paulson, was on duty in the *San Juan*'s radio room. It had been a busy day, and in a few minutes he expected to be relieved. "The first intimation I had of disaster was when the whistles first began to blow," he recalled. "I got up and looked out the door of the radio room, and saw a ship directly in front of us that loomed up like a mountain. She was almost upon us."[28]

Paulson did not feel a great jar, but heard the grinding sound of metal against metal. Immediately the ship was in complete darkness. Paulson returned to his desk in the radio room, switched on the emergency battery backup, and began tapping out a call for assistance. He heard a ship answer before water began gushing through the door. Paulson had no doubt the *San Juan* was finished: "As the water came around my legs, rising like a flood, I hammered out one S.O.S. A second later the water was over my head. Then I tried to fight my way to the door."[29]

Unemployed architect Martin Hanson and his family took a second-class accommodation:

> My wife, our sons Eric, 4, and Ola, 6, and I were in our cabin below deck when the crash knocked us to the floor. Startled at first, we did not know what to do.
>
> But realizing our danger, my wife and I wrapped a coat about each of the children and rushed up on the port side of the fore deck.

The *San Juan* was already listing to port. The big tanker was right off the port bow.[30]

Second steward William Gano was sitting on his bunk reading. Moments later, the world around him seemed to explode as the steel bow of the *S. C. T. Dodd* pushed into Gano's cabin, destroying the half of the bed that fortunately he was not using. The steward's room was plunged into darkness. Disoriented, he searched for his cabin door, which he could not find. However, his hand wrapped around a length of line dangling from somewhere above him. As he peered up, he saw that the rope led through a jagged space extending beyond the ceiling of his stateroom. He climbed hand over hand and found that it ended in the smashed remains of one of the *San Juan*'s lifeboats that had been on the deck above his cabin. In the short time Gano had been roused, the ship was listing heavily to port. The outcome, he knew, was inevitable. He dove from the upper deck into the sea.[31]

Unfortunately for the passengers, most had retired to their cabins when the collision occurred, while many of the crew of the *San Juan* were on deck because it was the change of watch. The speed with which the ship sank was difficult to believe. Charles Tulee, the first officer of the *San Juan,* recalled: "I was on the main deck when the crash came. And a minute and a half later my feet were in the water."[32]

Six-year-old Hollis Pifer was in his cabin when the collision occurred. "I was in bed when Mother came pounding on the door," Hollis remembered. "She wrapped a coat on me. . . ."[33] Then she carried him out on deck.

Insurance broker George Houghton retired to bed about nine o'clock, but had difficulty sleeping because of the constant blaring of the ship's fog whistle. A few minutes before midnight he heard the ship's whistle sound three times, the signal for reverse. Immediately the ship shook under the impact of a crash. Houghton estimated that the point of impact was on the other side of the ship, about amidships. "The crash didn't throw me from the berth but I scrambled out in a hurry. The lights went out a few seconds later. I found my trousers, vest and coat and had them on in a jiffy. I had no idea we had been struck by a boat but thought at first we had piled up on the rocks."[34]

In the darkness, Houghton found his life preserver under his bed, but could not find one shoe or his glasses. As he recalled: "The screams and noise were terrible."[35]

Houghton made his way out to the deck, where he saw a great gash on the stern quarter. He went back to his cabin, which was on the upper deck behind the bridge, and searched for his missing shoe. While he could not find it in the blackness of his room, he did discover his glasses. Even now, Houghton had no idea the danger he was in or how close the vessel was to sinking.

His cabin door leading to the saloon was open, and Houghton could make out a group of people near the dining room stairs. "They were shouting, crying and calling for life preservers. Some were praying. It reminded me of Dante's Inferno."[36]

Second Officer August Olson had stopped by the dining room to prepare for his watch. He had made himself a quick meal and had sat in the ship's pantry to eat a sandwich and drink a cup of coffee when the ship reverberated to the crunch of metal. The collision did not interfere with Olson's meal until the lights suddenly went out. Carrying his coffee and sandwich, Olson made his way to the deck: "Immediately I saw there was something wrong and I dropped my cup of coffee. Then I heard an order to man the lifeboats."[37]

FOURTH ASSISTANT ENGINEER G. W. Woolley of the *S. C. T. Dodd* stood on deck. "Almost immediately after we struck the *San Juan,*" he said, "the vessel came along our starboard side, our rails only a few inches apart."[38]

First Officer Tulee of the *San Juan* remained on the main deck as the ships swung together: "I shouted to the twenty passengers on deck to climb aboard the *Dodd,* as this could be done easily."[39] Few people did so, however.

Marjorie Pifer and her son were among the passengers straddling the *San Juan*'s rail, reluctant to risk the short leap to the other vessel. Woolley recalled:

When some one tried to push her over to our rail, I heard her cry: "Please, please—save my boy first."

Some one passed the child over to one of our men and then the ships drifted apart—too far for any of those poor people to jump. Mrs. Pifer went down with the *San Juan*.[40]

Sol Karansky, fourteen, of Los Angeles, had run away from home and shipped out as a deck boy on the *San Juan*. He was unprepared for what was about to happen: "I was in bed when the crash came, and ran to the deck in my nightgown. . . . Men and women were screaming and I could feel the ship tipping and reeling. I could see the bow of the *Dodd* dropping slowly away from us."[41]

As he gauged the gap between the two ships, it did not seem too far to jump. If he did not succeed, he would fall into the cold waters of the Pacific. "I'm a pretty good swimmer," he said, "but I didn't feel like getting wet that night."[42]

Something within Karansky also told him that this was his only chance to escape. "I took a run and a jump for it. My feet struck the rail—just making it. I was tripped forward to the deck. My face was badly scraped. But I was safe."[43]

After Karansky, a man attempted to cross and also made the deck of the other ship. The leap to safety, though, was becoming more difficult. Karansky recalled the horrifying scene: "Women with babies in their arms tried to make the jump, but the *Dodd* was drifting away and they fell in the water between the two ships. Their screams were awful. Men tried it, too, and fell short. They yelled, too, as they went down into the black water."[44]

Martin Hanson and his family stood near the *San Juan*'s rail: "I tried to shout above the terrible din to someone on the tanker to catch my boys. I wanted to throw them off. But I didn't have time."[45] The tanker was soon too far away.

By now the *S. C. T. Dodd* was lowering her lifeboats. Everything had happened so quickly that few people on board the *San Juan* had time to put on life preservers. Many had vanished before the rescue boats had cleared the falls.

THIRD ASSISTANT ENGINEER John McCarthy of the *San Juan* was finishing his watch. "I was on the ladder when the crash came, just leaving the engine room. The lights went out and a man passed me in the darkness. He knew the ship better than I. I went out on deck where the second mate [August Olson] and a seaman were at a lifeboat. I helped them to free the lashings of the lifeboat."[46]

A few passengers had come on deck and Olson had told them to wait a few seconds until the lashing had been removed and they could get in. "It was so dark I could not see to untie it," McCarthy said, "but the mate gave me a knife. Before the boat was ready the ship sank, and I went down with it."[47]

As Martin Hanson recalled: "Without warning, the *San Juan* rolled suddenly to port, and we were thrown into the water. I do not know what became of my wife and the boy she held. She was a good swimmer. I cannot swim. I held the other boy with one arm."[48]

Deckhand Caesar Ceballos was in his bunk below deck on the *San Juan* when the bow of the *S. C. T. Dodd* struck the liner. He wasted no time reaching the upper deck: "I'd hardly got to the rail, to see what had happened, when the stern of the ship, where I was, went down." As the ship sank, the deck began to break up, smashing his leg and pinning him against the metal rail. Water washed over the stern. "I went way down deep with the ship, but managed to get loose and swim."[49]

Jens Mehanner was also in his bunk at the time of the collision. The lights went out immediately, but the deckhand was so familiar with the ship that he reached the deck in seconds. There were few people on deck, but he could hear the screams of the terrified passengers trapped in the darkness below. Mehanner immediately went to his station on the starboard side to free his lifeboat, but the ship was going down too fast. "Before I could get it loose we were in the water."[50]

One of the first passengers to leave the stricken vessel was Maudie Dansby. "When the crash came I ran to the deck and, sensing the situation," she said, "dived overboard immediately and put as much distance as possible between myself and the sinking vessel."[51]

Theodore and Emma Granstedt were in their cabin. He reported hearing a terrific crunch of metal against metal. Then he was aware of being pulled down in a gigantic whirlpool.[52]

Like most passengers, Harry Kidder was in his cabin at the time of the collision. "I was in bed when I felt a dull thud. The lights went out right away and I rushed out on deck. Already the boat was listing, and as I rushed up the inclined decks the water followed me."[53]

The events of the next few minutes were fixed in Kidder's memory. "The cries of the children were awful to hear. Every one was screaming—I guess I was too. Suddenly the boat went down, and I was caught between two decks. I couldn't get out, but when I started to strangle on water I kicked."[54]

As insurance broker George Houghton recalled: "The ship quivered and I bolted for the deck. I saw some of the crew trying to launch one of the lifeboats, up forward. I think they got it off all right, but don't know what happened to it when it hit the water."[55]

On deck, Harry Wade and his friend L. B. Heatley were separated. A woman holding a small boy was near the saloon pleading with the others around her to find a preserver small enough to fit her son. Heatley went to find one, but when he returned she was gone.[56] Heatley then saw that the sea was rushing over the stern and up the saloon door. "I made a dash for the side and dived over. I guess I was in the water well over an hour and a half. I saw women struggling in the water crying—it was terrible. They were gasping and shrieking piteously for boats to come."[57]

Harry Wade was aware that the *San Juan* had little time left and had gone to the No. 1 boat station on the starboard side, where he and Quartermaster Luther Leathers began taking off the canvas cover. The two men quickly pushed four passengers standing nearby into the craft and began letting it down by its falls. As he recalled:

> Then while we tried to lower the lifeboat, the *San Juan* up-ended and slid under the water with a terrific roar.
>
> I was drawn down into the vortex. It seemed an age. Suddenly the boilers exploded with a deep, rumbling noise.
>
> I felt myself being shot up with terrific force to the surface and through the air. The fore topmast came up alongside of me end-on, and it and I went sailing skyward. The topmast fell close to me and I went under the water for a second time.
>
> When I came to the surface not a trace of the ship remained. She had disappeared, leaving piles of wreckage.[58]

As the ship disappeared below the surface, George Houghton remembered, "a thousand things ran through my mind and I must have lived an eternity in six or seven minutes. I felt the boat heave and the stern dipped under. I gave a jump, landed on the rail and jumped out as far as I could. The water was just below my feet then."[59]

Some of those who were pulled down with the ship never surfaced, while the wreckage injured others. Jens Mehanner was pulled deeper and deeper into the black sea. During the confusion, as he descended toward what appeared certain death, Mehanner was struck in the arm by some object. After a few minutes, he broke the surface of the water. "When I came up I grabbed onto a big chunk of wreckage."[60]

Theodore Granstedt struggled to the surface of the cold water. He counted seven others around him and the tanker was fortunately close. A rope from the *S. C. T. Dodd* was thrown over the side and came within reach of five of the swimmers. Granstedt was the only one to hold on long enough to be hauled on board the ship. He was barely conscious. Granstedt was never certain what happened to his wife, but believed that she had been trapped in their cabin when the liner went down.[61] Caesar Ceballos, the crew member who had been pinned against the ship's rail, had a difficult time swimming to the surface for his leg was badly crushed.[62] Sales representative Harry Kidder did not know how he had managed to free himself from the ship, but when he reached the surface he was near a plank. Swimming over to the piece of wood, he used it to support himself.[63]

Jens Mehanner floated, holding on to a few pieces of debris with one arm. "A woman with a life belt on her was floating near me, and I tried to get my wreckage over to her, but my free arm was broken and I could do nothing."[64]

When Third Assistant Engineer John McCarthy surfaced he was also able to hold on to a piece of wreckage. He remained in the frigid waters for about an hour before being rescued.[65]

Architect Martin Hanson said later:

> As I was trying to find something to cling to to keep me afloat, the *San Juan* rolled under. The center of it seemed to buckle and explode. I was sucked under. It must have knocked me unconscious.
>
> When I came to I was on the surface again. My boy was gone. A floating mattress came my way and I grabbed it. Someone on the tanker threw me a life preserver on a line and pulled me aboard.
>
> I wish I hadn't been saved. Everything I had is gone. Why couldn't I have died too?[66]

For young Sol Karansky on the *S. C. T. Dodd*, the "most awful" time during the drama unfolding before him was when the *San Juan* disappeared below the surface. "That moment was filled with the blood-curdling screams, which were followed by a moment of awful silence," he told the newspaper.[67] In another interview, he said: "For just three or four minutes I could see the *San Juan*—lower and lower and lower. Then down she went with a big whirl of waves."[68]

In true maritime tradition, Captain Adolf Asplund chose to go down with his ship. First Officer Charles Tulee and steward George Haines remained with him almost until the end.[69] Both men escaped the vortex and were picked up by boats from the *S. C. T. Dodd*.

ANOTHER SHIP was near enough to offer the *San Juan* aid. Following about three miles behind the *San Juan* was the McCormick Steamship Company (formerly the Charles R. McCormick Company) freighter *Munami*. Suddenly the crew on board the vessel heard a crash. Moments later the 20-year-old radio officer, William Staiger, picked up the message: "We are struck." This was followed by three SOS calls from the *San Juan*.[70]

At 11:55 P.M., Staiger wrote in his log, "Tanker *S. C. T. Dodd* rammed the S.S. *San Juan* eighteen miles south of Pigeon Point." Five minutes later the log noted, "*S. C. T. Dodd,* calling S.O.S., says 'sank *San Juan* immediately.' Tanker's boats out, rescuing survivors."[71]

After receiving the message from the tanker, Captain Gus Illig ordered his ship dead slow into the debris field. The *Munami*'s two lifeboats, under First Mate E. T. Swanson and Second Mate A. Winkel, were lowered. Captain Illig oversaw the rescue from his ship.

Swanson and his crew of four sailors attempted to nose the boat through the closely packed wreckage that littered the surface. A thick layer of oil pooled on the surface and covered everything and everyone in the water.[72] (The source of the oil was a mystery since the tanker was in ballast and it seems unlikely that the liner had been converted to oil-fired boilers.) The slippery substance made it difficult for survivors to cling to the pieces of wreckage. "Cries of 'save me' would come from a score at a time," Swanson recalled. "We could see hardly any of them, despite the searchlight from the *Dodd*, 500 yards away. . . ."[73]

For Winkel, the tragedy took a terrible turn. "I saw a baby floating on a mattress crying 'mama,' but when the boat approached the swell of the boat tipped over the mattress and the baby never was found."[74] The crew of the *Munami* would not quickly forget the events of the early hours of August 29. "To hear their cries and be impotent to save all of them was a maddening thing," said Captain Illig.[75] There were survivors who probably never completely recovered from the psychological wounds suffered during those hours of horror. Others, though, seemed hardly touched by the disaster.

Maudie Dansby, who had been in the water since a few minutes before the *San Juan* sank, continued to swim away from where the ship went down. "I'm a good swimmer, so I just kept moving and after a while some one, I don't know who, lifted me into a boat. So here I am and darned lucky to be here."[76] Dansby, who had gone overboard wearing not even a nightgown, was given a set of sailor's clothes on the *S. C. T. Dodd.* Once at San Francisco, she modeled her uniform for photographers. "Of course, I am terribly upset by the tragedy of all those poor people struggling in the water and the horror of it all," she told reporters, "but I feel fine myself. Really I enjoyed the swim."[77]

Harry Wade had been in the water less than an hour when the freighter *Munami* hove into sight and launched two of her lifeboats. On the ship, "I washed off the crude oil with kerosene and, except for a few slight bruises, I am feeling fine."[78]

Less than a dozen survivors were found during the three hours the *Munami*'s boats pushed through the debris. The two lifeboats were badly dented by the timbers floating in the water. The *Munami* continued to look for survivors until after 8 A.M., but no more were found. The steamer then transferred the injured to the Coast Guard cutter *Shawnee* for transfer to San Francisco. The *San Juan* tragedy claimed seventy-seven people. There were forty-two survivors; only two were women.

MANY PEOPLE had no idea whether their loved ones were on board the *San Juan.* The morning after the disaster, crowds converged at the shipping line's San Francisco office in the Arcade Building on Spring

Street. The same scene was repeated at the firm's Los Angeles office. A. H. Fay, local passenger agent at the Los Angeles office, recalled that Joseph Lee Pifer entered his office, read the names of his wife, son, and sister-in-law on the passenger list, and stumbled out murmuring, "They were there."[79] In a state of shock, it would be some time before Pifer discovered his six-year-old son Hollis survived.

Allegations concerning the feeble condition of the *San Juan* seemed to bring forward stories of other ships that sailed at the edge of disaster. One such account concerned the *City of Panama,* which had sailed the Central American route years earlier. (The *City of Panama* also served briefly as a replacement for the *Columbia* after the latter vessel wrecked in 1907.) The *San Francisco Call Bulletin* published a story of an alleged incident that took place before World War I in which the *City of Panama* returned to San Francisco "with passengers who told tales of broken seams, half the crew manning the pumps and other unseaworthy items."[80] So incensed were the passengers that they besieged the offices of the Steamboat Inspection Service, demanding that the *City of Panama* be taken out of passenger work. The inspectors surveyed the vessel, and the passengers were given the report that the ship was seaworthy. After a few minor repairs, the inspectors said, the aging hulk could be returned to service.

However, on board the *City of Panama* was a U.S. consular official who was being transferred to the State Department.

> He didn't stop in San Francisco. He went straight forth to Washington where he at once communicated with the highest influence of the steamboat service. He told that individual the same story [concerning the condition of the *City of Panama*].
>
> The result was that within a week the Pacific Mail had placed at auction a vessel that local inspectors only a few days before had said could be returned to the passenger service.[81]

When the vessel was auctioned off a few days later, "only junk dealers were there to bid. Accordingly, the vessel was sold merely for the iron in its engines."[82]

The account was nothing more than pressroom rumor, for there were no facts to back up the *City of Panama* story. What seems to be implied in this tale, however, is that the answer to safer passenger vessels would be found not in San Francisco, but in Washington.

The inquiry into the *San Juan* disaster under local inspectors Frank Turner and Joseph Dolan began within two days of the sinking. The newspapers had demanded answers to the question of the vessel's seaworthiness. Inspector Turner soon made his position clear. "I do not believe the age of the *San Juan* had much to do with the foundering. The *Titanic* was a new vessel and it went down when struck; the *Malolo* was brand new and it remained afloat when struck on its trial trip. . . . To compel the owners to put in modern double bottoms and other air-tight compartments would have cost more than the steamer was worth."[83] Turner, in effect, dismissed all questions concerning the seaworthiness of the *San Juan* and turned his attention on the officers on board the two ships involved.

Some of the survivors had charged the crew with neglecting the passengers to save their own lives. Among the passengers, only marine engineer Harry Wade was called to the stand. "The crew responded nobly but had time to do nothing to save passengers," Wade testified.[84]

Inspector Turner did not believe the crew was guilty of misconduct. "In an instance like this," he told the inquiry, "when a vessel is struck and sinks in three minutes, at midnight, nothing could be done by the crew in the way of lowering lifeboats or passing out life preservers."[85]

Third Assistant Engineer John McCarthy of the *San Juan* claimed that although many of the crew could have jumped to the other ship, many sailors held back and encouraged the passengers to save themselves.[86]

Contradicting the claims of the *S. C. T. Dodd*'s crew that the *San Juan* veered off course was Robert Papenfuss, the third officer of the liner. According to Papenfuss, it was a clear night when the collision occurred. He said: "When I saw the *Dodd* it was almost straight ahead, a degree to the left. I was on the bridge alone, the captain having gone below for lunch. I told the quartermaster to turn the ship slightly to the right when we were two miles apart so we could pass safely. I blew no passing whistle. The *Dodd*'s red light had been showing when suddenly the lookout reported her green light was in view indicating the tanker was heading toward us."[87]

The inquiry became mired in rumor and conflicting statements. In the end, Third Officer Papenfuss of the *San Juan* was found guilty of negligence and his license was revoked.[88] (Evidence adduced after the hearing showed that the *S. C. T. Dodd* had changed course, likely contributing to the collision.)

First Officer Charles Tulee of the *San Juan*, although overwrought by the loss of his ship, provided a clear account of the aftermath of the collision for the steamship inquiry. "I was not near the lifeboats and do not know as to whether any were lowered. I heard no signal to the crew to go to their stations. It all happened so suddenly—there was not more than ninety seconds from the crash to the sinking—that there was no time to lower the boats or put on life preservers."[89]

CURIOUSLY, fate had a double blow for the Los Angeles and San Francisco Navigation Company. About the same time the *S. C. T. Dodd* was burying her bow in the old iron liner, the *San Juan*'s sister ship *Humboldt* struck a fishing barge in Santa Barbara Channel. According to reports, the *Humboldt*'s bow knifed eight feet into the side of the barge. Because the *Jane L. Stanford* was constructed of wood instead of iron and had no engine or boilers, she did not sink. The barge crew was taken off by the *Humboldt* and put ashore. Why the *Humboldt* struck the barge remained unexplained. The barge's navigation lights were on.[90]

THE SINKING OF the *San Juan* seemed to crystallize the public's doubt about maritime safety standards. Although some West Coast lines operated well-maintained ships with properly trained crews that were highly regarded among travelers, cut-rate enterprises like the Los Angeles and San Francisco Navigation Company did much to undermine the public confidence in steamer safety. For the officers of the merchant marine and others with a personal stake in the viability of the passenger trade, the press was blamed for exaggerating the *San Juan* disaster. Newspapers were natural scapegoats, but such charges only clouded the issue. The press was simply reflecting the public's growing distrust of the West Coast shipping companies. Two days after the disaster, the *San Francisco Examiner* wrote: "Just why an antiquated vessel of the type of the *San Juan*, 47 years old, was permitted to carry passengers on the high seas was a question that nobody was prepared to answer yesterday."[91] Indeed, no government official ever properly answered the question.

The Steamboat Inspection Service was a branch of the Commerce Department, whose purpose was to promote the interests of business. Thus, the marine inspectors' main concern was to ensure that shipowners could entrust their vessels to competent officers. For this reason, the boards of inquiry were quick to discipline the officers adjudged negligent.

The actual safety of the vessels was regarded as a concern for the company itself. Although regulations existed, they were often inadequate, abstruse, and poorly enforced. Many of the accidents were unavoidable, but others were clearly the result of unseaworthy ships.

In part, it was the role of the Steamboat Inspection Service to shield the steamship companies and politicians from criticism. This was particularly true after the turn of the twentieth century, when the public began to expect higher standards of transportation safety. The perennial excuses given by local inspectors to account for the loss of "seaworthy" vessels were indeed wearing thin.

By the late nineteenth century, safety reforms had begun. The first tentative steps toward achieving international standards for passenger security on the high seas were proposed in an 1889 conference in London. The sinking of the *Titanic* in 1912 brought unprecedented attention to the question of safety at sea. Other conferences in 1914 and 1928 also addressed the problem.[92]

The interest in ship safety meant that improved lifesaving equipment on board passenger vessels became law. Now each passenger, regardless of sex or class, was guaranteed a place on an escape craft. For Pacific Coast shipowners, who had always regarded government regulations in the area of safety as an incursion into their business, the new regulations seemed a personal affront.[93]

However, the early safety reforms did nothing to assure the seaworthiness of the ships themselves. In 1929, a few ancient vessels continued to carry passengers on Pacific Coast routes. "Old or new, no matter how excellent her condition," John K. Bulger, now supervising inspector of steamships, would maintain, "no vessel can stand up under such a blow as the *San Juan* apparently received."[94] Yet it was not a question of standing up, but standing up *longer*. When a ship sank so quickly, the number of lifeboats on board mattered little, for there was simply no time to launch them.

Under the Department of Commerce, the Board of Steamboat Inspectors had been a loosely run organization open to patronage and corruption, and changes were slow in coming. President Woodrow Wilson signed the Seaman's Act in March of 1915, which required that over half of the crew on American passenger vessels be certified "able seaman." The regulations stipulated that sailors be qualified to meet minimum safety standards, such as launching and operating lifeboats. The responsibility for licensing ships' crews, though, did not go to the Board of Steamboat Inspectors. While the Steamboat Inspection Service had long been responsible for the certification of officers, the testing of thousands of sailors was beyond its resources.[95] The examination of crew members was given to the newly formed U.S. Coast Guard. Although under the Treasury Department, rather than the U.S. Navy, the Coast Guard was organized along military lines, with a strict code of discipline. While it would take many years to accomplish, the Coast Guard spelled the beginning of the end for the Steamboat Inspection Service.[96]

In the mid-1930s, the Atlantic Coast had a number of its own marine disasters. On September 8, 1934, the New York–bound *Morro Castle* caught fire while anchored in a severe storm off the New Jersey coast. Many passengers and crew were forced into the frigid water, with the death toll placed at 130. The tragedy became a public spectacle when 125,000 people arrived the next day by automobile and train at Asbury Park, New Jersey, to watch as the vessel continued to burn near the beach.[97] Less than two years later, the passenger ship *Mohawk* sank off Sea Girt, New Jersey, after veering in front of the Norwegian freighter *Talisman*. The probable cause was a defective steering mechanism. Tragically, 46 passengers and crew died.[98]

Although both vessels were less than ten years old, newspapers in the East raised many questions concerning ship construction. As a result, an extensive congressional investigation into the building and operation of American passenger ships was begun. Receiving much of the criticism for their failure to enforce existing regulations were the steamship inspectors.

The implementation of new standards meant that American passenger ships were built with public safety as a prime consideration.[99] However, for patrons on the West Coast liners, the changes came too late. The difficult economic conditions during the Great Depression and the emergence of the automobile and the bus as practical alternatives hastened the end of the coastal steamer service. For the wealthy, Trans World Airlines began service between the cities of Los Angeles and San Francisco using the newly developed Douglas DC-2 airplane. People who routinely took passenger ships along the coast were forced to make alternate plans in 1934, when labor unrest broke out in many West Coast ports. The San Francisco wharves were closed by the dockworkers for three months.[100]

In the 1930s, the end of coastal passenger service was at hand. The dominant Admiral Line discontinued coastal service in 1936. The Los Angeles and San Francisco Navigation Company ended an already limited passenger service using two freightliners, the *Wapama* and *Celilio,* in 1937. The McCormick Steamship Company offered passenger accommodation between Seattle and San Francisco on board its freighters until it was subsumed within the Pope and Talbot Lumber Company empire in 1940.[101]

Of necessity, steamships continued to connect Seattle and Skagway, Alaska. British Columbia, too, provided coastal links to Alaska via Prince Rupert and Vancouver. Ferry service between Seattle and Victoria, British Columbia, also continued (and continues today). Yet by the end of the 1930s, the principal maritime routes that promoted north-south commerce had all but passed out of existence. San Francisco, while still an important seaport, was no longer the hub of a West Coast maritime empire that stretched from San Diego to Portland, Seattle, Victoria, and on to Skagway.

The cruise ship may be seen as the successor to the Pacific Coast passenger vessels of generations ago, but this is not really the case. Few cruise patrons would deny that the cruise is more important than the vessel's destination. These great floating pleasure resorts have little in common with the coastal vessels of former days.

The period between the California gold rush and the beginning of the 1929 depression marked the golden age of coastal passenger travel. The working liners that once sailed this coast, carrying people and freight to the ports of the Pacific Northwest, have slipped below the surface of the present into the murky realm of the past. For the passengers and crews who lost their lives on these vessels, to be forgotten would be the greatest tragedy of all.

Notes

Introduction

1. *Seattle Daily Times,* February 15, 1898.

2. *Seattle Daily Times,* February 18, 1898.

3. An alternative explanation for the explosion on board the *Clara Nevada* was that she was carrying an illegal load of dynamite to Juneau, Alaska. There is little evidence to support such a claim.

4. A reasonable estimate of the death toll is about sixty-five. See *Seattle Daily Times,* February 18, 1898.

5. Clinton H. Whitehurst Jr., *The United States Merchant Marine: In Search of an Enduring Maritime Policy* (Annapolis, Md.: Naval Institute Press, 1983), 2.

6. Frederick E. Emmons, *American Passenger Ships: The Ocean Lines and Liners, 1873–1983* (Newark: University of Delaware Press, 1985), 148.

7. *Portland Oregonian,* July 25, 1906.

8. See Thomas R. Heinrich, *Ships of the Seven Seas: Philadelphia Shipbuilding in the Age of Capitalism* (Baltimore: Johns Hopkins University Press, 1997), 125.

9. One exception was the passenger service that connected Seattle with Alaska ports.

Chapter 1. *Yankee Blade:* Wreck of a Gold Ship

1. Erik Heyl, *Early American Steamers,* vol. 1 (1953; reprint, Buffalo: n.p., 1969), 463.

2. Donald G. Knight and Eugene D. Wheeler, *Agony and Death on a Gold Rush Steamer: The Disastrous Sinking of the Side-Wheeler "Yankee Blade"* (Ventura, Calif.: Pathfinder Publishing, 1990), 28–29.

3. *New York Daily Times,* August 20, 1853, cited in ibid., 29.

4. Denis Griffiths, *Steam at Sea: Two Centuries of Steam-Powered Ships,* Conway's History of the Ship, ed. Robert Gardiner (London: Brassey's Conway Maritime Press, 1997), 16–17.

5. *San Francisco Daily Alta California*, May 4, 1854. "Arrival of the New Steamship *Yankee Blade*." Maritime Heritage Project [cited January 23, 2000]; available online at http://www.maritimeheritage.org/PassLists/yb050454.html

6. *San Francisco Daily Alta California*, July 1, 1854.

7. *San Francisco Daily Alta California*, August 2, 1854.

8. *San Francisco Daily Alta California*, September 1, 1854, quoted in Maritime Heritage Project, "Goldrush Ships, Passengers, Captains." Coiba Island was the location of the woodcutting expedition.

9. *San Francisco Daily Alta California*, September 29, 1854, reprinted in Knight and Wheeler, *Gold Rush Steamer*, 45.

10. *Sacramento Daily Union*, October 5, 1854.

11. *San Francisco Daily Herald*, October 12, 1854.

12. *Los Angeles Southern Californian*, October 5, 1854. The actual number of passengers on board the *Yankee Blade* is a matter of debate, but the total far exceeded the 819 passengers claimed by the purser. Many of the voyagers were late arrivals who bought tickets at the time of sailing.

13. *San Francisco Daily Alta California*, October 10, 1854, unsigned correspondence. Much of the content of these frontier newspapers was made up of unsigned opinions and reports of its readers.

14. Ibid.

15. *San Francisco Daily Herald*, October 10, 1854, statement by Samuel Vought.

16. *San Francisco Daily Herald*, October 10, 1854.

17. *New York Daily Tribune*, November 11, 1854, excerpt of correspondence from G. A. Hart to his wife, quoted in Knight and Wheeler, *Gold Rush Steamer*, 70.

18. Knight and Wheeler, *Gold Rush Steamer*, 53.

19. *San Francisco Daily Alta California*, October 11, 1854, statement by Henry Randall.

20. Ibid.

21. California Historical Society, "Continuation of the Annals of San Francisco," *California Historical Society Quarterly* 15 (1936): 174.

22. *San Francisco Daily Herald*, October 11, 1854.

23. *San Francisco Daily Herald*, October 12, 1854.

24. Horace Bell, *Reminiscences of a Ranger* (Santa Barbara: Wallace Hubbard, 1927), 326.

25. *New York Daily Tribune*, November 11, 1854, excerpt of correspondence from G. A. Hart to his wife, quoted in Knight and Wheeler, *Gold Rush Steamer*, 72.

26. *San Francisco Daily Herald*, October 11, 1854.

27. Bell, *Reminiscences*, 325–326.

28. Ibid., 327–329.

29. *New York Daily Tribune,* November 11, 1854, excerpt of correspondence from G. A. Hart to his wife, reprinted in *San Francisco Daily Alta California,* January 29, 1855, and cited in Knight and Wheeler, *Gold Rush Steamer,* 74.

30. *San Francisco Daily Herald,* October 16, 1854.

31. *San Francisco Daily Herald,* October 11, 1854.

32. *San Francisco Wide West,* October 15, 1854.

33. *San Diego Herald,* October 26, 1854.

34. *San Francisco Daily Alta California,* October 17, 1854.

35. *San Francisco Daily Alta California,* October 25, 1854.

36. Ibid.

37. California Historical Society, "Annals of San Francisco," 185.

Chapter 2. *Brother Jonathan:* In the Teeth of the Dragon

1. Probably for this reason St. George Reef has been known locally as Dragon Rock.

2. Erik Heyl, *Early American Steamers,* vol. 1 (1953; reprint, Buffalo: n.p., 1969), 63–64.

3. *San Francisco Daily Alta California,* August 2, 1865.

4. Heyl, *American Steamers,* 63. Her draft was less than fourteen feet.

5. For an interesting account of the sinking of the side-wheeler *Central America* off the Carolina coast in 1857, see Gary Kinder, *Ship of Gold in the Deep Blue Sea* (Toronto: Random House, 1998). The shallow draft of the side-wheeler combined with the stress placed on a wooden hull by engine vibrations contributed to the loss of many vessels during violent storms.

6. Heyl, *American Steamers,* 64.

7. Ibid.

8. *Victoria Daily Chronicle,* August 4, 1865.

9. G. P. V. Akrigg and Helen Akrigg, *British Columbia Chronicle, 1847–1871* (Victoria, B.C.: Discovery Press, 1977), 106.

10. *Victoria Daily Chronicle,* August 4, 1865.

11. *San Francisco Daily Alta California,* August 5, 1865.

12. *Victoria Daily Chronicle,* August 4, 1865.

13. Ibid.

14. E. W. Wright, ed., *Lewis and Dryden's Marine History of the Pacific Northwest* (1895; reprint, New York: Antiquarian Press, 1961), 132.

15. See Don Marshall, *Oregon Shipwrecks* (Portland: Binford and Mort, 1984), 8.

16. *San Francisco Daily Alta California,* August 3, 1865.

17. *Victoria Daily Chronicle*, August 7, 1865.

18. Ibid.

19. *San Francisco Daily Alta California*, August 3, 1865.

20. James G. McCurdy, *By Juan de Fuca's Strait: Pioneering along the Northwestern Edge of the Continent* (Portland: Metropolitan Press, 1937), 58.

21. Ibid., 238.

22. Don B. Marshall, *California Shipwrecks: Footsteps in the Sea* (Seattle: Superior Publishing, 1978), 159.

23. *San Francisco Daily Alta California*, August 3, 1865.

24. Wright, *Lewis and Dryden's Marine History*, 132.

25. *Victoria Daily Chronicle*, August 29, 1865.

26. Wright, *Lewis and Dryden's Marine History*, 132.

27. *Victoria Daily Chronicle*, August 29, 1865.

28. Ibid.

29. Ibid.

30. Marshall, *Oregon Shipwrecks*, 7.

31. *Victoria Daily Chronicle*, August 29, 1865.

32. Ibid.

33. *Victoria Daily Chronicle*, August 3, 1865.

34. *Victoria Daily Chronicle*, August 29, 1865.

35. The August 2 dispatch from Crescent City stated that seventeen adults and three children survived, but only seventeen people are indicated on the list of survivors. According to Mrs. Stott, a Chinese woman and her child (probably Mrs. Lee and her infant, who are noted on the manifest) were two of the survivors. Their names do not appear among those saved. By this count, nineteen people survived.

36. *San Francisco Daily Alta California*, August 2, 1865.

37. Ibid.

38. *San Francisco Bulletin*, August 3, 1865.

39. *San Francisco Daily Alta California*, August 3, 1865.

40. Ibid.

41. Wright, *Lewis and Dryden's Marine History*, 134. Considerable discrepancy exists among various sources concerning the number of bodies recovered.

42. Ibid.

43. Bert Webber and Margie Webber, *Shipwrecks and Rescues off the Northwest Coast* (Medford, Ore.: Webb Research Group, 1996), 6.

44. Wright, *Lewis and Dryden's Marine History*, 134.

45. Marshall, *Oregon Shipwrecks*, 10.

46. M. S. Enkoji, "From Murky Depths, Sparkling History," *Sacramento Bee*, April 14, 1999.

Chapter 3. *Pacific:* The Final Whistle

1. *San Francisco Chronicle,* November 9, 1875.

2. *San Francisco Daily Alta California,* November 9, 1875.

3. *Olympia* (Washington Territory) *Standard,* November 13, 1875.

4. Erik Heyl, *Early American Steamers,* vol. 1 (1953; reprint, Buffalo: n.p., 1969), 331.

5. Ibid., 332.

6. David W. Higgins, "Into the Jaws of Death," in *The Mystic Spring* (Toronto: William Briggs, 1904), 323–324. See also Lucile McDonald, "The *Pacific*: A Jinxed Ship," *Seattle Daily Times,* April 7, 1968.

7. *San Francisco Examiner,* November 9, 1875.

8. *San Francisco Chronicle,* November 10, 1875.

9. *Victoria Daily British Colonist,* November 19, 1875.

10. *San Francisco Daily Alta California,* November 16, 1875.

11. Higgins, "Into the Jaws," 319.

12. *Victoria Daily British Colonist,* November 24, 1875.

13. *Victoria Daily British Colonist,* November 25, 1875. Both men were residents of Port Stanley, a small town near London, Ontario.

14. For backgrounds of the *Pacific*'s victims and survivors, see E. W. Wright, ed., *Lewis and Dryden's Marine History of the Pacific Northwest* (1895; reprint, New York: Antiquarian Press, 1961), 132; *Victoria Daily British Colonist,* November 13, 1875; *San Francisco Chronicle,* November 17, 1875, and other contemporary newspaper sources.

15. Bill Merilees, *Newcastle Island: A Place of Discovery* (Surrey, B.C.: Heritage House, 1998), 55–58.

16. *Victoria Daily British Colonist,* November 24, 1875.

17. *Victoria Daily British Colonist,* November 23, 1875.

18. Since the vessel was at an even keel when she entered Victoria harbor, but not so when she left, the cause was probably the result of the overloading of the ship with passengers and freight while in port. Freight stored on the upper deck would also have contributed to her instability. The condition is properly termed a "loll" rather than a "list."

19. Quoted in Higgins, "Into the Jaws," 325.

20. *Victoria Daily Standard,* November 12, 1875.

21. Higgins, "Into the Jaws," 332.

22. *Victoria Daily British Colonist,* November 19, 1875, and *Victoria Daily British Colonist,* November 20, 1875. There is no surviving transcript of this inquiry; however, the proceedings were thoroughly covered by the city's press. Henley's account of the tragedy was given during his testimony before the Victoria coroner's inquest.

23. *San Francisco Daily Alta California,* November 13, 1875.

24. Wright, *Lewis and Dryden's Marine History*, 226 n.

25. *Victoria Daily British Colonist*, November 20, 1875.

26. *Victoria Daily British Colonist*, November 21, 1875.

27. *San Francisco Chronicle*, November 9, 1875.

28. Quoted in ibid.

29. Quoted in ibid.

30. Ibid.

31. Quoted in the *San Francisco Chronicle*, November 13, 1875.

32. *San Francisco Chronicle*, November 9, 1875.

33. Wright, *Lewis and Dryden's Marine History*, 225.

34. Ibid.

35. *Victoria Daily British Colonist*, November 9, 1875.

36. *San Francisco Chronicle*, November 10, 1875.

37. The crew of the *Gussie Telfair* was highly regarded in the Northwest for undertaking the long and difficult search for those who had been on board the *Pacific*. No one on board the small vessel would take remuneration. Ironically, less than one month after the loss of the *Pacific*, the *Gussie Telfair* went aground on the Columbia River and sustained serious damage. No one on board was injured. See *Victoria Daily British Colonist*, November 30, 1875.

38. *Victoria Daily British Colonist*, November 11, 1875.

39. Ibid.

40. *San Francisco Daily Alta California*, November 10, 1875.

41. *San Francisco Chronicle*, November 9, 1875.

42. *San Francisco Chronicle*, November 10, 1875.

43. Editorial, *Victoria Daily British Colonist*, November 10, 1875.

44. Editorial, *San Francisco Chronicle*, November 16, 1875.

45. Editorial, *Victoria Daily British Colonist*, November 16, 1875.

46. *Port Townsend* (Washington Territory) *Weekly Argus*, November 20, 1875.

47. *Victoria Daily British Colonist*, November 19, 1875.

48. *Victoria Daily British Colonist*, November 20, 1875.

49. *Victoria Daily British Colonist*, November 14, 1875.

50. Higgins, "Into the Jaws," 333.

51. *Victoria Daily British Colonist*, November 23, 1875. Allen never made clear his reasons for taking a berth on the *Orpheus*, but work for ships' officers on the West Coast was difficult to obtain. He may have taken any job available.

52. *Victoria Daily British Colonist*, November 24, 1875.

53. Ibid.

54. Ibid.

55. Ibid.

56. *San Francisco Chronicle,* November 28, 1875. Captain Waterman's attitude was not surprising, for he had earlier earned an unenviable reputation as one of the most callous of shipmasters. In command of the clipper ship *Challenge* on a voyage from New York to San Francisco, he drove his crew unmercifully. Five men died in falls from the rigging. Eventually, the crew mutinied. With a belaying pin in hand, the captain killed two of his men and injured another. After the vessel tied up at a San Francisco wharf on October 29, 1851, the story of the voyage spread along the waterfront. A mob whose purpose was to lynch Waterman and the first officer was soon formed, but the two men escaped. While unpopular with his crew, Waterman was much sought after by shipowners, for the clipper ships he commanded set many speed records. He was eventually rewarded with an appointment to the San Francisco Board of Steamboat Inspectors.

57. Editorial, *Victoria Daily British Colonist,* January 14, 1876.

58. *Biographical Directory of the Governors of the United States, 1789–1978,* s.v. "Perkins, George Clement."

59. Higgins, "Into the Jaws," 335.

60. Ibid., 324.

61. *Tacoma News Tribune,* March 14, 1944.

62. Quoted in James G. McCurdy, *By Juan de Fuca's Strait: Pioneering along the Northwestern Edge of the Continent* (Portland: Metropolitan Press, 1937), 243.

63. Quoted in ibid.

Chapter 4. *Rio de Janeiro:* Death of a City

1. *San Francisco Call,* February 23, 1901.

2. The usual ease of bringing in ships made pilots careless, and since they were paid on a scale according to the size of the ship rather than hours worked, Jordan had every reason to finish the assignment as quickly as possible.

3. *San Francisco Call,* February 23, 1901.

4. Ibid.

5. *San Francisco Examiner,* February 26, 1901.

6. *San Francisco Bulletin,* February 26, 1901.

7. Randolf Arguelles, "Chronology of Significant Events Relating to the Career of Emilio Aguinaldo with Respect to the Various Imperialist and Anti-imperialist Campaigns in the Philippines" (N.p.: n.d.), http://www.bol.ucla.edu/~randolf/augichron.html, August 25, 1999. Rebel leader Emilio Aguinaldo, Randolf Arguelles observes, "initially arms his men with 2,000 rifles and hundreds of thousands of rounds of ammunition purchased by Aguinaldo for

P50,000 through American Consul General to Hong Kong Rounseville Wild-man. Neither a second shipment of arms, nor the P65,000 given to Wildman for the purchase of those arms, was ever returned; Admiral Dewey, however, provides Aguinaldo with 4,000 rifles for the rebels."

8. *San Francisco Examiner*, February 26, 1901.

9. *San Francisco Bulletin*, February 23, 1901.

10. *San Francisco Examiner*, February 23, 1901.

11. *San Francisco Call*, March 6, 1901.

12. *San Francisco Examiner*, February 24, 1901.

13. Frederick E. Emmons, *American Passenger Ships: The Ocean Lines and Liners, 1873–1983* (Newark: University of Delaware Press, 1985), 50.

14. *San Francisco Chronicle*, February 26, 1901.

15. *San Francisco Examiner*, February 24, 1901.

16. James P. Delgado and Stephen Haller, *Shipwrecks of the Golden Gate: A History of Vessel Losses from Duxbury Reef to Mussell Rock* (Lagunitas, Calif.: Lexikos, 1989), 76–78.

17. Andrew Rolle, *California: A History*, 5th ed. (Wheeling, Ill.: Harlan Davidson, 1998), 230.

18. *San Francisco Call*, December 17, 1900.

19. *San Francisco Call*, February 23, 1901.

20. Rolle, *California: A History*, 162–163.

21. *San Francisco Bulletin*, February 28, 1901.

22. *San Francisco Bulletin*, February 22, 1901.

23. *San Francisco Call*, February 23, 1901.

24. *San Francisco Bulletin*, February 22, 1901.

25. *San Francisco Examiner*, February 23, 1901.

26. Ibid.

27. *San Francisco Call*, February 23, 1901.

28. *San Francisco Examiner*, February 23, 1901.

29. *San Francisco Call*, February 28, 1901.

30. *San Francisco Examiner*, February 23, 1901.

31. *San Francisco Call*, February 23, 1901.

32. *San Francisco Bulletin*, February 22, 1901.

33. *San Francisco Call*, February 23, 1901.

34. *San Francisco Chronicle*, February 24, 1901.

35. *San Francisco Bulletin*, February 22, 1901.

36. *San Francisco Examiner*, February 23, 1901.

37. *San Francisco Chronicle*, February 24, 1901.

38. Ibid.

39. Ibid.

40. *San Francisco Call*, February 23, 1901.

41. *San Francisco Examiner,* February 23, 1901.

42. Ibid.

43. Ibid.

44. Ibid.

45. *San Francisco Bulletin,* February 22, 1901.

46. United States Life-Saving Service, District 13, "Wreck Report: *City of Rio de Janeiro,*" February 22, 1901, Bancroft Library, University of California, Berkeley.

47. *San Francisco Call,* February 23, 1901.

48. *San Francisco Chronicle,* February 24, 1901.

49. *San Francisco Call,* February 23, 1901.

50. *San Francisco Examiner,* February 24, 1901.

51. *San Francisco Chronicle,* February 24, 1901.

52. Ibid.

53. *San Francisco Call,* February 23, 1901.

54. *San Francisco Examiner,* February 23, 1901.

55. *San Francisco Call,* February 23, 1901.

56. Another passenger describes those on board this boat as steerage passengers, but it is almost certain they were Chinese crewmen enlisted to man the oars.

57. *San Francisco Call,* February 23, 1901.

58. *San Francisco Bulletin,* February 22, 1901.

59. Ibid.

60. This last violent act of the vessel has been attributed to the explosion of one of the boilers, but it was more likely the rapid release of air trapped in the hull.

61. *San Francisco Examiner,* February 23, 1901.

62. Ibid.

63. *San Francisco Call,* February 23, 1901.

64. Ibid.

65. Ibid.

66. *San Francisco Examiner,* March 2, 1901.

67. *San Francisco Call,* February 23, 1901.

68. *San Francisco Examiner,* February 23, 1901.

69. *San Francisco Bulletin,* February 22, 1901.

70. *San Francisco Examiner,* February 23, 1901.

71. *San Francisco Call,* February 28, 1901. Graham Coghlan provided different time estimates during other interviews and statements.

72. Ibid.

73. *San Francisco Call,* February 23, 1901.

74. *San Francisco Bulletin,* February 22, 1901.

75. *San Francisco Chronicle,* February 24, 1901.

76. *San Francisco Call,* February 24, 1901.

77. *San Francisco Examiner,* February 23, 1901.

78. *San Francisco Call,* February 23, 1901.

79. Ibid.

80. *San Francisco Call,* February 24, 1901.

81. *San Francisco Chronicle,* February 27, 1901.

82. *San Francisco Call,* February 26, 1901.

83. *San Francisco Examiner,* February 23, 1901.

84. Ibid.

85. *San Francisco Call,* February 23, 1901.

86. *San Francisco Examiner,* February 24, 1901.

87. *San Francisco Chronicle,* February 27, 1901.

88. *San Francisco Call,* February 24, 1901.

89. *San Francisco Chronicle,* February 24, 1901.

90. *San Francisco Call,* March 2, 1901.

91. *San Francisco Bulletin,* February 24, 1901.

92. Walter Lord, *A Night to Remember* (New York: Bantam Books, 1997), 111.

93. *San Francisco Call,* February 24, 1901.

94. *San Francisco Bulletin,* February 24, 1901.

95. *San Francisco Examiner,* February 28, 1901.

96. *San Francisco Call,* February 28, 1901.

97. *San Francisco Examiner,* March 9, 1901.

98. *San Francisco Call,* February 24, 1901.

99. *San Francisco Call,* March 28, 1901.

100. Ibid.

101. The *City of Rio de Janeiro* incident should be kept in perspective, for although the service certainly failed in its duty during the morning of February 22, 1901, at other times the prompt action of its surfers saved the lives of many people on board distressed ships along the Pacific Coast.

102. *San Francisco Bulletin,* March 7, 1901.

103. *San Francisco Call,* March 14, 1901.

104. *San Francisco Call,* January 28, 1902.

105. *San Francisco Chronicle,* November 26, 1902.

106. *San Francisco Call,* April 11, 1903.

107. *San Francisco Chronicle,* May 8, 1904.

108. San Francisco Bay is very deep. It is not as easy as it first may appear to locate a hull the size of the *City of Rio de Janeiro* on the ocean bottom.

109. *San Francisco Call,* February 23, 1901.

110. *San Francisco Examiner,* February 27, 1901.

111. *San Francisco Call,* February 23, 1901.

112. Don B. Marshall, *California Shipwrecks: Footsteps in the Sea* (Seattle: Superior Publishing, 1978), 99.

113. Bob Young and Jan Young, "Thirteen Minutes of Horror," *Westways* 53, no. 2 (February 1961): 24.

114. *San Francisco Examiner,* February 23, 1901.

Chapter 5. *Clallam:* The "Hoodoo" Ship

1. *Seattle Daily Times,* January 10, 1904.

2. For further information on Edward Heath, see Paul Spitzer, "Harsh Ways: Edward W. Heath and the Shipbuilding Trade," *Pacific Northwest Quarterly* 90 (Winter 1998–99).

3. *Victoria Daily Times,* January 9, 1904.

4. *Tacoma Daily Ledger,* April 16, 1903.

5. Gordon R. Newell, *The H. W. McCurdy Marine History of the Pacific Northwest: 1895 to 1965* (Seattle: Superior Publishing, 1966), 90. Even allowing for a stop at Port Townsend, it would appear that the *Clallam* rarely traveled much above ten knots.

6. *Victoria Daily Times,* January 9, 1904.

7. *Seattle Post-Intelligencer,* January 10, 1904.

8. *Tacoma Daily Ledger,* April 16, 1903.

9. *Seattle Post-Intelligencer,* January 10, 1904. There was a practical reason for a ship's stern-first launch: this was the best method to ensure that the rudder and propeller were not damaged by the drag chains as the hull reached the water. Small ships like the *Clallam,* though, were frequently launched sideways.

10. *Seattle Daily Times,* January 9, 1904.

11. Gordon R. Newell and Joe Williamson, *Pacific Coastal Liners* (Seattle: Superior Publishing, 1959), 110.

12. *Seattle Daily Times,* January 6, 1963.

13. Newell and Williamson, *Pacific Coastal Liners,* 110.

14. *Seattle Post-Intelligencer,* January 9, 1904.

15. British Columbia Archives, GR 431, File 6/6, Transcript of the "Inquest Regarding *Clallam* Wreck," 31.

16. *Victoria Daily Colonist,* January 10, 1904. (In 1893, the word *British* was dropped from the newspaper's masthead.)

17. *Seattle Post-Intelligencer,* January 10, 1904.

18. Ibid.

19. Ibid.

20. *Victoria Daily Colonist,* January 10, 1904.

21. *Seattle Daily Times,* January 11, 1904.

22. *Seattle Daily Times,* January 18, 1904.

23. *Seattle Post-Intelligencer,* January 10, 1904.

24. *Seattle Post-Intelligencer,* January 13, 1904.

25. *Seattle Post-Intelligencer,* January 12, 1904.

26. Diane F. Britton, *The Iron and Steel Industry in the Far West* (Niwot: University of Colorado Press, 1991), 62.

27. *San Francisco Chronicle,* January 11, 1904.

28. British Columbia Archives, GR 431, "*Clallam* Wreck," 47.

29. Ibid., 58.

30. Ibid., 14.

31. Ibid., 21.

32. *Seattle Daily Times,* January 10, 1904.

33. British Columbia Archives, GR 431, "*Clallam* Wreck," 134.

34. *Seattle Daily Times,* January 10, 1904.

35. British Columbia Archives, GR 431, "*Clallam* Wreck," 48.

36. Ibid., 32.

37. Ibid., 32–33.

38. Ibid., 48.

39. Ibid., 49.

40. *Seattle Daily Times,* January 10, 1904.

41. British Columbia Archives, GR 431, "*Clallam* Wreck," 90.

42. Ibid., 21.

43. Ibid., 52.

44. Ibid., 49.

45. Ibid.

46. *Seattle Post-Intelligencer,* January 12, 1904.

47. British Columbia Archives, GR 431, "*Clallam* Wreck," 90.

48. Ibid., 117–118.

49. *Victoria Daily Times,* January 12, 1904.

50. British Columbia Archives, GR 431, "*Clallam* Wreck," 131.

51. Ibid., 34.

52. Ibid., 59.

53. Ibid., 59–60.

54. *Seattle Post-Intelligencer,* January 10, 1904.

55. *Victoria Daily Times,* January 12, 1904.

56. British Columbia Archives, GR 431, "*Clallam* Wreck," 112.

57. Ibid.

58. Ibid., 35.

59. Ibid., 110.

60. Ibid., 36.

61. Ibid., 110.

62. Ibid., 62.

63. Ibid.

64. Ibid., 23.

65. *Seattle Daily Times,* January 10, 1904.

66. British Columbia Archives, GR 431, "*Clallam* Wreck," 53.

67. Ibid., 53.

68. Ibid., 39.

69. Ibid., 54.

70. Letter of Egbert F. Ferris to Charles Rennie, January 15, 1904, and published in the *Traverse City* (Michigan) *Herald,* n.d.; cited in the *Seattle Daily Times,* February 4, 1904.

71. *Seattle Daily Times,* January 10, 1904.

72. *Seattle Post-Intelligencer,* January 10, 1904.

73. British Columbia Archives, GR 431,"*Clallam* Wreck," 61.

74. Ibid., 40.

75. Ibid., 115.

76. *Seattle Post-Intelligencer,* January 10, 1904.

77. *Seattle Daily Times,* January 10, 1904.

78. *Seattle Post-Intelligencer,* January 11, 1904.

79. Ibid.

80. Ibid.

81. *Seattle Daily Times,* January 14, 1904.

82. Early on it was claimed that Daniel's body had been recovered, but the remains were that of his partner, Albert K. Prince.

83. *Seattle Post-Intelligencer,* January 11, 1904.

84. British Columbia Archives, GR 431, "*Clallam* Wreck," 87.

85. *San Francisco Chronicle,* January 15, 1904.

86. *Seattle Post-Intelligencer,* January 11, 1904.

87. *Seattle Post-Intelligencer,* January 10, 1904.

88. British Columbia Archives, GR 431, "*Clallam* Wreck," 92.

89. Ibid., 141–142. Other crew members claimed that the second rudder failed to operate properly during the *Clallam*'s last voyage.

90. Ibid., 42.

91. Ibid., 123–129.

92. Ibid., 9–10.

93. *Seattle Daily Times,* January 30, 1904.

94. The National Archives and Records Service, Pacific Northwest Branch, does not have a record of the *Clallam* Maritime Hearing; it was, however, well covered by Seattle newspapers.

95. *Seattle Daily Times,* January 20, 1904.

96. *San Francisco Chronicle,* October 5, 1904.

97. Lucile McDonald, "The Worse Disaster in the Strait," *Seattle Daily Times,* Sunday, January 6, 1963, magazine section.

98. *Seattle Daily Times,* January 22, 1904.

99. Gordon R. Newell, *Ships of the Inland Sea: The Story of the Puget Sound Steamboats* (Portland: Binfords and Mort, 1960), 145.

100. *Victoria Daily Colonist,* January 15, 1904.

101. George Musk, *Canadian Pacific: The Story of the Famous Shipping Line* (Toronto: Holt, Rinehart and Winston, 1981), 254. The *Princess Beatrice* was built at Esquimalt, near Victoria, in 1903.

102. *Seattle Post-Intelligencer,* January 12, 1904.

103. Britton, *Iron and Steel,* 70.

104. *Seattle Post-Intelligencer,* January 11, 1904.

Chapter 6. *Valencia:* Appointment with Death

1. *Seattle Post-Intelligencer,* January 26, 1906.

2. Department of Commerce and Labor, *Wreck of the Steamer "Valencia": Report to the Federal Commission of Investigation* (Washington, D.C.: Government Printing Office, 1906), 10.

3. *Seattle Daily Times,* January 24, 1906.

4. *San Francisco Chronicle,* January 26, 1906.

5. Ibid.

6. *Seattle Post-Intelligencer,* January 24, 1906.

7. *Seattle Daily Times,* January 24, 1906.

8. *Victoria Daily Colonist,* January 25, 1906.

9. *Seattle Post-Intelligencer,* January 24, 1906. See also Thomas R. Heinrich, *Ships of the Seven Seas: Philadelphia Shipbuilding in the Age of Capitalism* (Baltimore: Johns Hopkins University Press, 1997), 82.

10. Department of Commerce and Labor, *Wreck of the Steamer "Valencia,"* 8.

11. Ibid.

12. *Vancouver Daily Province,* November 1, 1901.

13. *Victoria Daily Colonist,* February 26, 1903.

14. By coincidence, on the day of the grounding of the *Valencia* on the rocks near Cape Beale, the Pacific Coast Steamship Company announced the construction of a new 450-passenger luxury coastal liner for the San Francisco–Puget Sound route. See *San Francisco Call,* January 22, 1906.

15. *Victoria Daily Colonist,* January 6, 1906. See also *San Francisco Chronicle,* January 24, 1906.

16. *San Francisco Chronicle,* January 24, 1906.

17. Ibid.

18. Department of Commerce and Labor, *Wreck of the Steamer "Valencia,"* 12.

19. Ibid.

20. National Archives, Pacific Region (Seattle), RG 41, Transcript of the Wreck of the U. S. [*sic*] *Valencia* Held before Bion B. Whitney and Robert A. Turner, Seattle, January 27, 1906, 48; quoted in the testimony of P. E. Pettersen.

21. *Seattle Post-Intelligencer,* January 26, 1906.

22. National Archives, Pacific Region, Transcript, 2.

23. *Victoria Daily Colonist,* January 26, 1906.

24. National Archives, Pacific Region, Transcript, 78.

25. Jack Wishaar, "People Spilled Like Pebbles in a Seething, Boiling Surf," *Seattle Post-Intelligencer,* January 26, 1906.

26. *Victoria Daily Colonist,* February 13, 1906.

27. Ibid.

28. *San Francisco Chronicle,* January 27, 1906.

29. National Archives, Pacific Region, Transcript, 17.

30. Ibid., 50–51.

31. *Seattle Post-Intelligencer,* January 29, 1906.

32. National Archives, Pacific Region, Transcript, 79.

33. Wishaar, "People Spilled Like Pebbles."

34. Ibid.

35. Ibid.

36. Boatswain Timothy McCarthy's testimony, quoted in National Archives, Pacific Region, Transcript, 29.

37. *Victoria Daily Colonist,* February 10, 1906.

38. First Engineer Thomas Carrick's testimony, quoted in National Archives, Pacific Region, Transcript, 10.

39. Wishaar, "People Spilled Like Pebbles."

40. Ibid.

41. *Seattle Post-Intelligencer,* January 26, 1906. See also *Victoria Daily Colonist,* January 27, 1906.

42. *Victoria Daily Colonist,* February 10, 1906.

43. *Seattle Post-Intelligencer,* January 26, 1906.

44. *Victoria Daily Colonist,* February 10, 1906.

45. *Victoria Daily Colonist,* January 23, 1906.

46. *Seattle Daily Times,* January 24, 1906. See also *Seattle Post-Intelligencer,* January 24, 1906.

47. *Seattle Post-Intelligencer,* January 26, 1906.

48. *Victoria Daily Colonist,* January 26, 1906.

49. *Seattle Post-Intelligencer,* January 26, 1906.

50. Ibid.

51. *Victoria Daily Colonist,* January 30, 1906.

52. *Victoria Daily Times,* February 6, 1906. Why a rescue party familiar with the dangers of the area would begin its journey without being adequately prepared has never been properly explained.

53. Ibid.

54. *Victoria Daily Colonist,* January 30, 1906.

55. *Seattle Post-Intelligencer,* January 26, 1906.

56. Ibid.

57. *San Francisco Chronicle,* January 28, 1906.

58. *Seattle Daily Times,* January 28, 1906.

59. National Archives, Pacific Region, Transcript, 24.

60. Rough seas and the icy waters of the Northwest Coast combined with a precipitous shoreline topography took the lives of both sexes. However, women at this time faced a number of disadvantages: they were only rarely taught to swim, were burdened by layers of clothing, and were conditioned socially to take a secondary role to men. When ill-trained crews on stormy waters handled lifeboats, the call for women and children first was often a death cry.

61. *Seattle Post-Intelligencer,* January 24, 1906.

62. Ibid.

63. *Victoria Daily Colonist,* February 13, 1906.

64. *Portland Oregonian,* January 26, 1906. Mrs. Ross's name was apparently incorrectly written as Mrs. Rose on the *Clallam*'s manifest.

65. *San Francisco Chronicle,* January 26, 1906.

66. *Vancouver Daily Province,* February 3, 1906. Several marines on board the *Queen* later denied the story.

67. *Vancouver Daily Province,* January 25, 1906.

68. *Seattle Daily Times,* January 28, 1906.

69. *Vancouver Daily Province,* March 20, 1906.

70. *Vancouver Daily Province,* February 3, 1906.

71. *Victoria Daily Colonist,* February 1, 1906.

72. Editorial, *Seattle Star,* January 31, 1906.

73. Editorial, *Seattle Star,* January 30, 1906.

74. Department of Commerce and Labor, *Wreck of the Steamer "Valencia,"* 7.

75. Ibid., 43.

76. Department of Marine and Fisheries, "Annual Report of the Chief Engineer of the Department of Marine and Fisheries," *Sessional Papers* 21–23 (1917): 25–30.

77. Editorial, *Seattle Star,* January 30, 1906.

78. Frederick E. Emmons, *American Passenger Ships: The Ocean Lines and Liners, 1873–1983* (Newark: University of Delaware Press, 1985), 153.

79. Ibid.

80. Giles T. Brown, *Ships That Sail No More: Marine Transportation from San Diego to Puget Sound, 1910–1940* (Lexington: University of Kentucky Press, 1966), 32–34.

81. *Portland Oregonian*, January 26, 1906.

Chapter 7. *Columbia:* Disaster off Shelter Cove

1. *San Francisco Examiner,* July 24, 1907. The honor of being the first electrified ship has been given to the *City of Berlin*, which was fitted out about the same time.

2. E. W. Wright, ed., *Lewis and Dryden's Marine History of the Pacific Northwest* (1895; reprint, New York: Antiquarian Press, 1961), 275.

3. Ibid., 274.

4. *San Francisco Examiner,* July 23, 1907.

5. Ibid. Shipping regulations calculated lifeboat and raft capacity in relation to a ship's tonnage rather than the maximum number of passengers a vessel was permitted to carry. The result was there were frequently more passengers than places on board the escape craft. It would take the *Titanic* disaster in 1912 to change the law.

6. Frederick E. Emmons, *American Passenger Ships: The Ocean Lines and Liners, 1873–1983* (Newark: University of Delaware Press, 1985), 150–152.

7. *San Francisco Chronicle*, July 23, 1907.

8. Ibid.

9. *Portland Oregonian*, July 23, 1907.

10. *San Francisco Bulletin,* July 25, 1907.

11. *San Francisco Examiner,* July 24, 1907.

12. *San Francisco Chronicle,* July 25, 1907.

13. Department of Commerce and Labor, Steamboat Inspection Service, Office of Supervising Inspector of First District, "Decision, August 31, 1907," reprinted in *Pacific Maritime Review* 4 (September 1907): 16.

14. Ibid., 15.

15. *Portland Oregonian,* July 25, 1907.

16. *San Francisco Examiner,* July 24, 1907.

17. Ibid.

18. *San Francisco Chronicle,* July 25, 1907.

19. Quoted in Department of Commerce and Labor, "Decision," 16. Other than from newspaper sources, there is apparently no surviving copy of the testimony of the witnesses.

20. *San Francisco Chronicle,* July 25, 1907.

21. *San Francisco Examiner,* July 24, 1907.

22. Ibid.

23. Ibid.

24. *Portland Oregonian,* July 23, 1907.

25. Ibid.

26. Ibid.

27. Ibid.

28. *San Francisco Chronicle,* July 25, 1907.

29. *San Francisco Bulletin,* July 25, 1907.

30. *San Francisco Examiner,* July 24, 1907.

31. Ibid.

32. Ibid.

33. Ibid.

34. *San Francisco Chronicle,* July 26, 1907.

35. *Portland Oregonian,* July 25, 1907.

36. Department of Commerce and Labor, "Decision," 18.

37. *San Francisco Bulletin,* July 23, 1907.

38. *San Francisco Examiner,* July 24, 1907.

39. Ibid.

40. Ibid.

41. Department of Commerce and Labor, "Decision," 16.

42. *San Francisco Examiner,* July 24, 1907.

43. Department of Commerce and Labor, "Decision," 16.

44. *Portland Oregonian,* July 23, 1907.

45. *San Francisco Bulletin,* July 25, 1907.

46. *San Francisco Chronicle,* July 25, 1907.

47. *Portland Oregonian,* July 25, 1907.

48. *San Francisco Bulletin,* July 23, 1907.

49. *Portland Oregonian,* July 25, 1907.

50. *San Francisco Examiner,* July 24, 1907.

51. *Portland Oregonian,* July 25, 1907.

52. *Portland Oregonian,* July 23, 1907.

53. *San Francisco Chronicle,* July 25, 1907.

54. *San Francisco Chronicle,* July 24, 1907.

55. *San Francisco Examiner,* July 24, 1907. The speed with which the *Columbia* sank drove most of the passengers who reached the deck over the rails. Apparently, this prevented a large-scale rush for the boats.

56. *San Francisco Chronicle,* July 26, 1907.

57. *San Francisco Examiner,* July 27, 1907.

58. *San Francisco Bulletin,* July 25, 1907.

59. Ibid.

60. *Portland Oregonian,* July 28, 1907.

61. Ibid.

62. *San Francisco Examiner,* July 27, 1907.

63. *San Francisco Chronicle,* July 26, 1907.

64. *San Francisco Examiner,* July 29, 1907.

65. Department of Commerce and Labor, "Decision," 16.

66. *Portland Oregonian,* July 25, 1907.

67. *Portland Oregonian,* July 28, 1907.

68. *San Francisco Chronicle,* July 28, 1907.

69. *San Francisco Examiner,* July 30, 1907.

70. *San Francisco Chronicle,* July 30, 1907.

71. *San Francisco Chronicle,* July 23, 1907.

72. Ibid.

73. *San Francisco Examiner,* July 23, 1907.

74. *San Francisco Bulletin,* July 25, 1907.

75. *San Francisco Examiner,* July 23, 1907.

76. Department of Commerce and Labor, "Decision," 16.

77. The official death toll did not include two children in steerage.

78. *Portland Oregonian,* July 24, 1907.

79. *San Francisco Examiner,* July 24, 1907.

80. *San Francisco Bulletin,* July 25, 1907.

81. *San Francisco Chronicle,* July 24, 1907.

82. Department of Commerce and Labor, "Decision," 17.

83. Ibid., 18.

84. Ibid.

85. *San Francisco Examiner,* July 23, 1907; *San Francisco Examiner,* July 25, 1907.

86. *San Francisco Chronicle,* July 26, 1907.

87. *San Francisco Examiner,* July 24, 1907.

88. *San Francisco Bulletin,* July 26, 1907.

89. *San Francisco Chronicle,* July 26, 1907.

90. *San Francisco Examiner,* July 23, 1907; *San Francisco Bulletin,* July 23, 1907.

91. *Portland Oregonian,* July 24, 1907.

92. *San Francisco Chronicle,* August 9, 1907.

Chapter 8. *Francis H. Leggett:* Battle Lost

1. *San Francisco Examiner,* September 20, 1914.

2. Ibid.

3. *Seattle Post-Intelligencer,* September 20, 1914.

4. *San Francisco Chronicle*, September 20, 1914.

5. *San Francisco Chronicle*, September 21, 1914.

6. *Portland Oregonian*, September 20, 1914.

7. *San Francisco Chronicle*, September 20, 1914.

8. *Portland Oregonian*, September 20, 1914.

9. *Astoria* (Oregon) *Astorian*, September 22, 1914.

10. *Portland Oregonian*, September 20, 1914.

11. *San Francisco Examiner*, September 20, 1914.

12. *Portland Oregonian*, September 21, 1914.

13. *San Francisco Examiner*, September 20, 1914.

14. Ibid.

15. *Portland Oregonian*, September 21, 1914.

16. *Portland Oregonian*, September 20, 1914.

17. Ibid.

18. *Portland Oregonian*, September 21, 1914.

19. Ibid.

20. *Portland Oregonian*, September 20, 1914.

21. Translated as *"Idzumo"* and *"Idzuma"* by other sources.

22. *Astoria* (Oregon) *Astorian*, September 20, 1914.

23. *Portland Oregonian*, September 21, 1914.

24. *Portland Oregonian*, September 20, 1914.

25. Ibid.

26. *Portland Oregonian*, September 21, 1914.

27. Ibid.

28. Ibid.

29. Ibid.

30. Ibid.

31. *Portland Oregonian*, September 22, 1914. See also *Portland Oregonian*, September 25, 1914.

32. *Portland Oregonian*, September 20, 1914.

33. Editorial, *Astoria* (Oregon) *Astorian*, September 22, 1914. The Plimsoll mark, which was adopted for British registered ships in 1876, appears at the center of the vessel and indicates the allowable loading levels for merchant vessels under different water conditions. Regulations governing the amount of freeboard on American merchant ships were tightened after the 1930 International Load Convention in London.

Chapter 9. *Princess Sophia:* A Grave Error

1. W. Kaye Lamb, *History of the Canadian Pacific Railway* (New York: Macmillan, 1977), 239–241.

2. There are many conflicting accounts about the loss of the *Islander.* The number of deaths is uncertain since it was known that there were many stowaways on board. It was not even established whether the ship struck in clear conditions or in fog. See Ken Coates and Bill Morrison, *The Sinking of the "Princess Sophia": Taking the North Down with Her* (Fairbanks: University of Alaska Press, 1991), 47–48; Betty O'Keefe and Ian Macdonald, *The Final Voyage of the "Princess Sophia": Did They All Have to Die?* (Surrey, B.C.: Heritage House, 1998), 32; and George Musk, *Canadian Pacific: The Story of the Famous Shipping Line* (Toronto: Holt, Rinehart and Winston, 1981), 252. For a more complete account of the loss of the *Islander* see Robert D. Turner, *The Pacific Princesses: An Illustrated History of Canadian Pacific Railway's Princess Fleet on the Northwest Coast* (Victoria, B.C.: Sono Nis Press, 1977), 42–47.

3. On August 26, 1914, in thick fog off Point No Point on Puget Sound, the *Princess Victoria* struck the liner *Admiral Sampson,* outward bound from Seattle for Alaska. While it was claimed that the *Princess Victoria* was proceeding at a cautious five knots, she almost cut the liner in half. Fire broke out immediately on the oil-burning *Admiral Sampson.* Panic-stricken steerage passengers scrambled from below deck and up a ladder lowered by the *Princess Victoria.* So eager were they to escape the burning ship that many climbed over the backs of slow-moving cabin passengers. Although most of those on board the stricken ship were taken on board the *Princess Victoria,* between eight and twelve people died. Within minutes, the *Admiral Sampson* had gone to the bottom. See *Seattle Daily Times,* September 20, 1914; Gordon R. Newell and Joe Williamson, "Canadian Pacific," in *Pacific Coastal Liners* (Seattle: Superior Publishing, 1959), 134; and Ruth Greene, "The Speed Queen, *Princess Victoria,*" in *Personality Ships of British Columbia* (West Vancouver, B.C.: Marine Tapestry Publications, 1969), 182–183.

4. Coates and Morrison, *Sinking of the "Princess Sophia,"* 48–49.

5. For an interesting account of the northern gold rush, see Pierre Berton, *Klondike: The Last Great Gold Rush, 1896–1899,* rev. ed. (Toronto: McClelland and Stewart, 1986).

6. James A. Gibbs, "Lighting Alaska's Waterways," in *Sentinels of the North Pacific: The Story of Pacific Coast Lighthouses and Lightships* (Portland: Binfords and Mort, 1955), 203.

7. Norman R. Hacking and W. Kaye Lamb, *The Princess Story: A Century and a Half of West Coast Shipping* (Vancouver: Mitchell Press, 1974), 302–303.

8. The CPR was not alone in this view. The Alaska Steamship Company, for example, continued operations between Seattle and the far North until 1954.

9. Coates and Morrison, *Sinking of the "Princess Sophia,"* 49–51.

10. Greene, *"Sophia, Princess of Death,"* in *Personality Ships of British Columbia* (West Vancouver, B.C.: Marine Tapestry Publications, 1969), 195.

11. *Victoria Daily Colonist,* October 27, 1918.

12. Ibid.

13. Coates and Morrison, *Sinking of the "Princess Sophia,"* 52–53.

14. *Vancouver Daily World,* October 28, 1918.

15. *Vancouver Daily Sun,* October 27, 1918.

16. *Victoria Daily Colonist,* February 11, 1919.

17. W. C. Dibble, letter of October 21, 1918, quoted in Greene, *"Sophia, Princess of Death,"* 208.

18. *Vancouver Daily World,* October 28, 1918.

19. See Robert Belyk and Diane Belyk, "No Armistice with Death," *Beaver: Exploring Canada's History* 68, no. 5 (1988): 43–49.

20. *Vancouver Daily Sun,* October 25, 1918. For additional information on the *Prince Rupert,* see Norman Hacking, *Prince Ships of Northern British Columbia: Ships of the Grand Trunk Pacific and Canadian National Railways* (Surrey, B.C.: Heritage House, 1995).

21. *Vancouver Daily Sun,* October 25, 1918.

22. Coates and Morrison, *Sinking of the "Princess Sophia,"* 63.

23. *Vancouver Daily Sun,* October 25, 1918.

24. *Victoria Daily Times,* October 23, 1918.

25. *Seattle Post-Intelligencer,* October 28, 1918.

26. Ibid.

27. Coates and Morrison, *Sinking of the "Princess Sophia,"* 30.

28. *Seattle Daily Times,* October 29, 1918.

29. *Seattle Post-Intelligencer,* October 27, 1918.

30. Berton, *Klondike,* 54, 64.

31. *Seattle Post-Intelligencer,* October 27, 1918.

32. *Vancouver Daily World,* October 28, 1918.

33. Coates and Morrison, *Sinking of the "Princess Sophia,"* 38–39.

34. *Victoria Daily Times,* October 28, 1918.

35. *Vancouver Daily World,* October 28, 1918.

36. *Seattle Post-Intelligencer,* October 27, 1918.

37. As was often the case after the loss of a gold ship, exaggerated rumors circulated claiming that millions of dollars in bullion were on board the vessel. "A Dawson Dispatch on Saturday [October 25] said that Klondike gold producers believed the *Sophia* carried about $1,000,000 being sent outside," noted the *Vancouver Daily Province* on October 28, 1918.

38. Coates and Morrison, *Sinking of the "Princess Sophia,"* 63.

39. Helen Wilson, letter to Alice Wilson Blair, Skagway, n.d., quoted in O'Keefe and Macdonald, *Final Voyage*, 54.

40. Quoted in the *Victoria Daily Times*, February 10, 1919. The messages between the Victoria office of the coast service and the *Princess Sophia* and other recipients were read into the record of the wreck inquiry held in Victoria on February 10, 1919, by James Troup.

41. See *Victoria Daily Times*, October 28, 1918.

42. Greene, "*Sophia,* Princess of Death," 195.

43. Coates and Morrison, *Sinking of the "Princess Sophia,"* 67.

44. Letter from Jack Maskell to Dorothy Burgess, October 24, 1918, Yukon Territorial Archives, Seddon Collection 86/49 part 1; rpt. Appendix A, Coates and Morrison, *Sinking of the "Princess Sophia,"* 171–172.

45. Coates and Morrison, *Sinking of the "Princess Sophia,"* 70–71.

46. *Vancouver Daily Province*, February 10, 1919.

47. *Victoria Daily Times*, February 10, 1919.

48. Ibid.

49. O'Keefe and Macdonald, *Final Voyage*, 130–131.

50. Ibid., 131.

51. Coates and Morrison, *Sinking of the "Princess Sophia,"* 71.

52. *Vancouver Daily Province*, January 31, 1919.

53. Quoted in ibid. The wireless message between the *Cedar* and the *Princess Sophia* was read into the record of the wreck inquiry by Captain John Ledbetter.

54. *Victoria Daily Times*, January 10, 1919.

55. *Vancouver Daily Province*, January 31, 1919.

56. Turner, *Pacific Princesses*, 117.

57. *Vancouver Daily Province*, February 1, 1919.

58. *Victoria Daily Times*, October 25, 1918.

59. *Victoria Daily Times*, February 10, 1919.

60. *Vancouver Daily Province*, February 1, 1919. Wireless messages between the *Cedar* and the *Princess Sophia* were read into the record of the wreck inquiry held in Victoria by Elwood Miller.

61. *Victoria Daily Times,* January 10, 1919. The text in the newspaper quotes Captain Miller as stating, "I remained at anchor until 5:20 the next morning. . . ." This is obviously an error and inconsistent with other sources. It should have read "that afternoon."

62. Ibid.

63. Ibid.

64. *Vancouver Daily Province*, January 31, 1919.

65. *Seattle Daily Times*, October 29, 1918.

66. *Vancouver Daily Sun,* October 28, 1918.

67. *Seattle Daily Times,* October 29, 1918.

68. *Vancouver Daily World,* October 31, 1918.

69. See *Vancouver Daily Province,* November 5, 1918; Coates and Morrison, *Sinking of the "Princess Sophia,"* 114–115; and O'Keefe and Macdonald, *Final Voyage,* 80.

70. Coates and Morrison, *Sinking of the "Princess Sophia,"* 121.

71. *Vancouver Daily Province,* November 5, 1918.

72. Ibid.

73. *Seattle Daily Times,* October 29, 1918.

74. See *Vancouver Daily World,* October 31, 1918.

75. *Vancouver Daily Province,* November 5, 1918. The newspaper incorrectly identified the body as that of C. W. Patrick.

76. Ibid.

77. *Victoria Daily Colonist,* January 25, 1919.

78. Coates and Morrison, *Sinking of the "Princess Sophia,"* 138–139.

79. *Seattle Post-Intelligencer,* October 28, 1918.

80. Richard Haws Jr., interviewed by Ruth Greene, in *Personality Ships,* 206.

81. *Seattle Post-Intelligencer,* October 27, 1918.

82. Ibid.

83. Quoted in *Vancouver Daily Province,* October 25, 1918.

84. *The Vancouver Daily Sun,* October 27, 1918.

85. Quoted in *Victoria Daily Colonist,* April 24, 1919.

86. See Greene, "*Sophia,* Princess of Death," 207–208.

87. *Victoria Daily Times,* October 28, 1918.

Chapter 10. *San Juan:* End of an Era

1. *Los Angeles Times,* August 31, 1929.

2. The estimates of her sinking time range from 90 to 300 seconds, but taking into account that few people had time to find and put on life preservers and that there was not sufficient time to launch even one lifeboat, it seems that she went down in less than 180 seconds.

3. Giles T. Brown, *Ships That Sail No More: Marine Transportation from San Diego to Puget Sound, 1910–1940* (Lexington: University of Kentucky Press, 1966), 144.

4. *Los Angeles Times,* August 31, 1929.

5. Ibid.

6. *San Francisco Examiner,* September 1, 1929.

7. *San Francisco Chronicle,* September 2, 1929.

8. *San Francisco Examiner,* September 1, 1929.

9. *Los Angeles Times,* August 31, 1929.

10. *San Francisco Examiner,* August 31, 1929.

11. *Los Angeles Times,* August 31, 1929.

12. *San Francisco Examiner,* August 31, 1929.

13. Maudie Dansby, "Shipwreck Too Tragic for Thrills," *Los Angeles Times,* September 15, 1929.

14. *San Francisco Examiner,* August 31, 1929.

15. Ibid.

16. Dansby, "Too Tragic."

17. *Los Angeles Times,* August 31, 1929.

18. *San Francisco Chronicle,* September 1, 1929.

19. *San Francisco Chronicle,* September 4, 1929.

20. *San Francisco Chronicle,* September 1, 1929.

21. *Los Angeles Times,* August 31, 1929.

22. *San Francisco Chronicle,* September 1, 1929.

23. *San Francisco Examiner,* August 31, 1929.

24. *San Francisco Chronicle,* September 4, 1929.

25. Ibid.

26. Harry Wade, "Survivor Describes Death Night Horror," *San Francisco Examiner,* September 1, 1929.

27. Ibid.

28. *San Francisco Examiner,* August 31, 1929.

29. Ibid.

30. Ibid.

31. *San Francisco Chronicle,* September 1, 1929.

32. *San Francisco Call Bulletin,* September 3, 1929.

33. *San Francisco Examiner,* August 31, 1929.

34. *Los Angeles Times,* August 31, 1929.

35. Ibid.

36. Ibid.

37. *San Francisco Chronicle,* September 4, 1929.

38. *San Francisco Examiner,* August 31, 1929.

39. *San Francisco Chronicle,* September 4, 1929.

40. *San Francisco Examiner,* August 31, 1929.

41. Ibid.

42. *Los Angeles Times,* September 1, 1929.

43. *San Francisco Examiner,* August 31, 1929.

44. Ibid.

45. Ibid.

46. *Los Angeles Times,* September 4, 1929.

47. Ibid.

48. *San Francisco Examiner,* August 31, 1929.

49. Ibid.

50. Ibid.

51. Ibid.

52. Ibid.

53. Ibid.

54. Ibid.

55. *Los Angeles Times,* August 31, 1929.

56. The woman was later identified as Marjorie Pifer.

57. Harry Wade, "Survivor Describes Death Night Horror," *San Francisco Examiner,* September 1, 1929.

58. Ibid.

59. *Los Angeles Times,* August 31, 1929.

60. *San Francisco Examiner,* August 31, 1929.

61. Ibid.

62. Ibid.

63. Ibid.

64. Ibid.

65. *Los Angeles Times,* September 4, 1929.

66. *San Francisco Examiner,* August 31, 1929.

67. *Los Angeles Times,* September 1, 1929.

68. *San Francisco Examiner,* August 31, 1929.

69. Ibid.

70. Ibid.

71. *Los Angeles Times,* September 1, 1929. The radio operator did not make it clear how he discovered that the second ship in the incident was the *S. C. T. Dodd.*

72. The oil was apparently from the *San Juan.* The *S. C. T. Dodd* was in ballast.

73. *Los Angeles Times,* September 1, 1929.

74. Ibid.

75. Ibid.

76. *Los Angeles Times,* August 31, 1929.

77. *San Francisco Examiner,* August 31, 1929.

78. Wade, "Death Night Horror."

79. *Los Angeles Times,* August 31, 1929.

80. *San Francisco Call Bulletin,* September 5, 1929.

81. Ibid.

82. Ibid.

83. *San Francisco Chronicle,* September 3, 1929. Completed in 1927, the 17,000-ton *Malolo* was the largest passenger ship ever built in the United

States. During her sea trials in 1927, she was rammed off Nantucket by the Norwegian freighter *Jacob Christian* and had to be towed to New York for repairs. See Frederick E. Emmons, *American Passenger Ships: The Ocean Lines and Liners, 1873–1983* (Newark: University of Delaware Press, 1985), 59.

84. *San Francisco Chronicle,* September 5, 1929.

85. *Los Angeles Times,* September 3, 1929.

86. *San Francisco Chronicle,* September 4, 1929.

87. *San Francisco Chronicle,* September 5, 1929.

88. Brown, *Ships That Sail No More,* 154.

89. *San Francisco Chronicle,* September 4, 1929.

90. *Los Angeles Times,* August 31, 1929.

91. *San Francisco Examiner,* August 31, 1929.

92. See Clinton H. Whitehurst Jr., *The United States Merchant Marine: In Search of an Enduring Maritime Policy* (Annapolis, Md.: Naval Institute Press, 1983), 34–35.

93. See Brown, *Ships That Sail No More,* 128. The owners, though, did not regard government subsidies as unwarranted incursions into the private sector.

94. *San Francisco Examiner,* August 31, 1929.

95. Robert Erwin Johnson, *Guardians of the Sea: History of the United States Coast Guard, 1915 to the Present* (Annapolis, Md.: Naval Institute Press, 1987), 41.

96. In 1943, the rapid wartime expansion of the merchant marine led the Coast Guard to temporarily assume most of the duties formerly performed by the Bureau of Marine Inspection and Navigation, the successors to the Board of Steamboat Inspectors. Commissions in the Coast Guard were given to those inspectors who wished them, despite the opposition of some officers within the maritime branch who did not believe the new inductees were suitable candidates. Rumors that inspectors accepted bribes had been circulating within the Coast Guard. In 1946, the duties of the steamship inspectors were permanently taken over by the maritime branch. See ibid., 200–201.

97. *New York Times,* September 10, 1934.

98. Emmons, *American Passenger Ships,* 129–131.

99. See Whitehurst, *United States Merchant Marine,* 34–35.

100. Andrew Rolle, *California: A History,* 5th ed. (Wheeling, Ill.: Harlan Davidson, 1998), 243–244.

101. Brown, *Ships That Sail No More,* 216–217.

Bibliography

Unpublished Sources

British Columbia Archives. GR 431, File 6/6. Transcript of the "Inquest Regarding *Clallam* Wreck."

National Archives, Pacific Region (Seattle). RG 41. Transcript of the Wreck of the U. S. [*sic*] *Valencia* Held before Bion B. Whitney and Robert A. Turner, Seattle, January 27, 1906.

San Francisco Daily Alta California, May 4, 1854. "Arrival of the New Steamship *Yankee Blade.*" Maritime Heritage Project [cited January 23, 2000]; http://www.maritimeheritage.org/PassLists/yb050454.html

United States Life-Saving Service, District 13. "Wreck Report: *City of Rio de Janeiro.*" February 22, 1901. Bancroft Library, University of California, Berkeley.

Published Sources

Aitken, Hugh G. J. *Syntony and Spark: The Origins of Radio.* New York: John Wiley, 1976.

Akrigg, G. P. V., and Helen Akrigg. *British Columbia Chronicle, 1847–1871.* Victoria, B.C.: Discovery Press, 1977.

Arguelles, Randolf. "Chronology of Significant Events Relating to the Career of Emilio Aguinaldo with Respect to the Various Imperialist and Anti-imperialist Campaigns in the Philippines." N.p.: n.d. http://www.bol.ucla .edu/~randolf/aguichron.htm. August 25, 1999.

Beaver, Patrick. *A History of Lighthouses.* Secaucus, N.J.: Citadel Press, 1971.

Bell, Horace. *Reminiscences of a Ranger.* Santa Barbara: Wallace Hubbard, 1927.

Belyk, Robert, and Diane Belyk. "No Armistice with Death." *Beaver: Exploring Canada's History* 68, no. 5 (1988): 43–49.

Benson, Richard M. *Steamships and Motorships of the West Coast.* New York: Bonanza Books, 1968.

Berton, Pierre. *Klondike: The Last Great Gold Rush, 1896–1899.* Rev. ed. Toronto: McClelland and Stewart, 1986.

Biographical Directory of the Governors of the United States, 1789–1978, s.v. "Perkins, George Clement."

Britton, Diane F. *The Iron and Steel Industry in the Far West.* Niwot: University of Colorado Press, 1991.

Brown, Giles T. *Ships That Sail No More: Marine Transportation from San Diego to Puget Sound, 1910–1940.* Lexington: University of Kentucky Press, 1966.

California Historical Society. "Continuation of the Annals of San Francisco." *California Historical Society Quarterly* 15 (1936): 174, 185.

Coates, Ken, and Bill Morrison. *The Sinking of the "Princess Sophia": Taking the North Down with Her.* Fairbanks: University of Alaska Press, 1991.

De La Pedraja, René. *The Rise and Decline of U.S. Merchant Shipping in the Twentieth Century.* New York: Twayne, 1992.

Delgado, James P. *To California by Sea: A Maritime History of the California Gold Rush.* Columbia: University of South Carolina Press, 1990.

Delgado, James P., and Stephen Haller. *Shipwrecks of the Golden Gate: A History of Vessel Losses from Duxbury Reef to Mussell Rock.* Lagunitas, Calif.: Lexikos, 1989.

Department of Commerce and Labor. *Wreck of the Steamer "Valencia": Report to the Federal Commission of Investigation.* Washington, D.C.: Government Printing Office, 1906.

Department of Commerce and Labor, Steamboat Inspection Service, Office of Supervising Inspector of First District. "Decision, August 31, 1907." Reprinted in *Pacific Maritime Review* 4 (September 1907): 16.

Department of Marine and Fisheries. "Annual Report of the Chief Engineer of the Department of Marine and Fisheries." *Sessional Papers* 21–23 (1917): 25–30.

Emmons, Frederick E. *American Passenger Ships: The Ocean Lines and Liners, 1873–1983.* Newark: University of Delaware Press, 1985.

Gibbs, James A. *Pacific Graveyard.* 3rd ed. Portland: Binfords and Mort, 1964.

————. *Sentinels of the North Pacific: The Story of Pacific Coast Lighthouses and Lightships.* Portland: Binfords and Mort, 1955.

————. *Shipwrecks of the Pacific Coast.* Portland: Binford and Mort, 1957.

Graham, Donald. *Keepers of the Light: A History of British Columbia's Lighthouses and Their Keepers.* Madeira Park, B.C.: Harbour Publishing, 1985.

Greene, Ruth. *Personality Ships of British Columbia*. West Vancouver, B.C.: Marine Tapestry Publications, 1969.

Griffiths, Denis. *Steam at Sea: Two Centuries of Steam-Powered Ships*. Conway's History of the Ship, ed. Robert Gardiner. London: Brassey's Conway Maritime Press, 1997.

Hacking, Norman. *Prince Ships of Northern British Columbia: Ships of the Grand Trunk Pacific and Canadian National Railways*. Surrey, B.C.: Heritage House, 1995.

Hacking, Norman R., and W. Kaye Lamb. *The Princess Story: A Century and a Half of West Coast Shipping*. Vancouver: Mitchell Press, 1974.

Heinrich, Thomas R. *Ships of the Seven Seas: Philadelphia Shipbuilding in the Age of Capitalism*. Baltimore: Johns Hopkins University Press, 1997.

Heyl, Erik. *Early American Steamers*. Vol. 1. 1953. Reprint, Buffalo: n.p., 1969.

Higgins, David W. *The Mystic Spring*. Toronto: William Briggs, 1904.

Johnson, Robert Erwin. *Guardians of the Sea: History of the United States Coast Guard, 1915 to the Present*. Annapolis, Md.: Naval Institute Press, 1987.

Kinder, Gary. *Ship of Gold in the Deep Blue Sea*. Toronto: Random House, 1998.

Knight, Donald G., and Eugene D. Wheeler. *Agony and Death on a Gold Rush Steamer: The Disastrous Sinking of the Side-Wheeler "Yankee Blade."* Ventura, Calif.: Pathfinder Publishing, 1990.

Lamb, W. Kaye. *History of the Canadian Pacific Railway*. New York: Macmillan, 1977.

Lord, Walter. *A Night to Remember*. New York: Bantam Books, 1997.

Marks, Paula Mitchell. *Precious Dust: The Saga of the Western Gold Rushes*. 1994. Reprint, HarperCollins West, 1995.

Marshall, Don B. *California Shipwrecks: Footsteps in the Sea*. Seattle: Superior Publishing, 1978.

————. *Oregon Shipwrecks*. Portland: Binford and Mort, 1984.

Marshall, Edison. *"Princess Sophia."* Garden City, N.Y.: Doubleday, 1958.

McCurdy, James G. *By Juan de Fuca's Strait: Pioneering along the Northwestern Edge of the Continent*. Portland: Metropolitan Press, 1937.

Merilees, Bill. *Newcastle Island: A Place of Discovery*. Surrey, B.C.: Heritage House, 1998.

Mullen, Kevin J. *Let Justice Be Done: Crime and Politics in Early San Francisco*. Reno: University of Nevada Press, 1989.

Musk, George. *Canadian Pacific: The Story of the Famous Shipping Line*. Toronto: Holt, Rinehart and Winston, 1981.

Neitzel, Michael C. *The Valencia Tragedy*. Surrey, B.C.: Heritage House, 1995.

Newell, Gordon R. *The H. W. McCurdy Marine History of the Pacific Northwest: 1895 to 1965.* Seattle: Superior Publishing, 1966.

————. *Ships of the Inland Sea: The Story of the Puget Sound Steamboats.* Portland: Binfords and Mort, 1960.

————. *SOS North Pacific: Tales of Shipwrecks off the Washington, British Columbia and Alaska Coasts.* Portland: Binfords and Mort, 1955.

Newell, Gordon R., and Joe Williamson. *Pacific Coastal Liners.* Seattle: Superior Publishing, 1959.

O'Keefe, Betty, and Ian Macdonald. *The Final Voyage of the "Princess Sophia": Did They All Have to Die?* Surrey, B.C.: Heritage House, 1998.

Paterson, T. W. *British Columbia Shipwrecks.* Langley, B.C.: Stagecoach Publishing, 1976.

Pickelhaupt, Bill. *Shanghaied in San Francisco.* San Francisco: Flyblister Press, 1996.

Rogers, Fred. *More Shipwrecks of British Columbia.* Vancouver: Douglas and McIntyre, 1992.

————. *Shipwrecks of British Columbia.* Vancouver: Douglas, 1976.

Rolle, Andrew. *California: A History.* 5th ed. Wheeling, Ill.: Harlan Davidson, 1998.

Scott, R. Bruce. *"Breakers Ahead!" On the Graveyard of the Pacific.* Victoria, B.C.: Sono Nis Press, 1982.

Spitzer, Paul. "Harsh Ways: Edward W. Heath and the Shipbuilding Trade." *Pacific Northwest Quarterly* 90 (Winter 1998–99): 3–16.

Starr, Kevin. *Americans and the California Dream, 1850–1915.* New York: Oxford University Press, 1973.

Turner, Robert D. *The Pacific Princesses: An Illustrated History of Canadian Pacific Railway's Princess Fleet on the Northwest Coast.* Victoria, B.C.: Sono Nis Press, 1977.

Webber, Bert, and Margie Webber. *Shipwrecks and Rescues off the Northwest Coast.* Medford, Oreg.: Webb Research Group, 1996.

Whitehurst, Clinton H., Jr. *The United States Merchant Marine: In Search of an Enduring Maritime Policy.* Annapolis, Md.: Naval Institute Press, 1983.

Woolf, Alexander. "The Loss of the *Rio de Janeiro.*" *Overland Monthly* 37, no. 4 (April 1901): 247–251.

Wright, E. W., ed. *Lewis and Dryden's Marine History of the Pacific Northwest.* 1895. Reprint, New York: Antiquarian Press, 1961.

Young, Bob, and Jan Young. "Thirteen Minutes of Horror." *Westways* 53, no. 2 (February 1961): 24.

Newspapers

Dansby, Maudie. "Shipwreck Too Tragic for Thrills." *Los Angeles Times,* September 15, 1929.

Enkoji, M. S. "From Murky Depths, Sparkling History." *Sacramento Bee,* April 14, 1999.

McDonald, Lucile. "The *Pacific:* A Jinxed Ship." *Seattle Daily Times,* April 7, 1968.

————. "The Worse Disaster in the Strait." *Seattle Daily Times,* Sunday January 6, 1963, magazine section.

Wade, Harry. "Survivor Describes Death Night Horror." *San Francisco Examiner,* September 1, 1929.

Wishaar, Jack. "People Spilled Like Pebbles in a Seething, Boiling Surf." *Seattle Post-Intelligencer,* January 26, 1906.

Index